A Solomon Islands Chronicle

As told by Samuel Alasa'a

Edited by Ben Burt and Michael Kwa'ioloa
with contributions from the Kwara'ae chiefs

Published for the Trustees of The British Museum by

THE BRITISH MUSEUM PRESS

First published in 2001 by The British Museum Press
A division of The British Museum Company Ltd
46 Bloomsbury Street, London WC1B 3QQ

ISBN 0 7141 2555 5

Designed and typeset by Ben Burt
Cover by John Hawkins Book Design
Printed and bound by Henry Ling Ltd, Dorchester, England

Contents

Acknowledgments

During the last twenty years we have been indebted to many friends, relatives and colleagues, both in Kwara'ae and elsewhere, for helping us in the research which underlies this book.

Samuel Alasa'a's words form the core of the book, but many other Kwara'ae people contributed the information which has enabled us to interpret and add to his account. They include: Adriel Rofate'e, Aisah Osifera, Silas Sangafanoa, Timi Ko'oliu, Johnson Rara, Andrew Gwa'italafa, Maefatafata, Clement O'ogau, Jonathan Didimae, Clement 'Au'au, John Langi. Sorry to say, many of these people, like Alasa'a himself, have since died, but we are pleased to be able to preserve a little of their knowledge in this book.

Others who acted as consultants and advisors on Alasa'a's account include: Frank Ete Tuaisalo, Sylvanus Maniramo, Kwalemanu 'Una, Uriel Mark Li'iga, David Timi, John Mani'a, Nelson Kwanabako, Ivery Arana, Dia Bagara, Benjamin Ramo, Michael Ngidui, Alec Rukia.

There are also important contributions from the Kwaio people, provided by David Akin, who generously helped us with valuable information and advice from his research among them. Others who have helped with the documents and photographs include: Judith Bennett, Graeme Golden, Andrea Tuisovuna, Barbara Henshall, Harry Persaud, Andrea Bannatyne, Lady Patricia Garvey, David Chow, staff of the South Sea Evangelical Mission.

Practical support and advice, particularly for Kwa'ioloa as an independent researcher, was provided by the staff of the Solomon Islands National Museum, including Lawrence Foana'ota, Edna Belo, John Keopo and Lawrence Kiko, as well as by Frank Lulu, Luluta and Lawrence La'ugere. Graham and Evelyn Baines have also provided welcome help and encouragement.

Funding for field research in Solomon Islands was provided by the British Academy, and the writing was supported by The British Museum.

The quiet and comfortable Grove public house in Balham (a.k.a. the Grave and the Balham Reading Rooms) deserves mention as a setting for much of the editorial work. Last but not least, we are grateful to Carolyn Jones of The British Museum Press for her sympathetic help in preparing the book for publication, and to Pauline Khng for copy editing.

For the benefit of Kwara'ae readers, we wish to make it clear that we will receive no royalties from the sale of this book and the sale price is to cover the cost of publication.

Ben Burt and Michael Kwa'ioloa

Foreword
Michael Kwa'ioloa, Secretary, Kwara'ae House of Chiefs

I, Michael Kwa'ioloa, am born of Samuel Alasa'a, who is believed to have been born in 1886, and died in his home village of Anofiu in East Kwara'ae, Malaita Province, Solomon Islands, on Wednesday 28 October 1987. He is the person whose account is documented in this chronicle.

I come from the island chain of Melanesia, which consists of many different lands and cultures as ancient as any in the world. We have culture (*falafala*), law (*taki*) and knowledge (*liato'o*) as special as any other, as a reading of this book will prove to be true. Our history did not begin when Europeans came to our lands and it is racist to think of what happened before contact as pre-history. Melanesian history began when our first ancestors set foot on our soil long ago. To me, we Melanesians are rich and beautiful, not in financial wealth but in riches and beauty which are natural and indigenous. This goes beyond the riches and beauty of any other race or culture.

My father Alasa'a's chronicle is an exact account of an original history from centuries ago, clearly identifying the desires, longings, aspirations and determination which show who, where and what a Solomon Islands man is. Most of the history gives an account of the amazing wisdom, knowledge, understanding and skill passed on to him from my great-great-grandfathers long ago. As his son, when he died and my elder brother Maesatana also died, I took over the leadership, and I feel it an honour and a humble duty to write this Foreword.

Introductory remarks to such a document, speaking in the voice of contemporary society, are helpful, useful and powerful pronouncements to present and future generations. I therefore feel obliged to explain that the keynote of this document, which Ben Burt and I agree on, should be 'Our culture is the soul of our society.' Reading this chronicle will keep reminding indigenous Solomon Islanders not to drift dangerously backwards. This written account from my father means that present and future generations will be set right by experiencing their original background. For if Ben Burt and myself had not documented this information today, then those of tomorrow would have nothing to go on, or even to correct. This Foreword is written some years after these various materials, and it is written in full knowledge of possible criticisms. As editors, we have documented not what we thought to add, but exactly what was in my father's own account.

Michael Kwa'ioloa, 1997
Photo by Saul Peckham

In many parts of Solomon Islands the differences between our many different cultures are highlighted by progress. The present book will help us understand the kind of adaptation which has already occurred in Solomon Islands during the past 150 years. Much of our knowledge of these adaptations is incomplete, and we hope that many other people will fill in the gaps in the future. From twenty-two years of working with Ben Burt to research the Kwara'ae region, I myself feel and understand that it is impossible for anyone to produce a book of this nature without much support from their traditional senior chiefs, pagan priests, senior women, etc. and we are indebted to those who have provided us with valuable information.

I must also take into account that my father, the late Samuel Alasa'a, as the main source, had a good memory which stored what he produced for this chronicle. He was unable to read or write but was magically educated by his grandfathers, mothers and fathers. My father's contribution makes our research worthwhile and beneficial, for he is really helpful to everyone, and even though a person was from another clan he provides their histories and genealogies. He told me "I must impart the knowledge given to me to everyone before I die. Also, I need to see that a system of government by traditional culture is recognised by central government."

Comparing life at present with the past, things are less co-operative. In my experience, in the past my fathers lived by means of exchange. For example, when a relative needed a pig, we would provide it for a garden plot of taro; if relatives offshore needed taro, we provided it while they provided fish. When someone paid brideprice for their son, everyone gathered together and contributed shell-money. When someone built his house, everyone helped to build it, and when cleaning the village area, the chief ordered everyone to work together.

Nowadays, since the British colonised us, we live in a trading system based on cash. People who are employed or produce for the market are the only ones who survive. That classifies us into three categories: (1) officials (2) people in the middle, not very rich and not very poor (3) the grass-roots level. It results in the saying 'the rich become richer, the poor become poorer.' This is contradictory to my traditional culture, in which everyone is concerned for each other.

It is a failing of our governments of past days that they have not properly managed the affairs and the well-being of our traditional culture by providing financial support to document the knowledge of our many senior chiefs who have passed away. This chronicle therefore highlights 'traditional culture' to promote the responsibilities of traditional leaders as a basis for the education of others. In this respect there are proposals to record and revive the best qualities of our cultural heritage, in order to cement our society through these important qualities which have served our people so well for so many centuries past. In particular, the Solomon Islands Traditional Culture and Environment Conservation Foundation recognises the important role of traditional leaders and chiefs in our societies, and recommends the recognition of tradition and an advisory role for traditional leaders at all levels of the government system of Solomon Islands.

This work is an extension and development of our earlier research. In the course of our research, Ben Burt has been more than a brother to me, making it possible to bring me to London to work on our book drafts, and his wife Annette is an in-law to me. I also presented him to my father, overcoming his fear and enabling him to pass on the original knowledge transferred to him by our forefathers. The reason was to document the full account, lest it be buried six foot underground. It was a golden chance that anthropologist Ben Burt was available for us to write this book. Its purpose is to record how a senior elder from Malaita Province, Solomon Islands, honoured the obligations of his traditional culture.

Introduction

Ben Burt, British Museum

In the 1980s a Pacific Islands elder, Samuel Alasa'a, decided to pass on the knowledge he had gained over a long lifetime by recording some cassettes of history for his sons. He told the story of how the ancestors of their people, the Kwara'ae of Solomon Islands, first arrived in their homeland on the island of Malaita about twenty-five generations ago, explained the genealogical histories of their own clan homelands, and described the arrival of the Europeans, as experienced in his youth.

Alasa'a's words form the core of this book, presenting one Solomon Islander's perspective on the history of his own people. This introduces a broader view of the past based on other sources which help both to interpret his account to those unfamiliar with his cultural background and to compare it with alternative historical perspectives. As editors, myself an anthropologist who has researched with the Kwara'ae for many years, and Michael Kwa'ioloa, who is Alasa'a's son, we have drawn on local knowledge, anthropological research and early colonial records to present a many-sided account of a Pacific Islands history.

Alasa'a's life and times

Until Alasa'a's fathers' generation, the Kwara'ae had always lived in independent local communities, as farmers of the inland forests, seldom travelling beyond the territory of the neighbouring sea peoples on the coasts. Their history mainly concerned the doings of their own clan ancestors, their feuds and migrations, marriages and land claims.

Alasa'a's chronicle begins with the arrival of the first settlers at their original home of Siale and the dispersal of their descendants throughout Kwara'ae and beyond. He goes on to trace the ancestors of his own clan of Tolinga, from the settlement of their ancient lands in the central inland to their descendants of the present. He introduces the clan of Fairū in East Kwara'ae into which his Tolinga ancestors married and details the turbulent history of that local community in recent generations. Running through all these histories are the genealogies which link Alasa'a to his relatives and neighbours through common ancestors long ago.

Alasa'a's fathers witnessed the arrival of the first 'whitemen' (*ara 'ikwao*, as the Kwara'ae call us) in ships which carried men away to lands then unknown in Fiji and Queensland (from the 1870s). After spending years abroad as plantation workers, many returned home with novel goods, technologies and ideas to a way of life still governed by the stormy politics of inter-clan feuding, to which they contributed by importing guns. From the day of Alasa'a's birth at Kwaruakalo in Latea (some time around 1890), this feuding cast a shadow over his early years. But as a youth he also saw returning labour migrants, including some of his own relatives, establish a more peaceful regime in the first Christian communities in the district, supported by Australian missionaries (in the 1900s). Eventually he himself went to work abroad on the neighbouring island of Isabel, leading him into a frightening encounter with the colonial authorities of the British Solomon Islands Protectorate (in 1918). After returning to Malaita he saw the colonial government impose its law upon the feuding warriors of his Kwara'ae homeland (in 1919).

Alasa'a's recordings show how conscious he was of being one of the last surviving links between the world of his youngest descendants, secure in the peace and relative prosperity of modern Solomon Islands, and the self-sufficient but precarious lifestyle of feuding local communities of his own childhood and ancestors since ancient times, which he saw European colonialism bring to an end. The history passed down from his forebears and the contrasting experiences of his own life and times each inform the other in his narratives and commentaries, revealing a sense of continuity and coherence which belies the changing times.

Alasa'a's narrative ends about 1920, but Solomon Islands continued to change ever more rapidly as his life went on. In about 1940 he married Arana, daughter of a notorious warrior, Arumae Bakete. Alasa'a used to stay with their family at Saia in 'Ere'ere and was encouraged to elope with Arana by her aunt; something which would have been extremely dangerous in the days when men were still free to kill those who compromised the virtue of their womenfolk. But as it was, brideprice was paid, a marriage feast was held and the couple went to live at Fauboso in Latea. Arana bore eight children before she died in 1957, of whom four lived to adulthood. Alasa'a was already middle-aged by the time the Second World War reached Solomon Islands in 1942, and the people of Malaita attempted to regain their independence through the island-wide Maasina Rul movement in the late 1940s and early 1950s.

From here the story is taken up by Michael Kwa'ioloa, born in 1953, whose own published autobiography provides a background to his father's later life (Kwa'ioloa & Burt 1997). While Alasa'a was brought up in a society governed by the spiritual power of ancestral ghosts, becoming a 'tabu-speaker' (*fataābu*) or priest before joining the South Sea Evangelical Mission (SSEM) in the 1940s, Kwa'ioloa encountered these ghosts in the 1970s as a (lapsed) Christian. He went to school, then learnt the skills and trades of urban life in Honiara, the new post-war capital of Solomon Islands on Guadalcanal island. Returning to Malaita, he took his own part in the development of new local government and church bodies, as Solomon Islands was prepared to become an independent state in 1978.

It was in Honiara, where Kwa'ioloa and his elder brother John Maesatana were living in the 1980s, that they recorded their father's memories, in the midst of a clan of grandchildren living in a Malaitan suburb very different from their Kwara'ae homeland. In those last years Alasa'a travelled often between Honiara and Malaita, where he lived with his sister's daughter Maefatafata at Anofiu in East Kwara'ae. He died at Anofiu in 1987 at a great age, perhaps about a hundred.

Presenting Alasa'a's chronicle

I first met Alasa'a in 1979, when Michael Kwa'ioloa introduced me to his father on my first research visit to Solomon Islands. On my second visit in 1984 Kwa'ioloa tried to persuade his father and his elder brother Maesatana that I should document the old man's knowledge for my own research into Kwara'ae tradition and Christianity. They were more sceptical and less willing to trust a whiteman, and Alasa'a declined to recount to me the things he regarded as most important until I returned to Solomon Islands on my third visit in 1987. By then he had retired to Anofiu, where he was fading away as he sat by the hearth of a small house, blind, tired and ready to die. He had decided to open everything he knew to me, through Kwa'ioloa, in the hope of preserving it. The account I recorded from him then proved a useful addition to the earlier recordings, but I only learnt of these afterwards, when Kwa'ioloa transcribed and gave them to me. It was then that I realised the importance of what Alasa'a had to say, not to a foreign anthropologist but to his own sons, and I persuaded Kwa'ioloa that it would be worth publishing.

However, Alasa'a is only one of innumerable voices in the Kwara'ae oral tradition. While he was undoubtably an authority on the history he recounted, so are many others, and they are not always in agreement. To make this point, and to benefit from some other perspectives without interrupting Alasa'a's monologue, we have presented his words in parallel with what others have dictated or written on the same subjects. Most of these voices are also of Kwara'ae people known to Alasa'a but, in later chapters, they include also the foreigners who have become involved in Kwara'ae history in recent times. Some of these sources contradict Alasa'a, often in small particulars which may be more significant to them than to most readers, although we have tried to avoid including statements which may inflame local controversies on issues such as land claims. More obvious differences in perspective emerge from colonial sources, although these are likely to present less problems as far as Kwara'ae readers are concerned.

By presenting this complementary information as texts and documents, linked by editorial comments and explanations and illustrated by maps, diagrams, photographs and drawings, we also hope to convey something of the atmosphere of the times and places in which historical events occurred and the way knowledge of them has been preserved and researched. But a fuller understanding of Alasa'a's chronicle requires above all some consideration of his cultural background and his reasons for relating it as he did.

History as social precedent

Alasa'a's historical perspective is very local, often parochial, but it echoes cultural themes widely shared in Kwara'ae and beyond, some of which can be traced to a cultural heritage far older and wider than the history he relates. One of his main concerns is for origins, the foundation of his own ancestral clans and lands and their relationship to Kwara'ae and the island of Malaita as a whole. In this, Alasa'a epitomises a widespread Austronesian attitude to the past: "That it is knowable and that such knowledge is of value, that what happened in the past has set a pattern for the present, and that it is essential to have access to the past in attempts to order the present." (Fox 1996:5). In responding to the changing circumstances of a Christian country undergoing rapid political and economic change, Alasa'a voices a perspective on Kwara'ae history and culture firmly rooted in this notion of precedent set in the times which 'came before' (*ma' i na'o*), in an identity established by descent from ancestors traced through many generations.

This identity is at once corporate and personal, with Alasa'a often referring to his ancestors as 'I' rather then 'he' or 'they', while speaking on behalf of their descendants of the 'profound group' (*fū'ingwae*) which is a Kwara'ae clan. This term may apply to an ancestor's descendants in any line of descent, whether two or twenty generations ago, from a family to the whole of Kwara'ae. Alasa'a's history will only make sense with some understanding of what his audience took for granted about kinship and descent in Kwara'ae community organisation.

The Kwara'ae live in extended family 'homes' (*fanoa*), clusters of houses seldom large enough to be called villages (although a 'home' can also mean a homeland or community, from a hamlet to a town or a country). These settlements are usually based on small clan groups of fathers, brothers and sons, whose wives and mothers have come from other clans and whose daughters and sisters likewise go to marry elsewhere. While all men and women theoretically have a claim on all relatives descended from any of their ancestors, it is these clan groups of men descended in the male line who have the strongest claim to represent them and their ancestors. Precedence and leadership are claimed on the basis of seniority of birth in a genealogical hierarchy which ranks elder brothers and their descendants before younger ones, whether they are born of the same parents or of ancestors five, ten or twenty generations ago. Hence the lengthy genealogies in Alasa'a's history, mainly comprising lists of fathers, brothers and sons, explain relationships between widely dispersed local clans which can have implications for the rank and status of their present-day leaders.

But while the principles of precedence are agreed, effective claims to seniority may have to be negotiated and are frequently challenged. While most Kwara'ae agree on the common descent of their people from one group of founding ancestors, there are many contradictions among the genealogies of major clans of ancient common ancestry. Formerly, when Kwara'ae society was riven and fragmented by chronic feuding, when enmities were remembered as long as genealogies but genealogies were confidential, lore-masters had less opportunity to compare and check their common knowledge than at present. So Alasa'a's account of the ancient common origins of the Kwara'ae clans may be disputed by those whose ancestors passed on different versions, particularly if this seems to affect claims to seniority in the genealogical hierarchy.

The fact that there is not more disagreement on the shared ancestry of different major clans reflects the importance of ritual procedures under the ancestral religion, in which the ghosts of the dead were worshipped for the power they held over their living descendants. Local clans were obliged to send pigs back to be sacrificed at the burial places of the ancient common ancestors whose homes they had left, often long ago and far away. This ritual system linked local clans dispersed throughout Kwara'ae to certain ancient shrines, such as Siale, the founding shrine of Kwara'ae in Alasa'a's history. Such sacrificial procedures are still cited as evidence of the relationships of clans to one another and, most importantly, to their lands.

History as land claims

The land which people can 'claim' (*firia*) as their own by inheritance from the common ancestors who settled and claimed it before them is what gives them their identity and name as a clan. These shared claims are validated by the kind of genealogical histories featured in Alasa'a's chronicle and by the sacrifices formerly offered to ancestral ghosts at shrines on these lands, as Kwara'ae histories both describe and prescribe.

At the time when Alasa'a related his stories, if not in the times they describe, land claims had become a central concern of Kwara'ae history as the crucial values established and bequeathed by their ancestors. Alasa'a told much of his history for the explicit purpose of validating his inherited claims to certain lands, for the sake of his sons and future generations of descendants. The vital evidence which he was passing on to them and putting on record concerns the births, marriages and deaths of their ancestors, the homes where they lived, the places where their bones were deposited after death, and the genealogies which link the dead to their descendants and the living to each other. This was intended to validate claims to the lands of his ancestors and, in some cases, to be senior or leader among those who share the right to live and work on the land.

Although people may disagree on land claims which go back to a few generations after the first arrivals on Malaita, disputes are likely to be most serious between neighbours, who usually share a number of much more recent ancestral connections. Alasa'a's histories demonstrate the complexity of descent relationships within local clan communities, where families of a neighbourhood may trace separate clan origins to places far away but share land with neighbours who are related to them through female rather than male ancestors, maybe through many generations of intermarriage. When there is competition for leadership and control of land, descent in the senior male line may be only one of the principles invoked, particularly in the absence of clear and unbroken male lines of succession.

This is the underlying theme of much of Alasa'a's clan history, which relates the origins of continuing relationships among the various people who share claims to his lands. Some of this history, with accompanying rhetoric, is actually presented as if he were giving evidence in one of the acrimonious land disputes which take up so much time and energy in the Solomon Islands courts. Alasa'a's name does indeed appear several times in the court records for East Kwara'ae, disputing land claims with his neighbours.

Such land claims have a special significance in a society, and a country, where forces for commercial development, channelled by a Western-educated elite, are challenging the principles and practice of communal tenure of land and resources upon which Kwara'ae society was founded. While Alasa'a was concerned in his histories first of all with the lands his own descendants would inherit, the way such local clan histories are represented and understood has wider implications for the future of traditional land tenure systems in Malaita and Solomon Islands.

Despite the emphasis which the Kwara'ae place on inheritance of seniority and leadership for land in the male line, Alasa'a's land claims confirm the underlying principle that everyone inherits the right to live and garden on the land of both their parents and all their previous ancestors. Much of his account is concerned with seniority for the lands occupied by his more recent ancestors on the basis of descent through a series of women of a clan which had no descendants in the male line. This kind of claim contradicts arguments within Kwara'ae and beyond for converting a flexible system of communal land tenure into more exclusive patrilineal patterns of inheritance, by land registration based heavily on 'primary rights' inherited in the male line. This might be more compatible with Western models of rural economic development but it is not necessarily in the best interests of rural communities. Alasa'a's history is the kind of evidence which should be taken into account in this important debate (as discussed further in Burt 1994b).

History as local politics

Disputes over land have become notorious for dividing and disrupting Kwara'ae communities since at least the 1960s, with Alasa'a's home district as a particular hot spot. But the histories which Alasa'a relates in support of land claims also illustrate other tensions and conflicts in the life of Kwara'ae communities, which had more serious consequences in earlier times. While the Kwara'ae were yet unconstrained by government from pursuing disputes and grievances with violence, much of their history concerned assaults and killings, armed raids, sorcery attacks and the resettlement of fugitives. These are the subjects of tales known as *'a'emae*, told for interest and entertainment and formerly also related as rhythmic chants (*kana*).

'A'emae means the 'basis' of death, feuding and bands of men (all covered by the word *mae*) and these tales are both dramatic and violent. They involve named local communities and places, although the characters are not always identifiable in the genealogies, and the tales are not necessarily told as the clan history of the storyteller. Alasa'a alludes to such tales as part of the historical legitimation for his land claims and clan identities. Without relating them in detail, he uses the tales to explain the social landscape of a community which continues to respond to relationships formed by the deeds of their ancestors.

These tales also offer glimpses of pre-colonial politics, dominated by the actions of proud and wilful men pursuing grievances at the expense of other people's lives, often of those innocent of offence. The legal principles involved, the 'law' (*taki*) which the Kwara'ae proclaim as the foundation of their culture, are based on the concept of tabu, which pervades Alasa'a's chronicles.

Tabu (*ābu*) can be understood as the requirement to treat persons, human or spiritual, with the respect appropriate to their status and situation, forbidding acts which would damage or denigrate them. Relationships with ancestral ghosts (*akalo*), the most exalted and powerful members of society, were governed by particularly rigorous rules of tabu which characterised the ancestral religion. These focused on the separation of ghosts, and the men responsible for their worship, from the defiling qualities of women, particularly their reproductive functions. All offences against persons are in some sense breaches of tabu which have to be made good; the living seek restitution or compensation by use or threat of force, while ghosts required pigs to be baked as sacrificial offerings, to prevent them causing sickness and ill-fortune.

Not surprisingly, it is the exercise of the most drastic sanctions which dominate Alasa'a's history, rather than presentations of shell-bead money or pig-bakings to preserve peace and good fortune. On the principle that families and clans are collectively responsible for their relatives, everyone in a community found themselves under threat of death for grievances caused by one of their members, and they were obliged to retaliate in the same fashion. One killing was likely to lead to another, bringing periods of chronic insecurity whenever ill feeling turned to violence. Alasa'a gives some telling comments on what it was like to live under this political system, from the experiences of his own youth.

History as change and continuity

This insecurity goes some way to explain both the acceptance of colonial rule by many Kwara'ae, and resistance to it by the warriors who gained their influence from feuding. It is the subjugation of these warriors and the imposition of colonial law which marks the triumph of colonialism in the latter part of Alasa'a's chronicle.

This subjugation occurred almost fifty years after the Kwara'ae first became involved in the colonial economy, from the early 1870s. After their first encounters with European labour recruiters, Malaitans soon became dependent on industrial goods, particularly tools and weapons, obtained by going to work overseas. But for a long time, even after the British established a Protectorate over Solomon Islands in 1893 and began to offer plantation work within the Solomons in the early twentieth century, inland Malaitans like the Kwara'ae retained their political autonomy.

Significantly, these early colonial developments do not feature in Alasa'a's clan histories, except in the appearance of guns in the weaponry of local fighters. With his focus on feuds, migrations, land claims and genealogies, the chronicle seems unaffected by developments beyond the bounds of Kwara'ae. The sense of continuity from ancient times is reinforced by Alasa'a's habit of interrupting his narrative to mention genealogical links between persons two or three generations before and their present-day descendants. From the first arrivals to the events of his fathers' times, Alasa'a's history concerns only the origins and identity of his own local community.

Alasa'a treats the advent of colonialism as a separate topic, focused on the personal experiences of his own youth. Some of the events he recalls do have implications for his land claims, but in recounting the impact of Christian missions and British government he seems more concerned to make a record of the remarkable transformations he witnessed. Of these the most significant to him seem to have been the peace, security and freedom from want attributed to Christianity and government. But despite his own generally positive view of colonialism, we can see from his account that others fought hard to oppose it, surrendering their political and religious autonomy only when forced to do so by a combination of government force and the failure of the spiritual power of their ancestors.

Something else that changes as Alasa'a's chronicle reaches the colonial period is the availability of new voices to complement his and other Kwara'ae perspectives, particularly the reports of government officers and missionaries. Taken alone, of course, these would give a very partial account of Kwara'ae history, ignorant of events beyond their own spheres of influence and coloured by their particular interest in controlling and changing Kwara'ae society and culture. But when compared with Kwara'ae versions of events, from Alasa'a and others, the two kinds of sources illuminate one another most effectively. Not only do the colonial accounts explain much of what Alasa'a could not have known or understood, but some contemporary reports, written within days of the events they describe, corroborate his recollections of some sixty years later in remarkable detail. This gives added credibility to Alasa'a's account of events for which colonial records cannot be found, including those which the potential authors may have preferred to forget.

History as tradition

Although Alasa'a's experiences of the colonial period mark a departure from the parochial history of earlier times, he incorporated them into the same historical paradigm of origins, precedents and legitimations. Despite some doubts about modern times and the youth of today, Alasa'a saw colonialism as restoring the original 'tradition' (*falafala*) or 'custom' as he calls it (Pijin *kasatomo* or *kastom*) of the Kwara'ae people through the work of the Christian missions, which converted almost the whole of Kwara'ae during his lifetime. Like other Kwara'ae historians, he traced the origins of his people and their culture back to a biblical tradition which their forefathers changed into ancestor worship after they arrived in Malaita, as the beginning of his chronicle explains.

Kwara'ae interest in the biblical foundations of their society and the indigenous foundations of their Christianity reflects some important present-day concerns. In particular, it supports their determination to assert cultural and political autonomy in opposition to colonial or state control. Kwara'ae activists seek to govern their own communities according to the laws and values of ancestral tradition, under the authority of their own leaders, sanctioned by God and the church rather than government. This is one theme underlying the tradition which Alasa'a reflects upon, which he was working with others to revive through the Kwara'ae organisation of 'chiefs' or community leaders at the time he recorded his chronicle. Tradition or custom in this sense has been the focus of Kwara'ae popular movements for independence from the colonial institutions of missions as well as government since at least the Maasina Rul movement of the 1940s. As such it played an important part in developing a devolved system of local and provincial government within the Solomon Islands state.

Equally important to senior men like Alasa'a is the role of tradition in authority and morality at the domestic and local level of family and clan. In the talk which concludes his chronicle, Alasa'a lectures younger generations on obedience to their parents in matters of personal behaviour, as a responsibility to their relatives. The repeated killings suffered by the people of their Fairū clan in his histories emphasise the seriousness of his warnings about the consequences of disregarding the law in former times. The continuing risk of violence in retaliation or restitution for offences is equally well illustrated by the experience of his son Kwa'ioloa, whose autobiography (Kwa'ioloa & Burt 1997) also demonstrates the respect for parental authority and ancestral wisdom which is so highly valued in Kwara'ae culture.

For his sons and grandsons, his intended audience, Alasa'a's recorded talks set out both the history which underpins their identity and land claims, and the values by which they and their contemporaries should live. He describes the changes experienced in his youth, now so far in the past, from a personal or local perspective which emphasises his and his family's roles in the events which had such an impact on the wider community of Kwara'ae and beyond. Alasa'a's own intention in his chronicle was plainly to carry forward the cultural tradition established by his ancestors for the benefit of his descendants in generations to come.

But while the values Alasa'a preaches derive from ancestral tradition, the spiritual support he invokes is Christian, and he concludes with a prayer to God. In his commitment to Christianity during his last years, after periods of wavering faith since his first conversion in the 1940s, Alasa'a actually repudiates much of what his history describes, the spiritual legacy of his ancestral ghosts, or 'satans' as he refers to them. In this way he makes his own accommodation to the transformation of Kwara'ae society and culture experienced during his long lifetime.

History in print

While we may acknowledge Alasa'a's intentions and attitudes in recording this chronicle for his sons, others will not respond to it as they did. Kwara'ae readers with their own stake in the history he recounts may have reason to question Alasa'a's words, or our presentation of them, where they contradict their own ancestral traditions or present-day interests. Others, particularly Western readers, may query some of what he says for reasons of their own cultural approaches to history. We hope that most readers will see Alasa'a's chronicle as a study in Pacific Islands local history, informed by the culture, world-view and historical perspectives of a past generation, too easily forgotten in the changing times.

But a book like this does raise questions about the nature and purpose of historical research and publication. The best outcome of such critical queries would be a debate on the constitution of local history in Kwara'ae, Solomon Islands or Melanesia. It is a quarter of a century since academics at the University of Papua New Guinea began to acknowledge publicly the obligation to write for, as well as about, the peoples of Melanesia (see *Research in Melanesia* 1975). Yet our research is still largely inaccessible to most islanders, particularly to the majority who lack the education to benefit from academic works written in English. Besides, the fact that most Melanesian history is contained in oral traditions which are subject to local cultural conventions has important implications for the creation of a written record (see Burt 1998 for further discussion of these issues).

In a later contribution from the University of Papua New Guinea, *Oral Tradition in Melanesia* (Denoon & Lacey 1981), historians pointed out that oral traditions are part of ongoing social processes and that in published form they may serve new purposes which affect the oral tradition itself by fixing and disseminating information which was formerly adaptable and restricted. As with Alasa'a's chronicle, oral traditions may be recounted to serve vital interests in the present and their significance may be diminished by making knowledge openly accessible, or enhanced by the legitimating power of print. Either may have serious implications for the lives both of those who provide the texts and those they are talking about. At the same time, it is generally assumed that oral traditions are being weakened by the social and cultural changes which increasingly separate younger generations of Melanesians from their own cultural heritage. This encourages some, like the Kwara'ae people who have contributed to this book, to regard documentation and publication as a way of maintaining traditional knowledge and values by new techniques suited to the changing times.

The implications of transforming an oral into a written tradition are no clearer than the future of Melanesian culture under Western cultural hegemony or globalisation, but bringing the oral tradition into local literature must surely improve the prospects for people to build upon their own experience of the past. By publishing Alasa'a's chronicles in the local language as well as in English, we hope to contribute to the ongoing reconstitution of local culture by providing something for local people to read. But in doing so we need to consider how they may understand and evaluate such oral traditions, and try to anticipate the questions raised by publication.

As Alasa'a's chronicle illustrates, in Kwara'ae much cultural knowledge, whether genealogies or historical stories, moral codes or ritual procedures, is valued for the practical benefits it confers, such as advancing claims for seniority for land or political status, improving personal morality and life skills and, formerly, gaining support and protection from ghosts. Such knowledge is more likely to be guarded and shared strategically than broadcast around. Even when imparting the basic morality which everyone recognises, parents shut other people's children out of the house to prevent them benefitting from the teaching they give their own children. Formerly crucial ritual knowledge, such as genealogies and invocations for sacrifices, would be confided in secret by a father to a chosen son.

Alasa'a's recordings for his sons share some of this confidentiality and were not intended for general circulation. As heir to his father's knowledge, Michael Kwa'ioloa has taken a difficult decision in having them published, for once privileged knowledge is made public the privilege is lost. However, Alasa'a dictated much of his historical information for purposes which may be advanced by publication, putting on record versions of events, particularly concerning land claims, which others have disputed. Both he and his opponents were also quite prepared to recite genealogical histories publicly and have them entered in the public record when their land disputes came to court (and extracts from these court records are included in this book). Besides, despite the tradition of confidentiality, Kwara'ae activists and community leaders have been compiling and comparing their neighbours' genealogies for more than thirty years, and lists of laws for even longer. More recently, they have organised programmes to map clan lands in order to resolve historical disputes over land claims and facilitate economic development.

One problem these Kwara'ae enterprises share with this book is the fact that the historical traditions of different clans so often contradict one another. It is not easy for the heirs to this knowledge to come to terms with the realisation that historical recollections or records may not be infallible but can contradict one another in good faith (as distinct from being falsified, as disputants so often accuse one another of doing). Kwara'ae men find it hard to admit that the versions passed down to them from their own forefathers could be wrong, and 'my father told me so' tends to mean 'it must be true'. For some at least, casting doubt would entail questioning the veracity of those who have become ghosts, with spiritual means of knowing the real historical truth which ancient stories are believed to reflect. Sometimes ghosts even communicate such truths directly through dreams and revelations which are taken to legitimate or elaborate on received knowledge. This epistemology has been inherited with the oral history by Christians who accept the reality and power of ancestral ghosts even though they decline to worship them.

So Alasa'a's chronicle may be received with scepticism or even hostility by some Kwara'ae readers who are close enough to him to have an interest in his stories, but not close enough for these interests to coincide with his. To them we can only say that publishing Alasa'a's words does not prove whether or not they are true, and that they will at least find some signs of alternative opinions in the book. By presenting Alasa'a's stories in parallel with other texts which not only expand on his words but also offer alternative perspectives, we hope to encourage our readers, Kwara'ae and others, to reflect that there is always a multitude of voices which have something to say about any single history.

Alasa'a's chronicle and other local histories

It is only thanks to the many such voices which have already been published as contributions to the history of Malaita and Solomon Islands that we are able to publish Alasa'a's chronicle as we have. This book follows a long list of publications which have made his island one of the best documented in Melanesia. Most of them have been written by 'whitemen' (and some women) and most present their own interpretation of history rather than the views of those they were writing about, but their voices provide an important background to much of Alasa'a's own account.

Some of the earliest authors describe their own experiences of colonialism, which include events of great significance for islanders, although with rather little insight on the islanders' perspectives, let alone into what was going on in their local communities. Colonial officers and travellers published autobiographical journals with sensational titles like Douglas Rannie's *My Adventures Among South Sea Cannibals* (1912), actually an excellent account of the nineteenth-century Queensland labour trade with perceptive observations on Malaitans and other islanders. Even books marred by the sensationalist and racist distortions current in the early colonial period may contain useful historical information, like *The Savage Solomons* by the Protectorate Commissioner of Lands, S.G.C. Knibbs (1929) and *Bride in the Solomons* by Osa Johnson (1944), illustrated by her husband's 1917 photographs, which also appear in this book.

Other important sources of both historical information and early photographs are the missions. Reports published in their journals, the South Sea Evangelical Mission's *Not In Vain* and the Anglican Melanesian Mission's *Southern Cross Log*, are particularly informative, while books include autobiographies such as *Pearls from the Pacific* by Florence Young (1925), still famous in Malaita as founder of the SSEM. Some Anglican missionaries also wrote as anthropologists, the first to research the cultures of Malaita. They produced reference works of lasting value, like Walter Ivens' *Melanesians of the Southeast Solomon Islands* (1927) on southern Malaita and *The Island Builders of the Pacific* (1930) on the Lau, north of East Kwara'ae. Although for a long time anthropology was more concerned to deny the history of Solomon Islanders by presenting their cultures as trapped in some ancient primitive state, the Malaitan interest in oral histories and genealogies does come through in some of these early works. The first detailed study to acknowledge the colonial transformation promoted by the missions came in the 1930s, with Ian Hogbin's account of the To'abaita people of north Malaita and their so-called *Experiments in Civilization* (1939).

Since then, anthropologists have researched most of the language groups of Malaita, making it the most studied province of Solomon Islands, mainly because it is the most culturally diverse and conservative. During the 1960s there was a virtual invasion of anthropologists, resulting in many publications in the 1970s and 1980s. Harold Ross wrote on the social ecology of Baegu (1973), Pierre Maranda on the religion of Lau (1970), Matthew Cooper on the religion of Langalanga (1972), and Remo Guideri on the ritual organisation of Fataleka (1980). Apart from Kwara'ae, this covered most of the culturally similar peoples of north Malaita. In the same period, Daniel de Coppet arrived to research the pre-colonial society and cosmology of 'Are'Are in south Malaita, and Hugo Zemp to study their music (eg. de Coppet & Zemp 1978).

But although these cultural studies are essential for understanding the local histories of Malaita, none of them are really situated within the historical traditions of the communities concerned, and some give hardly more attention to the published colonial history. The first major contribution to Malaitan local history came from East Kwaio, immediately to the south of Alasa'a's home district across the boundary between the northern and southern culture areas of Malaita. Here another of the 1960s arrivals, Roger Keesing, used Kwaio voices as well as colonial sources to document the colonial history of one of the most conservative communities on Malaita, as summarised in his book *Custom and Confrontation* (1992). The autobiographies of his friends 'Elota (Keesing 1978) and Jonathan Fifi'i (Fifi'i & Keesing 1989) describe from personal experience the kind of feuding history which Alasa'a's chronicle traces back several generations for his clan of Fairū, and an experience of colonial conquest far more traumatic than that of their Kwara'ae neighbours. This conquest is also the subject of *Lightning Meets the West Wind* (Keesing and Corris 1980), a book comparing Kwaio and colonial sources on the life and death of William Bell, the District Officer who subdued East Kwara'ae (as Alasa'a describes in Chapter 5), before he was killed by Kwaio warriors in 1927. The book caused a public controversy in Solomon Islands, a reminder of the relevance of local history to contemporary politics (further explored by Akin 1999).

Keesing's collaborator on this book, the historian Peter Corris, represents a parallel development in Solomon Islands studies; the use of oral history to complement documentary sources and contribute a local perspective to colonial history. This helps to make Corris' *Passage, Port and Plantation* (1973) a major source on the history of the nineteenth-century labour trade. From a contrasting perspective, Graeme Golden publishes a wealth of oral history from his subjects, *The Early European Settlers of the Solomon Islands* (1993) which complements the recollections of the islanders they dealt with (including Alasa'a's plantation employment in the 1910s).

Another anthropologist working in Kwaio, David Akin, has also made an important contribution to this book with information from his own research. Akin's analysis of Kwaio local and colonial history (n.d.) illuminates the tensions between ancestral tradition and religion on the one hand, and Christianity and colonial development on the other, which have been a major force for social change throughout Malaita during the twentieth century. The Kwaio strategy of renegotiating relationships with their ancestral ghosts represents an alternative to the Kwara'ae rejection of their ghosts in favour of Christianity, reflecting the two people's contrasting access to the centres of wealth and power in the Solomon Islands colony and state.

Alasa'a's stories of Kwara'ae origins, Christian conversions and colonial subjugation, confirmed in his concluding personal statement of allegiance to God, represent the more general Malaitan response to colonisation. This is the subject of my own research in Kwara'ae from 1979. *Tradition and Christianity* (Burt 1994a) traces the religious and social transformation of East Kwara'ae through its local and colonial history. The consequences of this transformation for life in Kwara'ae in the second half of the twentieth century are further illustrated in Michael Kwa'ioloa's autobiography, *Living Tradition* (Kwa'ioloa & Burt 1997), which stands in contrast to his father Alasa'a's experiences of a long generation before. David Gegeo and Karen Watson-Gegeo have also written on Kwara'ae culture, particularly child-rearing and family relationships, and on recent local history (e.g. 1996).

One thing which distinguishes Alasa'a's chronicle from most other Malaita or Solomon Islands histories, even the local voices of autobiographies and oral histories, is of course its presentation in the local language, which most of its readers will be unable to understand. There are some other Solomon Islands histories in local languages, like Akin's series of oral traditions published to promote literacy and cultural development in Kwaio (eg. Ma'aanamae 1993), and more with English translations, such *Six Stories of Rapu'anate* (Aihunu 1978) and *Custom Stories of the Marovo Area* (Hviding 1995). Alasa'a's chronicle has most in common with Rolf Kuschel's *Vengeance is their Reply* (part 2 1988), a volume of edited and annotated oral history in the local language and English, which chronicles the political history of the small Polynesian island of Bellona. The scarcity of such books is hardly surprising considering the small potential readership. Despite Kwara'ae suspicions to the contrary, sales of books on small local communities in the Pacific Islands, with much of the text in a language unintelligible to the vast majority of potential readers, are not likely to recover the cost of printing them. We are fortunate that British Museum Press is prepared to bear the added expense of including the Kwara'ae language texts in this book for the sake of local readers.

Editing Alasa'a's chronicle

Not only will most readers of Alasa'a's chronicle find about a quarter of the text unintelligible, but they will also find aspects of his narratives so parochial and obscure that they might be tempted to dismiss them as irrelevant to their own experience. It has been our task as editors to arouse the curiosity which most people have in the lives and cultures of others different from themselves, by interpreting the voices of Alasa'a and his relatives and neighbours, and of the foreigners who intruded into their lives. We hope we have helped their stories not only to inform Kwara'ae readers in their own history, but also to capture the imagination of other people in Solomon Islands and in countries far from the Pacific Islands.

This task has required some rearrangement of Alasa'a's dictated narratives. How many hours he actually recorded is uncertain, but this chronicle draws on five cassettes, some of which include more than one recording session. The order the recordings were made in is not always clear, and the quality is not improved by occasional fading batteries and over-recording by grandchildren who did not realise the importance of the cassettes they were playing with. Alasa'a was not attempting to compose the continuous history presented in this book, but followed a number of themes, some of which he repeated in different recordings. It has not been too difficult to edit these into chronological order, to cut out less-detailed duplicate versions of stories and genealogies, and to divide the whole into chapters which broadly reflect the themes of his narratives. Where material from one recording session adjoins another, or the sequence of the original text has been changed, this is shown by * * * (as distinct from . . . where text is omitted). In some cases this means that small amounts of significant information have been inserted from an alternative text on the same subject.

This has done little violence to Alasa'a's own historical perspectives or to the messages he was intending to convey. The more difficult editorial decisions concern what he had to say about some of his neighbours and his land. Much of Alasa'a's history is given as evidence against other people's land claims and he is not only proclaiming the seniority of his own ancestors and the truth of his own clan histories but also denouncing opponents for contesting his claims. We have cut out some stronger comments on these disputes, not to question the rights and wrongs of claims by either party but rather as a necessary attempt to avoid provoking more trouble in future. Although Alasa'a and most of the other old men who spent so much time arguing with him about land are now long dead, the disputes between them are still very much alive among their descendants.

Of course, these controversies will mean very little to most readers, and nor would most of the information with which Alasa'a supports his claims, if it were not explained and clarified. Even Kwara'ae readers may find much of the genealogical information confusing, particularly when he recited lists such as 'A begot B begot C begot D' in language which could indicate either a line of fathers and sons or a series of sons of one father. But in a society like Kwara'ae, such genealogies provide the essential social framework for history, as well as its only chronology. To convey and clarify this feature of Alasa'a's chronicle we have summarised genealogies in diagrams, and in many cases it has been possible to compare and include information from alternative sources to resolve ambiguities in Alasa'a's account. Readers who are not related to any of the ancestors concerned may not find some of the details of great interest, but if they reflect that Alasa'a remembered all this genealogical information, and more, without any written aids, it may help them to appreciate the scope of Kwara'ae oral history.

To give a visual impression of the people and places Alasa'a describes, we can draw on a rich archive of photographs, early and recent. Most photographs in this book are certainly or probably of Kwara'ae people, but only the most recent, taken by myself during the last twenty years, are from Alasa'a's own district of Kwai or East Kwara'ae. These are the ones where the origin of the photograph is not mentioned. Photographers visited Malaita from the 1900s onwards, but most of them missed the Kwai area on their tours of the east coast, or went only to the west. Of course, all these images represent their own times, mostly decades or centuries after the events they are used to illustrate here. But most are from Alasa'a's own lifetime and the earlier ones in particular represent the kinds of sights which would have informed his imagination of former times. These photos, combined with extracts from colonial documents and books, reproduced where possible in their original appearance, are intended to convey something of the wealth of historical information which exists about the island of Malaita.

Although Alasa'a's chronicle spans many centuries and ends three generation ago, it should be read as the recollections and opinions of an old man of the 1980s. His perspective, and that of the other Kwara'ae voices in this book, are those of the late twentieth century, and their words address the concerns of their own times, with particular views of how the times which came before should be reflected in the present and future. As the book goes to press, some thirteen years after Alasa'a's death, his people are in the midst of the most violent communal conflict to have afflicted them since the beginning of the colonial period; Malaita against Guadalcanal and both against the Solomon Islands state. Never has it been more important for Solomon Islanders to reflect upon their own history as they struggle to shape a very uncertain future. We hope that what Alasa'a and the other contributors to this book have to say will be of interest and value to readers in Kwara'ae, Solomon Islands and beyond.

1
Na Fulilana Fanoa 'i Malaita

'Io, nau ku ala'a sulia bubunga 'i Malaita ne'e nai ala'a isada. Daolana fanoa lō 'i Malaita, noa'a ta ngwae 'iri tuatuafia, buri ana na red si nini'a, sa Noa saunga'inia faka ma god ka kurua 'ania fanoa ne'e. Ngwae kī kira saea ne'e fasi rō fungu'a kī fa'inia rō gwa'unga kī, ka noa'a. Te'e gwa'unga'a nini'a, fungu'a nai'ari nini'a, god kurūa go'o aelana nini, fanoa nini 'i ano ta'ifau go'o 'ania kafo fūri. Kira kurū ka leleka ka sui, sa Noa go'o, 'afe nia, ulu ngela nia kī, ulu funga nia kī, kira mauri, kira ka ta'ea fanoa ne'e. Ka noa'a ta ngwae 'iri tuatua ana bubunga ne'e kī, ni'i teo 'o'o. Leleka nia ka gwa'u na'a, god ka tuatua saena fanoa 'i langi, ka lia saena fanoa nini 'i ano, ka 'uri "O reala, bubunga ne'e kī nini'a gwa'u ka teo go'o 'ani. Ma fa'uta nini'a kira ka fikulia na'a fanoa nini'a 'i Aisia? Nau ku ogā ti ngwae ke leka 'uana ti bubunga la'u."

God ka fata fuana sa Gebriel. Rō ainselo kī loboni'a: sa Maekol tua fuana keresilana ngwae ne'e saea rū ka soke, nia ka keresia. "Aia'a, Gebriel 'oe koso, koso ko dao fuana sa Bilitigao." Akalo nai na'a nari, nau ku saea birisi, birisi god. "'Oko fata 'uri fuana: god saea 'oe leka. 'Ae ngalia kwalu fū'ingwae kī, ko leka saena felofelo fūri. Fiu bubunga kī ne'e ke teo, kwaula ne'e rū 'oe." 'Unari sa Bilitigao ka dangi ofodangi ka saea, sa Haman Rosa, sa ngwane'e fa'i na'ona'o lo'oko, ka 'uri, "Sai, ainselo ne'e fa'uta ne'e naisi lisia kwa? Aigelo di'ia nia dao ka fata kulu ke lisia ta'ifau go'o." Nia tuatua, go'o aigelo koso. Sa Abarahama, sa Haman Rosa, sa Bilitigao, sa Rosa, sa Bilitirosa, to'a nai'ari nari, to'a ne'e kira tuafia fanoa nari 'i Aisia nairi'a. 'Unari kira ka lisida go'o ta'ifau, kira ka fiku ta'ifau, ka 'uri na'a "God saea sa Bilitigao ke leka." Nia ngalia kwalu fū'ingwae kī, ka leka 'uana kwalu bubunga kī.

1
The Founding of the Homeland of Malaita

Yes, I'm talking about the island of Malaita, and I'll begin talking. At the arrival at the country[1] of Malaita, no-one had lived in it since that Red Sea, when Noah built a ship and god[2] drowned the country with it. People talk as if there were two floods and two subsidings, but no. There was one subsiding, that was the flood when god drowned this island, this whole country on earth, with that water. They all drowned and then eventually just Noah, his wife, his three sons and his three daughters-in-law were alive and they revived the country. No-one was living in these islands, they were doing nothing. While they were empty and god was living in the country above, he looked at this country on earth and said "Hey, there are empty islands just lying there. How is it they're crowding this country of Asia? I want some people to go to other islands."

God spoke to Gabriel. There were two angels over there; Michael was there to write down a person who told a lie, he wrote it down. "Well Gabriel, you go down, go down for Bilitigao." That was my ghost, I'll say priest, a god priest.[3] "You say this to him: god tells you to go. You take eight clans and go in that sail-ship. There are seven islands, and the eighth one is yours." So then Bilitigao, next day in the morning, told Haman Rosa, the man who was first-born there, and he said, "Hey, that angel, how is it I didn't see him? If the angel comes and speaks let's all see him." He stayed until the angel came down. Abraham, Haman Rosa, Bilitigao, Rosa, Bilitirosa, those were the people, the people who lived in that country of Asia. So then they all saw it, they all gathered and said "God is telling Bilitigao to go." He took eight clans and went to eight islands.[4]

1 'Country' is one way of translating *fanoa*, which means a 'home' or 'habitation', or its 'inhabitants'. *Fanoa* may be a small family hamlet, a town, a clan homeland, an island, or the community living there.

2 Alasa'a uses the English word 'god' not as a personal name (*sa* God) but as if it were a generic term for the Christian deity, just as ghost (*akalo*) is for the Kwara'ae ones.

3 By the English term 'god priest', Alasa'a distinguishes Bilitigao from so-called 'devil priests' who worship their dead ancestors, referred to as 'ghosts' (*akalo*) by the Kwara'ae, but as 'devils' by the white missionaries.

4 'Eight' is a standard number for a group or batch of things, and can be as imprecise as 'dozen' in English.

The arrival

Alasa'a begins the history of Kwara'ae with the ancient ancestors who first settled the island of Malaita, about twenty-five generations ago according to his genealogies.

The ancestors of the Kwara'ae and other Solomon Islanders were among the Austronesian peoples who migrated from Southeast Asia into island Melanesia from about 3,000 years ago, according to anthropologists and prehistorians. When the Kwara'ae themselves trace their origins to Asia, they usually mean the biblical Holy Land. This distant country has been a subject of particular interest ever since their ancestors began to learn about Christianity from missionaries on the plantations of Queensland in the 1880s. The Bible soon became their most important source of world history, even for those like Alasa'a who never learned to read.

Samuel Afutana Alasa'a in 1984. Alasa'a posed for this portrait to demonstrate the ornaments worn in his younger days, as an illustration of Kwara'ae tradition.

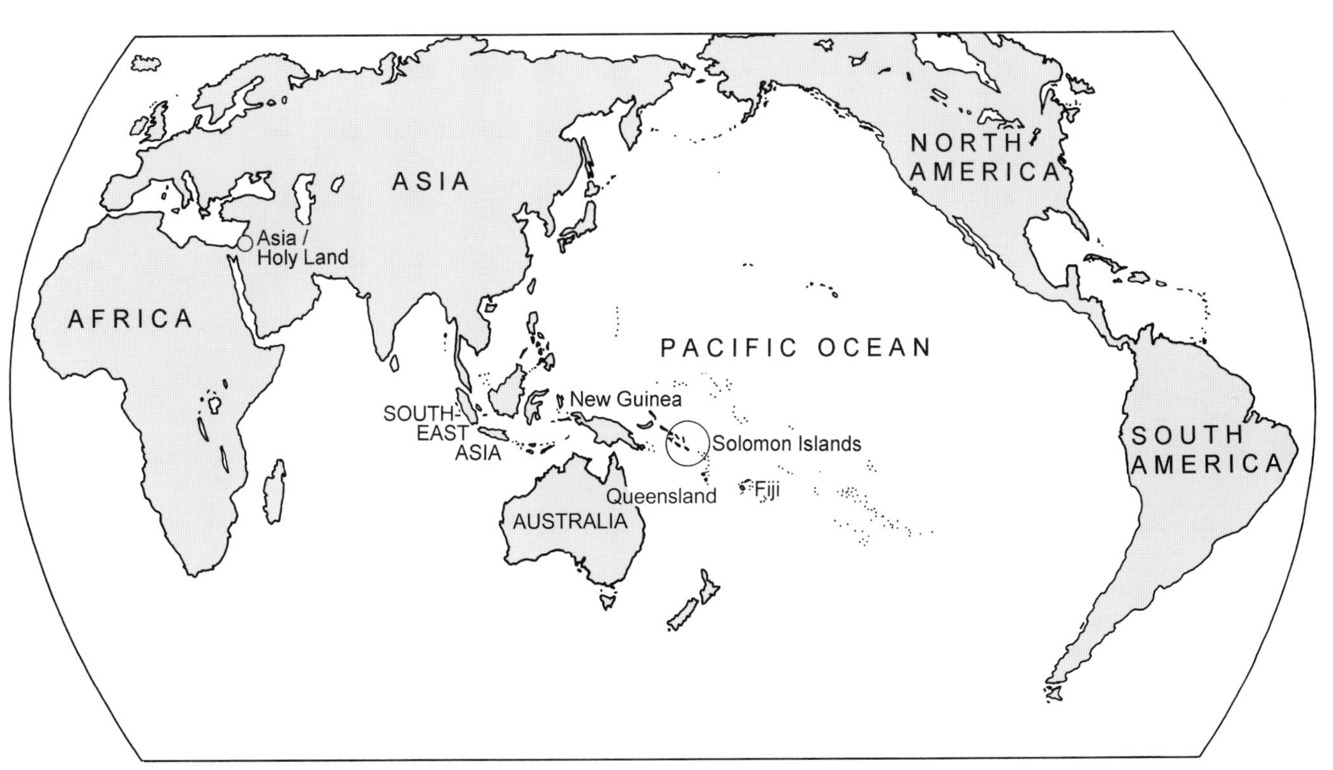

Rū ne'e ke rora, fanoa 'i Malaita nini nau ku ala'a 'i sulia, ne'e nau ku sai ana. Nau ku īa ma'i lo'oba, ita ana sa Atama ka leka ma'i ka dao ana sa Noa ana fa'i 'ego ka tata'e 'i nai'ari ana ūlu ngela nia kī. Sa Abarahama ga'a ana ma'a nia sa Noa teo kukusu a'asia latona, nia ne kaili ka siroro'a na'a, kaili ka gwā.

Aia'a 'unari, kira fi'i lisia aigelo fuiri sa Gebriel. Sa Bilitigao ka 'uri "Sali god saea nai leka ma nai liu 'i fa'i kwa? Noa'a ta ta'itala. Di'ia 'i tolo ma nai donga go'o tala 'i tolo, ma di'ia saena asi ne'e nai leka ki liu fa'uta?"

Ne'e rua lisia, oli, oli ka leka. Ūla nia ka koso ka fata 'uri, "God saea, 'oke ngalia kwalu fū'ingwae kī, ko tua sulia kwalu bongi kī, ko fikua fanga 'oe kī, ko fikua rū 'oe kī leleka ka sui, saena la'ula'u fuiri." Ne'e kira saea 'ania faka 'i na'o, ne'e saena tolo 'i Malaita kira saea 'ania felofelo, nia di'ia 'aba felofelo kī, ka di'ia 'aba la'ula'u kī. Go'o sa Bilitigao ka lisia na'a ka fata' uri ana, "'Ira ma, ta'itala fa'ua?" Sa Gebriel ka 'uri "'Oke tua sulia kwalu bongi kī, kwaula bongi sina ke sū, ta'itala 'oe ka ra'e. 'Oke ra'e saena faka ne'e, ma'a 'oe ne'e nia 'i buira, mulu leka ngalia ma'i akata'i ma'e fata'a na'i 'afe nia fa'inia." 'I Melita lokoni'a lo kira saea 'ania bubunga lo'oko, nini'a ki feoa ki saea 'ania 'i Malaita, aelana loko nau. Sa Rosa ne'e 'ingata'i ngwae, sa Bilitirosa ne'e ai sulia, nau'a ūla ngwae.

'Unari kira ka ra'efia ola lo'oko, kira ka tuafia faka lo'oko leleka ka sui, kwalu bulubulu fukiri ka tata'e ka ra'e. Kwalu bulubulu ne'e kī ne'e ki saea 'ania sa Kwalukwalikwali, sa Rosa nari satana, na bubunga lo'oko kira fa'asatā 'ania sa Rosa. Aia'a 'unari, nia ka fata 'uri, "Kaumulu ra'efia ka sui na'a, 'ae'o Bilitigao 'oke ngalia gwa'i noto to'ia ne'e, ko tua 'i māna faka ne'e. Aia'a ma'a 'oe ka ngalia akata'i ma'e fata'a ne'e ka tua 'i buira faka ne'e. 'O 'afe 'oe fa'ini'o 'i māna faka ne'e 'i ke 'olo'olo, ma'a 'oe ke tua 'i buira faka ne'e 'i ke 'olo'olo.

Lest there be mistakes, it's the country of Malaita I'm talking about, which I know of. I'm tracing it from back there, beginning with Adam and coming on to Noah, to the inundation which arose there, to his three sons. Abraham laughed at his father Noah lying curled up and deforming his genitals, that's why we're poor and we're black.

Well, so then they saw the angel Gabriel. Bilitigao said "If god says I'm to go, where am I going to? There's no path. If it was inland I'd follow the inland path but if it's by sea I'm to go, how are we going?"

It was the second sighting, he returned and went. On the third he descended and said "God says you are to bring eight clans, stay for eight days, gather your food, gather your things completely, into that cloth." That's what they called a ship formerly, which inland on Malaita they called rattan, it was like rattan leaves, like pieces of cloth.[1] Then Bilitigao saw him and said to him, "So then, which way is it?" Gabriel said "You are to stay for eight days and on the eighth day when the sun sinks, your pathway will come up. You climb into the ship, your father at the back, you all go and bring those ten sayings[2] which are with his wife." She was Melita, who they called that island after, which we twisted to call it Malaita, that's my island. Rosa was the principal man, Bilitirosa was the next one and I was the third man.[3]

So then, they climbed into the canoe, they stayed in the ship, then eventually the eight stars arose and ascended. The eight stars are why we call him Kwalukwalikwali [Eight-morning-stars], that was Rosa's name, on the island they named him Rosa. Well, so he said "You have all climbed in; Bilitigao, you take the boulder, cradling it, and sit at the front of the ship. Well, your father takes the ten sayings and sits at the back of the ship. Your wife and you at the front of the ship to be right, your father sits at the back of the ship to be right.

1 That is, ships were referred to by the cloth of their sails, which were likened to the shape of rattan leaves.

2 These were ten 'laws' (*taki*) or commandments, as explained on page 15.

3 By 'I', Alasa'a means 'my ancestor', in this case Bilitigao. The Kwara'ae commonly identify with their ancestors by referring to them in the first person.

The Bible in Kwara'ae history

The Kwara'ae often identify their history with that of the Old Testament and find many similarities between their own pre-Christian culture and that of the ancient Jews. Although Alasa'a followed the ancestral religion for the first forty or more years of his life, he would have been familiar with biblical traditions since his youth, from the preaching of his Christian relatives and neighbours (as mentioned in Chapter 4).

The story of Noah which Alasa'a refers to comes from Genesis 9:22-25. Noah's son *Ham, the father of Canaan, saw the nakedness of his father . . .* and Noah said *Cursed be Canaan; a servant of servants shall he be unto his brethren.* Alasa'a echoes the way some early white colonials used this story to justify their exploitation of black people as the descendants of Ham, the 'hewers of wood and drawers of water', 'poor' and 'black'.

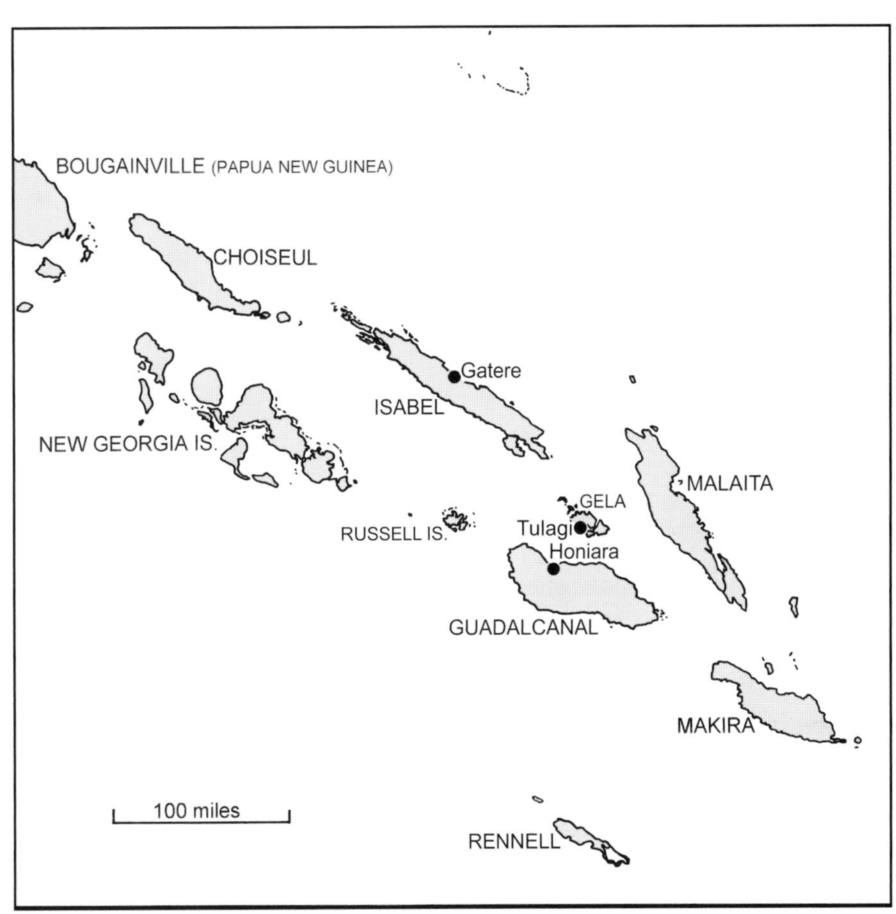

Solomon Islands, showing the main islands and some places mentioned in this book

Some say that the Kwara'ae first arrivals came by raft; others, like Alasa'a, speak of a ship or canoe. This fleet, photographed some time in the 1910s or 1920s, is from Santa Ana at the eastern end of Makira island, but the canoes look just like those once used by the sea peoples of Malaita for voyages to other islands.
From the South Sea Evangelical Mission archive

Kamu ke ra'e kamu kesi lia la'u 'i burimu'a, kamu ke lia na'a 'uana 'i māna, leleka ka dangi, faka ne'e māna teo ka teo na'a. 'Oko lisia ta bubunga ta ma bubunga nai'ari 'oke tara ana, 'oko alua ta fū'ingwae 'i ne'ana." Ta bulubulu ka no'ana, kwalu kwalikwali fuiri kī ba'ea, ta'i ba sa Kalulu ba'a teoteo ka fi'i no'ono'ona go'o. Kira leleka kira ka tara ana bubunga nai'ari, kira ka tua 'i nai'ari, ta bulubulu ka no'ana. Tata'e kira ka leka la'u sui, sa Gebriel ka dao ka "Mulu leka la'u", tala'ida ka dao ana fiuna bubunga. Tua ka fa'asia. Leleka kira ka dao 'i ne'e 'i Solomone, fiu aelana kī ne'e sui 'i ne'e 'i Solomone, boromes lan god lokoni'a, aelana nia, aelana 'isi'isi.

Loko kira fi'i 'idua olo'a nai'ari ka olo 'i Kwailafa, kira fi'i fulia 'i Su'ufau. Kira ka tua 'i Su'ufau fasi kira ke tua na'a 'ada 'i Su'ufau. Sa Gebriel ka dao ka 'uri "Noa'a, moro leka," ka fa'asida 'i 'Ailako, nia ne, nia fi'i no'ana. 'I 'Ailako ne'e babala 'i alo go'o, kaili fiku go'o ana, kira fi'i 'idu ma'i 'i Aisia 'Ainitolo, nia ne Siale go'o, kira fiku 'i ne'e. Kira ka tua 'i ne'e kira ka saunga'inia alta ne'e, birisi sa Bilitigao, kilu gwa'u nia nia teo go'o 'ana, nia teo go'o 'ana nini'ari. Aibuira sa 'Ainigao kira ka tua 'i nai'ari, kira ka etangia sukulu 'i nai'ari, sukulu ka leka 'i ne'e, ka noa'a ta kōgwata'a, ka noa'a ta kwaitaofi'anga, ka noa'a ta kwaitaranga'inga, ka noa'a ta rū. Kira etangia bubunga ne'e 'ania god. God ogā bubunga ne'e ka ra'e logo nini'ari, ka bolo fa'inia. * * *

Dao'a ne'e kira bōngia fanoa ne'e 'ania ten komand fani bibi. Kira ka bōngia 'ania rō fa'i loi kī fani rō kilu mani kī. Tai nia 'i Alasa'a, tai nia saena Masu'u. Na rō kilu mani nai'ari kī ni'i teo go'o 'ani. Ma nau ku 'ingo 'uri noa'a ta ngwae kesi soke kaumulu go'o 'uana ngalilana mani saena fanoa ne'e. Si ne'e ta ngwae kata ngalia ka tua le'a ana ma kaumulu ka noa'a. . . .

You all climb in and don't look behind you, look to the front until day and the front of the ship has come to rest. If you see an island, that's an island you can land at, you can put a clan there." A star disappeared, of the eight morning-stars which led them, one, Kalulu, came to rest and disappeared. They went on and landed at that island, they stayed there and a star disappeared. They set out and went on again, then Gabriel came and said "Go on again", leading them to the seventh island. Then he left. Eventually they arrived here at Solomon [Guadalcanal], the seven islands ended here at Solomon, god's promised land was the one over there [Malaita],[1] his island was the last island.

There they moved the landing and landed at Kwailafa and then founded Su'ufau. They stayed at Su'ufau as if they were to remain at Su'ufau. Gabriel came and said "No, go on" and left them at 'Ailako, then he disappeared. 'Ailako was just a taro [garden] shelter we gathered at, and they then moved to Asia 'Ainitolo, that is Siale, they gathered there. They stayed there and built the altar there, the priest Bilitigao, just his empty grave remains, it remains there at present. The younger brother 'Ainigao and others stayed there, they began the mission there, the mission went on there, there was no pig-baking, no cursing, no swearing, none of those things. They began the island with god. God wanted the island improved at that time, to suit him. * * *

At the arrival they secured this country with ten commandments and a stabiliser.[2] They secured it with two vipers and two pits of money. One is at Alasa'a, one is in Masu'u. These two pits of money still remain.[3] And I pray that no-one will deceive you to take the money in this country. Lest someone take it and live well from it, and you don't. . . .

1 Guadalcanal is 'here' and Malaita 'there' because Alasa'a recorded this talk at his sons' home in Honiara.

2 This 'stabiliser' (*bibi*) is the boulder which the settlers brought with them from Asia, which remains in the old shrine at Siale and is sometimes said to have writing on it. A *bibi* is a marker to hold something in place, symbolically or magically, ensuring stability and security.

3 Many people believe, or hope, that there is a hidden treasure, maybe gems or valuable minerals, somewhere on Alasa'a mountain in the Kwara'ae interior. Alasa'a speaks of this in terms of traditional valuables, the strings of shell-bead money used for ceremonial payments such as bridewealth and restitution.

The founding shrines

Once they had been guided to Malaita, the new arrivals established themselves in the mountainous interior of the empty island, at places from whence their Kwara'ae descendants now trace their origins.

Of these ancient sites, Siale is widely regarded as the founding shrine for the Kwara'ae people as a whole, especially by those, like Alasa'a, who belong to the clans which continued to be closely associated with it in recent times. 'Ainitolo nearby was the home site of the original Siale group. 'Ailako was the focal shrine for another group of clans, most strongly represented in West Kwara'ae. They would not agree with Alasa'a that 'Ailako was "just a taro [garden] shelter."

No doubt archaeological research would confirm the antiquity of these sites, but this is something the Kwara'ae chiefs are unlikely to permit.

The ten commandments

It is said that the first ancestors brought with them a set of 'laws' or rules (*taki*), the 'sayings' which Alasa'a refered to earlier. These formed the basis of the culture they established in their new home and are often likened to the biblical ten commandments.

In the 1940s Justus Jimmy Ganifiri, a Head Chief in the anti-colonial Maasina Rul movement, compiled a list of these laws as an alternative to those imposed on Malaita by the British colonial government. Ganifiri's notebook was kept by Paramount Chief Adriel Rofate'e, who continued the work of upholding Kwara'ae traditional law from the 1960s.

Ganifiri's book begins with the headings under which he lists traditional moral values and offences. These are intended to apply under both the ancestral religion and Christianity. Ganifiri himself was a senior figure in the South Sea Evangelical Mission (SSEM) and in 1965 he became General Superintendent of the newly independent South Sea Evangelical Church (SSEC).

Malaita, showing language groups and some places mentioned in this chapter.

AKWALA TAKI		*TEN LAWS*
1 FO'OÑA'A	[fo'onga'a]	*PRAYER*
2 FA'AMBUA	[fa' ābu'a]	*HOLINESS (treating as tabu)*
3 MALADALAFA'A	[maladalafa'anga]	*ACTING DISRESPECTFULLY*
4 FAI ASOA AMBU KI	[fa'i asoa ābu kī]	*HOLY (tabu) DAYS*
5 ROÑOA SULIA TO'A DOE KI	[rongoa sulia to'a doe kī]	*OBEYING IMPORTANT PEOPLE*
6 SAUÑWAEA	[saungwae'a]	*KILLING*
7 USUA	['usu'a]	*ILLICIT SEX*
8 BELIA	[bili'a]	*THEFT*
9 SURANDUA	[suradu'a]	*SLANDER*
10 KWAIOGAIÑA	[kwaiogai'anga]	*COVETOUSNESS*

From Kwara'ae document with original spelling, conventional spelling and translation added.

Iu, nau'a Samuel Alasa'a, nau ku ala'a sulia ābu'a ana akalo 'i Siale. Etangilana ma'i noa'a ta ābu'a, bore ma sukulu go'o, na siosi go'o, etangilana ma'i 'i Siale. Etangilana rū etaeta saena sukulu ne'e sa Bilitigao. Noa'a kisi kōgwata ana. Ngwae 'i Mānadari, ngwae sa Nakisi, sa Umaābu, nia lekaleka 'i Guadalcanal, ka oli ma'i ka alua sa Masuri, Tufu'iba'e. Fasi kira ke saungia, nia ka tafi ma'i ka ru'ufi nau, ngwae sukulu lala, kira ka fonea ma nia ke tafitafi. Nia ka tafi ka koso saena kilu mani loeri, lo kira 'ilia fuana fa'i loi loeri, ka tua fani mani 'i saena. Nia ka ngalia 'eo lo 'i Siale ka tua fani. Kira ka dao, kira ka ū kalikalia fa'i loi loeri, kira ka lafua gwa'i fau, ka koso saena kilu, 'unari ta ngwae liu, go'o ma'e 'eo. Tai ka liu go'o, ma'e 'eo ka siki ka to'ea. Leleka kwalu-talanga'i ma'e 'eo kī ka sui, mae ka koso saena ededea, ka ra'e ana ta bali. Na rū loeri ka ra'e ka ū ka 'ada kokolana, "Mulu leka 'aumulu, limaku aka'u na'a. 'Ae'o ngwae nia mala 'amu 'oko teo fani 'afe 'oe saena rodo ta'ena." Kira ka oli ma'i kira ka lulu, nia ka ū 'usia kilu fuiri. Kira ka lululu ka noa'a logo kira ka leka 'ada, ma nia ka buri saena kilu loeri. Leleka sa Kafiako, na aiburina sa Masuri ba, nia labua. Sa Kafiako ta'e ka lulua ka leleka nia ka dao to'ona ne'e nia ke agoago go'o saena kilu ne'e. 'Unari nia ka leka saena kilu loeri ke ra'e tafa, go'o nia ka ta'e ka fanasia 'ania sua loeri. Sui nia ka 'asi saena kilu loeri, ka ngwaka saena kilu ma noa'a ta ngwae kesi lisia ta kula ana.
* * *

Yes I, Samuel Alasa'a, I'll talk about the tabu of ghosts at Siale. In the beginning there was no tabu, but there was the mission, the church, from the beginning of Siale. In the beginning the first thing in the mission was Bilitigao. We didn't bake pigs to him. The man at Mānadari, Nakisi's man Umaābu,[1] he went to Guadalcanal, came back and begot Masuri, Tufu'iba'e. They would have killed him, he fled and came in with me, a mission man, they stopped him and he fled. He fled and went down into that money pit which they dug for the viper to stay in with the money. He took the poison of Siale and stayed with it. They came and stood around the viper, they lifted the boulder and went down into the pit, so then as a man passed, there came a poisoned arrow. As one passed a poisoned arrow flew and pierced him. Eventually after a batch of poisoned arrows, the band went down into the deserted valley and climbed the other side. The so-and-so climbed and stood and shouted his call, "Off you all go, my hand's caught you. You'll have to be a real man to sleep with your wife tonight." They returned and searched and he was guarding the pit. They searched in vain, they went off, and he remained in the pit. Eventually Kafiako, the younger brother of that Masuri, speared him. Kafiako set out and searched until he came upon him hiding in the pit. So then, he went into the pit and climbed out, then he got up and shot him with a spear. Then he fell into the pit and rotted inside the pit and no-one saw any more of him. * * *

Dao'a ne'e, kira dao 'i 'Ailako, kira ka lia talana, ifita'i 'ai ne'e sa ngwane'e 'Unigao, ka nia saena Masu'u. To'a nai'ari Aisia 'Ainitolo tu Siale, tata'e ta'ifau kira ka o'olia. Kira ka 'ilia fununa gwaurau lōri fuana mole'e 'afe lōri ka fiku 'i saena, fuana o'olilana. O'olilana ka leleleka, ta'e ma'i saena fanoa nai, kira o'olia 'i Siale, kira tua 'i Siale. Sa Siligao, sa Ofoniu, kira oli la'u 'uana 'i lo'oba 'i Solomone.

At the arrival when they arrived at 'Ailako and they looked for a place, the bole of the tree was that man 'Unigao, and he's in Masu'u.[2] Those people of Asia 'Ainitolo to Siale all set out and gardened. They dug in the posts of that shelter for the crowds of women to gather inside, for gardening. The gardening went on and on, coming into my home, they gardened at Siale and lived at Siale. Siligao and Ofoniu returned again over to Solomon [Guadalcanal].

1 That is, the ancestor of Nakisi, a senior man of the Mānadari clan, who died at a great age in 1984.

2 Unigao, who died and was worshipped at Masu'u in southern Kwara'ae, was the senior ghost in the pantheon of Kwara'ae ancestors, father of Bilitigao in Alasa'a's account.

Osifera with the staff of Bilitigao, 1983

Osifera and the staff of Bilitigao

Bilitigao's staff is said to have guided his journey into the interior of Malaita. He would stick it in the ground wherever he came to live and when it fell over he had to move off in the direction it pointed, until it led him to Siale. The staff was passed down by the priests of Siale until the last of them became Christian, and it was then inherited by Osifera.

Osifera is mentioned in Alasa'a's chronicle as a leader for land given to his ancestor by Alasa'a's ancestor (pages 33-34), and he also contributed some of the information in this book. He was a strong, sometimes militant, advocate of traditional values and a leading figure in Kwara'ae politics. But he was also a gentle, kind and humble person, in the best tradition of the Kwara'ae community leader or 'important man' (*ngwae 'inoto'a*). He died in 1997, in his late eighties.

Kwara'ae 'money'

Malaitans use strings of shell beads to exchange for goods, services, persons and land, including some things for which they now pay cash. The value of this shell-money derives from the labour required to shape, drill and polish the beads and from the scarcity of certain kinds of shell.

The Kwara'ae seldom make shell-money themselves but usually buy it from neighbouring peoples for garden produce, pigs or cash. One kind, used throughout north Malaita, is made by the sea people of Langalanga on the west coast and its major denomination is the 'ten-string' (*tafuli'ae*). Another kind, used by peoples to the south, comes from their inland neighbours in Kwaio, and includes the *bani'au,* roughly equivalent in value to the ten-string.

Formerly short lengths of shell-money, especially of the southern kind, could buy small items and many artefacts had more or less standard exchange values. But it was most important for major presentations, involving the large denominations like ten-strings. These were, and still are, essential for the bridewealth which a man's family has to present in exchange for his wife, and for restitution or compensation payments to make good offences against others, from swearing or theft to killing. For this reason shell-money is regarded as a symbol of peace, creating or restoring amicable relationships between people and communities.

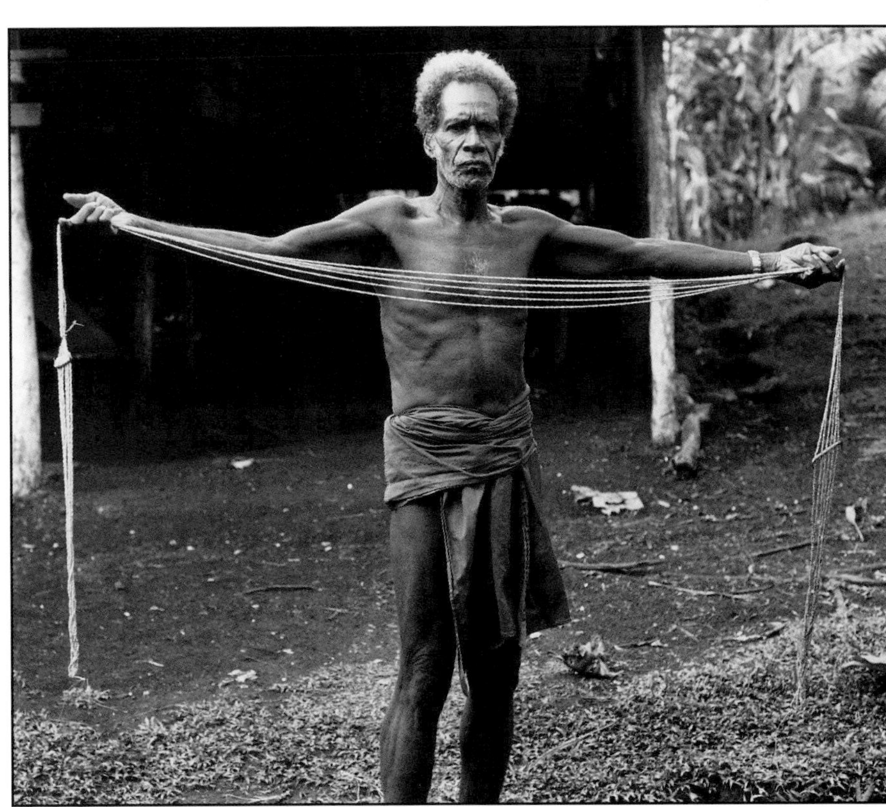

Marcus Bualimae of Tolinga displaying a bani'au *unit of the southern kind of shell-money, in 1991. Bualimae is a 'son' of Alasa'a, descended from a common ancestor four or five generations ago (as shown in the second genealogy on page 53)*

Oli ka dao ma sa Bilitigao birisi mae na'a, sa 'Ainigao ka mae na'a. Kira sukulu sade ka leleka, akalo sa Nakisi sa Siligao, kira saea 'ania sa Ifumeo. Ngwae sata 'ania mo, ngwa'i to'a fuiri lisilada ifuda meo ta'ifau go'o. Ta'e ka lisia 'olota lōri, Aisia 'Ainitolo tu Siale, ka 'uri "Kulu bolebolea kulu ke fo'ofo'osia go'o god, ngalia gwata ki kōngia lala ana birisi mae na'a." Buri'ana go'o, sa Niugao, nia 'i Faualifia, ngalia gwata ka kōngia na'a ana birisi fani ma'a nia, sa 'Ainigao. Sasadili nai atolada lala 'i nai'ari, nia go'o nai.

Aia'a, kōngia gwata ana sulina sa 'Aini, rodorodo go'o salo ne'e ka uku ta'ifau na'a, gwā ta'ifau na'a. Rodo go'o uta ka to'ona, kwanga-kwanga ka rada na'a, kauburu ka 'oi na'a. Go'o ka taka 'ania tua'a lo 'i Siale nai kwa. Kwa'i sulia rodo ka rorodo ka dangi, nia ta'e ka tafitafi ka oli 'i Otesao. Ta ngwae 'iri tua 'i to'oba. Ka kwa'i sulia asoa ne'e leleka ka rodo, ka kwa'i sulia rodo leleka ka dangi go'o, ka mū na'a. Tua'a tua ta'ifau 'i Otesao, ta ngwae 'iri oli 'ala'a, kira fiku ta'ifau 'i Otesao; 'i Mānadari ne'e 'aena go'o 'i Siale. Feraābu go'o nai rū sa Nakisi, nia go'o nai.

Kauburu mū 'unari, 'iu, sa 'Unigao nia na'a saena 'i Masu'u, 'ifita'i'ai. 'Una'ari, Toligao, ngela sa Bilitigao, birisi, nia oli 'ala'a 'uana 'i Siale. Sa Niugao oli 'ala'a 'i Siale. Sa Gaonimidi oli 'ala'a 'uana 'i Siale. Sa Bilitirosa oli 'ala'a 'uana 'i Siale. To'a kira ka oli go'o 'ala'a na'iria, ma koso ta'ifau kira ka fiku 'i Mānadari, ki saea 'ania 'i Otesao. Oli na'a, kira tabua na'a fanoa loeri. Sa Gaonimidi nini'a sa Rofa saka ana 'i Gwauna'ongi. Sa Bilitirosa nini'a ābu fa'inia fa'i lo'i, ka 'iri ara'i, daemon lokoni'a mani ana, nia saena fanoa. Sa Niugao ngwae nini 'i Kwarutasi nini'a koso ka nia 'i Faualifia. Aia, kauburu lōri ago ka leleka, god ka fa'atani aku, nia fa'asatā go'o 'ania kauburu 'Elafaudumu. Kauburu lo fa'alia 'i Siale nari go'o. Sa Siligao koso, nia 'i Mānadari, fanoa nia na'a ne'e 'i Mānadari. Sa Gaonimidi, sa Rofa ne'e ū fuana, nia na'a 'i Gwauna'ongi, ka noa'a na'a 'i Siale.

When they came back Bilitigao the priest was dead and 'Ainigao was dead. They went on with Sunday church, and Nakisi's ghost Siligao was called Red-Hair. Why was the man so named, when that group of people's hair all looked red? He got up and looked at that altar at Asia 'Ainitolo to Siale and said "You're all mad to pray to god, take a pig and let's bake it to the dead priest instead." After that Niugao, at Faualifia, took a pig and baked it to the priest and his father, 'Ainigao. The Sasidilis, that was their sacrifice there, that was.[1]

Well, he baked the pig for the bones of 'Aini and next day the clouds all gathered, it was all black. As it got dark rain fell, thunder flashed, a gale broke out. Then it scattered the family at Siale. It blew through the night and when it was day they got up and fled and returned to Otesao. No-one stayed up there. It blew through the day until night, it blew through the night until day, then broke off. The family all stayed at Otesao, no-one went back up, they all gathered at Otesao, at Mānadari which is just at the foot of Siale. That tabu-sanctum belongs to Nakisi, that's it.

So when the gale broke off, yes, 'Unigao was in Masu'u, the tree bole. So then, Toligao, son of Bilitigao the priest, returned up to Siale. Niugao went back up to Siale. Gaonimidi returned up to Siale. Bilitirosa returned up to Siale. The people returned up there and all came down gathered at Mānadari, which we call Otesao. On returning they cleared a home there. It was Gaonimidi who Rofa emerged from at Gwauna'ongi.[2] It was Bilitirosa who was tabu with the viper, he didn't marry, that diamond was used as money, it's at home.[3] Niugao was the man at Kwarutasi who went down and was at Faualifia. Well, that gale was hidden until god showed it to me, he named the gale 'Elafaudumu. That was the gale which destroyed Siale. Siligao went down, he was at Mānadari, his home was at Mānadari. Gaonimidi, Rofa stands for him, he was at Gwauna'ongi, not at Siale.

1 Alasa'a is saying this was the first sacrifice made by the ancestors of the Sasadili clan.

2 'Rofa' is Paramount Chief Adriel Rofate'e (see portrait on page 37).

3 This is another reference to the idea of hidden treasure. Some say the snake with gold or a shining diamond on its head lives on Alasa'a mountain.

The first ancestors

In 1974 Alasa'a dictated some information on the first ancestors for the records kept by the local historian Adriel Rofate'e of Gwauna'ongi.

Unigao is the first to stand before any other generation is concerned. His second name is Saungai. His brother is Bilitirosa known as a bachelor. Unigao begat Bilitigao, 'Ainigao, Fanegao, Siligao, Afelaua, Midigao, Tufuigao, Manuaha, Gaonimidi, Ariakao. These ten brothers including their father Unigao and their second father Bilitirosa this form up the 12 tribes of Siale. Unigao brought ten commandments or laws in this island. His brother Bilitirosa brought a snake with money or gold on its head. His first-born Bilitigao brought a piece of metal or iron and its still there at Ainitolo and the long grave of Bilitigao.

From English manuscript, spelling amended

The dispersal from Siale

There are many stories of how the ancestors of Kwara'ae arrived in Malaita and then dispersed from Siale to settle the lands belonging to their descendants today. Besides explaining the derivation of the Kwara'ae clans, these stories also deal with important cultural origins, such as baking pigs as sacrifices to ancestral ghosts, as in Alasa'a's account.

Andrew Gwa'italafa of Ubasi summarised incidents from a number of stories when he dictated his version in 1984.

I really come from a man called Bilitigao. At the beginning of our history he came and settled at a place called Ruafatu on Guadalcanal. Then he came on a raft and landed at a place called Su'ufau in West Kwara'ae. So after this man had settled there for a while he took off into the bush and lived in several different places. Then when he looked down towards the sea he saw it was nearby and he was afraid in case people might come after him and kill him. So he moved further up into the inland and when he reached the central inland he looked and there was no sea around him, he looked up at the hills concealing him and he started to clear a settlement there. He named that place Siale. Siale is right in the centre of Malaita.

When Bilitigao settled there he had some children and a big group who came with him. I know that I come from the line of one of his children, Umarara. He had others I don't know, but the clans which derive from Siale know which child came from which man and if he was really born of Bilitigao and his wife Miriaba. So they settled there for a long time and my grandfather told me a big gale broke everything down and they started to move away. Another story I heard is that Bilitigao killed his grandson and it was that which made the settlement at Siale split up. Yet another story I heard from my grandfather is that someone defiled the stream at Siale and that was why Bilitigao was angry and they began to split up.

While they were there they used to have one language and if I'm correct, maybe it was none other than Kwara'ae. Well, maybe when their father died and they started to spread out, one went to West Kwara'ae, one to North Malaita, one to 'Ari'ari, one to Kwaio, they began to forget their original language. My ancestor Umarara went up to 'Aimomoko, quite close to Siale, and begot the people of 'Aimomoko.

Translated from Pijin and abridged

Bilitigao's grandson

This well-known story, referred to by Gwa'italafa, was dictated by Adriel Rofate'e in 1979.

While they lived at Siale, Bilitigao lived with his sons until a big gale blew and smashed Siale, so he went down to live at a safer place, Mānadari. While living there one of his sons, Umarara, had a small child. So once Bilitigao went to bathe. Well, his hair was covered with a cloth or something and it was tabu for anyone to see. So that time he took his grandson and they went down to the water. The child sat on a stone, looked down at his grandfather Bilitigao and had a surprise: "Hey, your head, what's that?" Then he was angry, he finished bathing, came up and said "What did you ask?" "Hey, I saw your head, it's, it's really red!" So then Bilitigao, also called Red-Hair, Ifumeo, was angry and pushed his finger into the boy's head and killed him outright. Then his son Umarara was angry and didn't want to stay with him and he returned to Ruafatu. He lived there, then another time he came back to Malaita, arrived at Gwa'idala and came up, but he didn't stay at Siale. He went back to live at Anomula [Masu'u]. He died there, his burial place is there and they worship him there.

Translated from Pijin and abridged

Sa ngwane'e Munigao, nia na'a 'i Ualakwai, ka dao ka tuafia na'a fanoa nai'ari nai, sa Tafanga nari. Sa Midigao nia na'a 'i Atare, sa Maelekini na'iri'a. Sa ngwane'e Tufuigaodoe ta'e ka tuafia 'i Kwarui, ka mae ka teo 'i Kwarui. Sa Fanegao ta'e ka nia na'a 'i Fūna'aibulu, ka mae ka nia na'a 'i nai'ari, kira ka kō na'a ana 'i nai'ari. Ngwae nai'ari kī leka kwau kira na'a 'i To'abaita, nau ku kwatea na'a ai kira 'i 'Aoke, kira ka ngalia na'a. . . .

Oli ma'i, oli na'a ma'i. Sa Bilitigao nini'a Siale na'a. Sa ngwane'e Niugao faina na'iri'a, atokale na'a fuana Sasidili, ato na'a fuana sa Kwarua, ato na'a fuana 'i Fa'arau, ato na'a fuana 'i Fu'usai, nia nai, nau ku koso na'a nai. 'Unari, sa Manuafa koso ka nia na'a 'i Ra'ofai. Sa 'Afelaua korea kwalu 'afe kī ana te'e ala'anga, leka ka nia na'a 'i Kwaio, ka fulingani na'a Kwaio. Nini nia nau ku oga fasi sa O'ogau dao ma'i, kero'o ke 'inia leleka ke sui, nia ka leka saena buka 'i kira ke rita'inia saena kastomo. Aia'a, sa Iligao ra'e ka nia 'i Alasa'a fani mani lo koso saena kilufau lōri. Nia a'arai. Go'o ka lu'ia rō ngwae kī nini kera'a to'o ana rō mani kī, rō fa'i loi kī, kera'a 'iri ara'i, 'afe kira kī kata arefo 'ani'i ma kira ka lisi'i. Sa Bilitrosa, sa Iligao, sa Iligao nia 'i Fauangwafi. Nau ku toli susuburi sa ngwane'e 'Unigao nini'a sa 'Arikao. Nia ta'e ka nia saena Masu'u, ka ra'e ka nia 'i lōri 'i Tolosi. Akalo sa Niuni nini. To'a doe ne'e dao 'i ne'e ma ka sui na'a, nini'a kira fulia bubunga ne'e. Noa'a naisi liu na'a ana ta kula, nau ku liu nai soke na'a. . . .

Nia ka fa'asida 'i Su'ufau, god ne'e fa'asida. Ka lafua tua'a ne'e ka aluda 'i 'Ailako. Sa Fulaigao nini'a nia 'i Su'ufau, sa To'i ne'e ū fuana. Sa I'anigao nini'a, leka ka nia 'i Moarodo, sa tai ne'e ū fuana. Sa Manigao nini'a, leka ka nia 'i Oloda'aābu, ka alua sa Ifurere. Sa Ifunagao nini'a, leka ka nia 'i Da'i, alua Tufunigini. Dao'a saena bubunga ne'e kira alua ka sui dangalu saena limaku, nau ku daua, ne'e ki saea saena kasatomo, ne'e ta ngwae ne'e ke ngenge la'u ma ka kwa'i la'u. Fatalaku nari dao na'a 'unari. * * *

That man Munigao, he was at Ualakwai, he came and settledthat homeland, he's [the ancestor of] Tafanga. Midigao, he was at Atare, that's Maelekini. That man Tufuigaodoe set out and lived at Kwarui, he died and lies at Kwarui. Fanegao set out and was at Fūna'aibulu, he died and was there, they baked to him there. The men who went away and are now at To'abaita, I've given out theirs at 'Aoke, they've taken it.[1] . . .

Back, let's go back. Bilitigao, he was Siale. That man Niugao was the fourth, the forebear of the Sasidilis, forebear of Kwarua, forebear of the Fa'araus, forebear of the Fu'usais, who is one I'm descended from. So then, Manuafa went down and was at Ra'ofai. 'Afelaua [Wife-grabber] married eight wives by one account, he went and he was in Kwaio, he founded Kwaio. That's why I want O'ogau[2] to come here so we can pick it out and then eventually it can go in a book so they can read the tradition. Well, Iligao went up and was at Alasa'a with the money which went down into the pit in the rock. He was married. Then he forbade the two men who had the two moneys, the two vipers, they couldn't marry in case their wives took surprise if they saw it. Bilitirosa and Iligao, Iligao was at Fauangwafi. I'll set down the last-born of that man 'Unigao, who was 'Arikao. He set out and was in Masu'u, he climbed and was up at Tolosi. He's Niuni's ghost. That's the big people who arrived here finished with, that's how they founded this island. I won't go on to other parts, if I did I'd be lying. . . .

He left them at Su'ufau, god left them. He lifted the family and left them at 'Ailako. It was Fulaigao who was at Su'ufau, To'i stands for him. It was I'anagao who went and was at Moarodo, whoever stands for him. It was Manigao who went and was at Oloda'āabu, he begot Ifurere. It was Ifunagao who went and was at Da'ia and begot the Tufuniginis. The arrival in this island they put completely into my hands, I hold it and what I'm telling is in tradition, what people argue about and act on. That's where my talk comes to. * * *

1 Many Kwara'ae trace the origin of all Malaitans to Siale, and Alasa'a is saying that he explained the origins of the To'abaita people of North Malaita to them at the Malaita provincial capital of 'Aoke.

2 Clement O'ogau is a senior Kwara'ae man related to the Kwaio people to the south, whose portrait appears on page 69.

The first ancestors of Kwara’ae

Alasa’a lists some of the ancestors who dispersed from Siale after the gale, with the places they went to and some of their living representatives. The sites where they lived and died continue to mark their descendants’ claims to the land they settled until today. Compiling such information about ritual and social organisation has been an important concern of Kwara’ae political leaders for many years, as they work to unite their people as descendants of a single ancestral family and to resolve disputes over the inheritance of land.

The diagram below is a Tolinga clan version of relationships between some of the ancient ghosts said to be the ancestors of all the Kwara’ae people. Other clans might not agree which ancestors are brothers or fathers and sons to each other, and they might include other names not shown here. Some, like the historian Adriel Rofate’e, have tried to find a version of this genealogy which all major clans would agree on. But as each clan inherits its own version from its own ancestors, this may prove to be impossible.

Kwara’ae names

In Kwara’ae many names of people and places are descriptive and could be translated into English, but we have done so (in brackets) only when this is relevant to the narrative. Some people are named after personal characteristics, like the ancestor Bili’a (Dirty). Places are often named after natural features, especially trees, like ’Ainitolo (Tree-of-the-inland).

Personal names often end in *doe* (big) or *te’e* (small), when children have been named after senior relatives. Hence Samuel Alasa’a was Alasa’adoe (Alasa’a senior) in relation to his sister’s son Alasa’ate’e (Alasa’a junior). *Ko’o* at the beginning of a name implies grandparent, especially for an ancestor (although it also means grandchild). But names may be shortened by omitting *doe*, *te’e* and *Ko’o* or by dropping other syllables.

Clans and communities are named after the places where they live or derive from and identify with. Hence the first ancestors could be called the Siales (Siale kī), just as their descendants are the Kwara’ae(s).

A genealogy of the first ancestors

according to Samuel Alasa’a

In this and other genealogies, personal names are in capitals and place names in lower case.

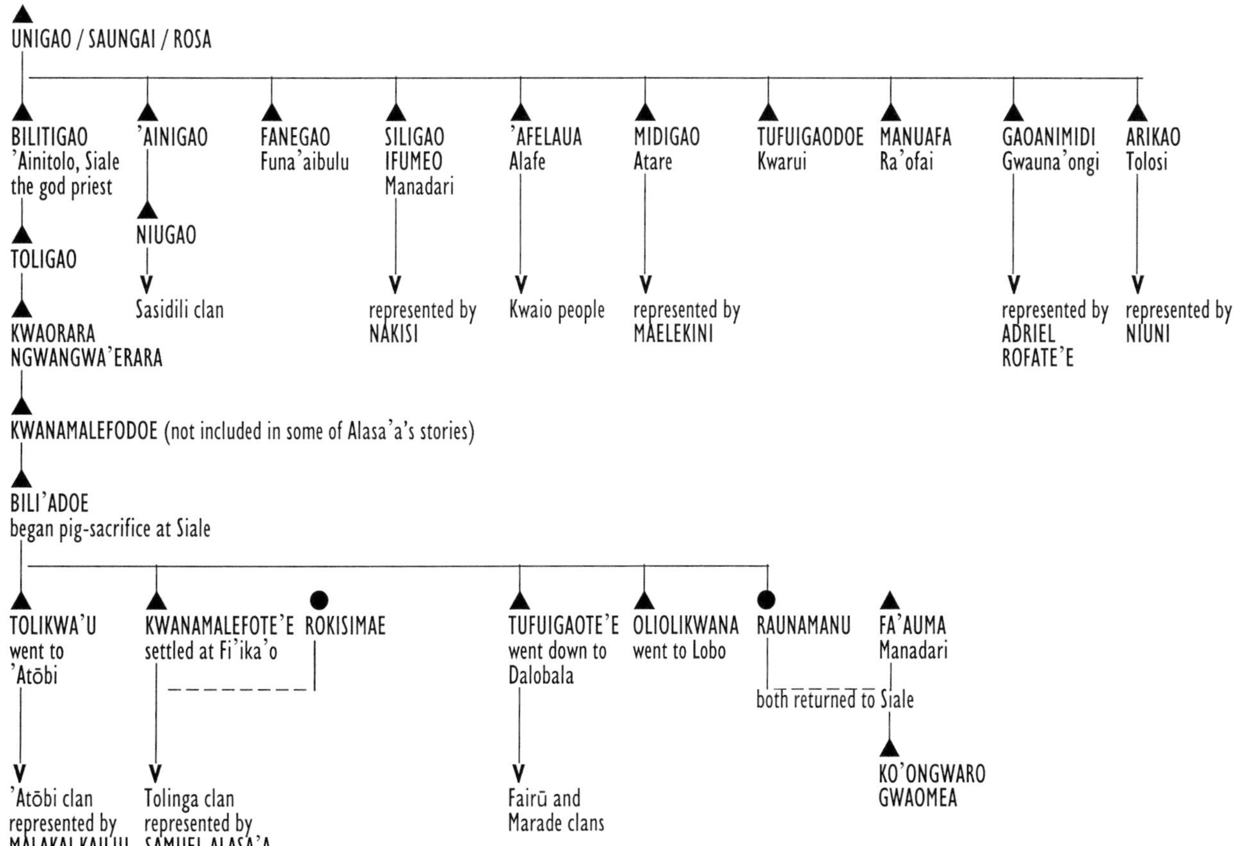

This diagram is based on Alasa’a’s stories, but he also mentions many ghosts whose relationships to one another are unclear and there are some inconsistencies between his accounts. For instance, in one story he says that Kwanamalofodoe was the son of Kwaorara and father of Bili’adoe (as shown here) but in another that he was the son of Bili’a (that is, the man shown here as Kwanamalefote’e).

Ta'ena nau ku oga nai ala'a sulia 'i Siale. Sa Bili'adoe ne'e fataābu etaeta mala kō'a ka fi'i fuli. 'Unari mala kō'a ana akalo ka fi'i fuli. Sa Bili'adoe ka kōngia tafulu gwata'anga fa'asia fera to'oto'o kī. 'Unari kōgwata'anga nia eta fuli aku 'i Siale. Leleka sa Bili'adoe ka 'uri "Nia le'a fuana kulu ke daro'ia nama kulu ke atongia feraābu kī. 'I ne'e ta ngwae ke kō nama ana feraābu nia, fuana tua'a nia." Kira ka to'o fa'i leka'a. Ta ngwae fani to'a nia kira leka tua ana ta ma'e fanoa fani fataābu kira. Ka leleka ka sui ana sa Timi Ko'oliu 'i 'Ere'ere. Ngwae kī kira leka kō to'oto'o bore kira ke olitani nama gwata kira kī 'i Siale. Iu, na etangilana kō'a ana akalo nia eta aku 'i Siale ana sa Bili'adoe.

Now I want to talk about Siale. Bili'adoe was the first tabu-speaker and only then did [sacrificial] baking begin. So only then did baking to ghosts begin. Bili'adoe baked ten pigs from each sanctum. So pig-baking originated with me at Siale. Eventually Bili'adoe said "It's best for us to share it out and divide up the tabu-sanctums. So a man will have to bake at his own tabu-sanctum, for his family." They each took a journey. Each man and his people went to live in a home with their tabu-speaker. Eventually it ended with Timi Ko'oliu at 'Ere'ere. Men went to bake separately but they had to send back their pigs to Siale. Yes, the beginning of baking to ghosts began with me at Siale with Bili'adoe.

Sa Tolikwa'u ka atongia Atōbi, sa Kailiu ū fuana. Kwanamalefodoe ne'e 'oia 'i Fi'ikao. Nau'a ne'e ū 'i fulina fani logo Tolinga. Sa Tufuigaote'e nia oia 'i Dalobala, Fairū ne'e ū 'i fuila. Sa Oliolikwana leka ka 'oia 'i Lobo nia alu ngwae fuana 'i Fiu. 'I Raunamanu nia 'afe 'i Mānadari fuana sa Fa'auma, ka oli 'uana 'i Siale, ka fi'i alua sa Ko'ongwaro, ta sata sa Gwaomea, ka fi'i alua sa Kona 'i Umulana. Kira saea 'ani Konadoe. 'I 'Ofa'ikwai nia 'afe 'i Kwauasifai, ka atokale fuana Kwaurafi. Iu, na ābu'a ka 'uri, fanoa 'i Siale ke 'asi ke teo 'ana, noa'a ta ngwae kesi sū 'uana.

Tolikwa'u set out Atōbi and Kailiu stands for him. Kwanamalefodoe settled Fi'ikao. I stand in his place, and also for Tolinga. Tufuigaote'e settled Dalobala, the Fairūs stand in his place.[1] Oliolikwana went and settled Lobo and begot men for Fiu. Raunamanu was married at Mānadari to Fa'auma, she returned to Siale and then gave birth to Ko'ongwaro, also named Gwaomea, then bore Kona at Umulana. They call him Konadoe. 'Ofa'ikwai married at Kwauasifai and was forebear of the Kwaurafis. Yes, tabu said the country of Siale would become and remain as it is and no-one can dispute it.

Na gwata fuana saena Masu'u ne'e gwata doe mala. Na kō'a 'i saena Masu'u ne'e nia 'ato liu fuana fataābu. Sulia ta'i ngalia go'o, ta fita gwata bore fataābu ke to'osi'i ta'ifau go'o 'i gwauna 'abana, nia ka ngali'i 'uana kula ana kō'a. Fataābu ke unuunulia gwata kī ke sui ka afatafangi'i ka sui mala ka fi'i do'ofi'i. . . .

Iu, na dao'a nini'a 'i Siale noa'a la'u ti ngwae ana akalo nini'a. Bore ma ngwae sukulu kī lala. Ta rū la'u, na kwalu ngwae kī 'i Malaita kira afeda saena tatafe 'ai, kira ka olo 'i Gao. Ka sui kira ka saungia kwalu fafanga kī mala, kira ka fi'i korea kwalu kini kī ma ka ngalida 'uana 'i Malaita. Iu, kira ka ta'e ma'i saena te'e iolo, iolo ne'ari nia teo ka ili'i fau'a ka dao 'i ta'ena, sa Ludalalamua.

The pig for Masu'u is a really big pig. The baking in Masu'u is very difficult for the tabu-speaker. Because in one taking, however many pigs, the tabu-speaker loads them all on his shoulder and takes them to the baking place. The tabu-speaker singes the pigs, then he cuts them open and after that he cooks them. . . .

Yes, at the arrival at Siale there were none of these men of the ghosts. There were mission men instead. Something else, eight men from Malaita floated on a raft of wood and landed in Gao.[2] Then they killed eight cannibals and then they married eight women and took them to Malaita. Yes, they set out in one canoe and this canoe remains, turned to stone until today, called Ludalamua [Load-in-enemies].

1 Alasa'a takes up the story of Fi'ika'o and Tolinga (his ancestors on the male side) in Chapter 2, and of Fairū (his ancestors on the female side) in Chapter 3.

2 Gao is at the east end of the neighbouring island of Isabel. Some say that the first Kwara'ae arrivals came to Malaita via Gao (which may account for the *gao* suffix of their names).

Shrines and sacrifice

Kwara'ae worship-places, both shrines for ancestral ghosts and Christian churches, are called *feraābu*, tabu-*fera*. A *fera* is a restricted abode or sanctum and under the traditional religion it meant the men's house of a settlement, which was tabu and forbidden to women. Men, boys and male visitors would spend much of their time there, although they also shared the ordinary dwelling house (*luma*), which was the women's domain. A tabu-sanctum or shrine, an enclosure not always including buildings, was particularly tabu to women, whose presence would defile it. It was even tabu to men who did not follow strict rules separating themselves from women.

In Alasa'a's history the sanctum of each settlement represents the men of the local clan, the group of fathers, brothers and sons whose wives and mothers come from other clans and whose daughters and sisters likewise go away to marry. He explains how the clan sacrificial system of Kwara'ae originated, as men dispersed from Siale and founded their own local tabu-sanctums. These were the shrines where their descendants kept the skulls, bones and relics of those who lived and died there, generation after generation. At these shrines the living sacrificed pigs to the ghosts of their dead, while also continuing to send pigs back 'up' to Siale and the other ancient shrines they derived from, as sacrifices to their more ancient ancestors.

Pig sacrifice is usually referred to as 'baking' (*kō*), meaning cooking in an oven of hot stones, as a sacramental meal to be eaten by the priest and men of the community. These and other dealings with important ghosts had to be conducted by a priest or 'tabu-speaker' (*fataābu*). This man was generally the eldest son of the senior male line but as he had to be specially chosen by his ancestral ghosts a younger son or a man descended from a woman of the clan might be appointed instead.

Timi Ko'oliu of Sasadili, last senior priest in Kwara'ae, in 1979. Until his death in 1984 he looked after the ancient shrine of Masu'u (Anomula) for the people of 'Ere'ere, the last major congregation in Kwara'ae to worship their ancestral ghosts.

Kwara'ae priests have never allowed photographs to be made of sacrificial rituals or the shrines where they were held. But a pig is baked for a sacrifice in the same way as for other feasts. Here Adriel Rofate'e cuts the baked pig into strips as portions for guests at a feast in 1983.

Kira ka oli ma'i 'uana 'i Lobo. 'Unari kira ka salingani akalo ana talo'a 'uana 'i Siale. Kira ka dao 'i Siale ma kira ka ri ka fata 'uri, "'Oke ngalia akalo ana ramo'a 'oe ko leka fani fa'asia fanoa nau. Sulia nau ku dao na'a fani akalo ana talo'a nau."

Na ābu'a ne'e rū 'i Siale ma toto'a ne'e rū 'i Siale. Sulia . . . kira kwatea toto'a 'ania talanga'i mani, to'onī'a ma fai tafulu, kami ka ngali'i go'o 'i Labu'isata. Ta toto'a ne'e nia 'i Anotototo. 'Unari 'afe nai'ari 'i Rokisimae ka fi'i tua ka alua go'o rō ngwae kī, go'o nia ka mae. 'I Rokisimae, fada 'ania ne'e nia rokisia mae. Na ma'a nia ne'e sa Ra'ena nia dao ka fa'aābua fanoa nau, fanoa sukulu lala. Ngwae Umulana dao ka ngalia akalo ni talo'a fu 'i Lobo, kira ka saungia ka sui, mala ābu'a fi'i saka 'i Siale. 'Unari ābu'a fi'i angwa'i to'oto'o saena fanoa ne'e.

Kaida'i ana daolana fa'i ābu 'i Siale kira fa'amāliua ngela kī. Ka leleka sina ka fane ngasi mala o'a fi'i angi ka fūlangani mola'a. Kaida'i ana ābu'a noa'a ta kini kesi ra'e 'i Siale fani ngwae dalafa kī. Di'ia 'afe ra'e nia mae na'a, noima di'ia ngwae go'o 'ana ra'e ma nia mae logo. Na ābu'a eta ma'i 'i Gao sulia kini 'i Gao ne'e 'afe ma'i fani fuana sa Oliolikwana. Nia nini'a ābu'a suasua ka teo saena fanoa 'i Siale. 'I na'o ana dao'a ne'e noa'a ta ābu suasua'anga sulia ngwae sukulu kī. 'I na'o di'ia ngwae ne'e tarasina 'usia fanoa ma nia'a na'a ne'e ramo. Di'ia ngwae ne'e akalo filia fuana kō'a ma nia'a na'a ne'e fataābu. Ngwae nai'ari akalo filia na'a ne'e ke kō akulu. Noa'a ta ngwae kesi sū 'uana fataābu'anga. * * *

'Unari ka leleleka, etana sa Bilitigao, ruana sa Toligao, ūla sa Kwaorara, faina sa Kwanamalefodoe, limana sa Bili'a, kōgwata'anga fi'i saka 'i nai'ari. Nia nai kōgwata'a ne'e saka ana nau'a. . . . Kōgwata'a fi'i saka 'i nini'ari ana sa Bili'a. Bili'a ka fi'i alua Kwanamalefote'e, mae fi'i afole 'i nai'ari. Kwanamalefote'e nini'a ra'e ka to'osia go'o Lobo 'osi'ana sa Niuni, ka laua 'afe nia, ka osia 'ania. Fanoa 'i Siale nia 'unari.

They came back to Lobo. So then, they transferred the ghost of fame to Siale. They arrived at Siale and they shouted, saying "You take your ghost of war and go away from my home. Because I have come with my ghost of fame."

Tabu belongs to Siale and death compensation belongs to Siale. Because . . . they gave death compensation of a hundred moneys, a thousand dolphin-teeth and forty pigs, we took them at Labu'isata. Another death compensation was at Anotototo. So then the woman Rokisimae bore two sons, and she died. Rokisimae means that she exchanged death. Her father was Ra'ena who came and made my country tabu, instead of a mission country. An Umulana man came and took the ghost of fame down at Lobo, they killed him, and it was then that tabu emerged at Siale. So then, tabu spread to each place in this country.

When time came for the tabu period at Siale they'd send the children to sleep. Later on, once the sun was fully risen, the gong cried to announce normality. At the time of the tabu no woman could climb up to Siale, nor undisciplined men. If a woman climbed up, she was dead and if a man climbed up, he was dead too. Tabu started from Gao because a woman from Gao came with it in marriage to Oliolikwana. That's why such an extreme tabu lies on the country of Siale. Formerly, at the arrival, there was no extreme tabu because they were mission people. Formerly, if a man protected the community, he was the warrior. If he was the man a ghost chose for the baking, it was he who was the tabu-speaker. The man who the ghost chose would bake for us. No-one could insist on being a tabu-speaker. * * *

So then, it went on and on, the first was Bilitigao, the second Toligao, the third Kwaorara, the fourth Kwanamalefodoe, the fifth Bili'a, and pig-baking then emerged. That's when pig-baking emerged with me. . . . Pig-baking emerged at that time with Bili'a. Bili'a then begot Kwanamalefote'e and feuding then broke out. It was Kwanamalefote'e who went up and overthrew Lobo because of Niuni, he seized his wife and destroyed it. The country of Siale was like that.

Tabu

When persons or things are tabu (*ābu*) this means that they are sacrosanct, or holy as the Kwara'ae usually translate it, as distinct from merely 'normal' (*mola*). They should be guarded from forbidden actions which might somehow damage or despoil them. Hence tabu separates ghosts and the men who worship them from the normality of everyday life, particularly from defilement by women.

As Alasa'a implies, tabu was a focal concept of the ancestral religion. Baking sacrifices to ghosts was a particularly tabu activity requiring special procedures to return to normality afterwards. At sacrificial festivals (*maoma*) the health and prosperity of the whole community depended on correct observance. The strict rules of tabu for Siale reflected the special powers of its ghosts and the prestige of those who worshipped them.

The ghosts of Siale

Certain ghosts brought fame (*talo'a*) through their power to promote peace and prosperity. This enabled a clan to hold great festivals which broadcast the names of the men who organised them far and wide. Ghosts who gave warrior or feuding powers (*ramo'a, mae*) protected the community but also caused fighting, incompatible with fame.

The stories of the ghost of fame and of Rokisimae, which Alasa'a only mentions in passing, were dictated in 1983 by Johnson Rara, an elder of the 'Aenakwata clan. The two experts disagree on some of the details, but both use the story to explain the origins of rituals which they witnessed in their younger days, up to the 1930s.

Alasa'a says a man of Umulana took the ghost, meaning Bulu'a of 'Aimomoko (whom he mentions again later), and that it was Kwanamalefodoe who married Rokisimae, while Rara says that the same man, Kwanangwailo, did both. Alasa'a says the father of Rokisimae, who came to live with her at Siale and was worshipped there, was Ra'ena, while Rara says he was Bili'a.

Lobo, where the ghost of fame came from, is in West Kwara'ae; as Rara says, it originated near 'Aoke, the Malaita capital.

My ghost was a man from Dalobala called Nwa'erobo and his sons were Maengali and Ko'obibi. Maengali went to live at Lobo and had sons Oleolekona, Ri'obobo and Obola'isau, and a daughter Ofanagao. Eventually everyone at Lobo died off. Ofonagao had married away to Siale and when they heard that the Lobos were finished her son Kwanangwaelo went to get the ghost from Lobo. It was a ghost for peace, to replace the ghosts of Siale.

This ghost was a bonito fish. It came up following a stream and the people of Lobo took it to worship. It wasn't a fish, it was a stone which looked like a bonito, and a tabu-speaker dreamed and went to get it from the Ta'ilalo stream near 'Aoke. They worshipped it at Lobo and they heard about it at Siale: "Oh, this is a good ghost, let's bring it here to make our home peaceful." Because it was a ghost for fame, for making big feasts for everyone to come and be happy, at the tabu-sanctum at Siale.

When Kwanangwailo reached Lobo he saw a cripple woman and asked "Where are the ghosts here?" and the cripple said "Go into the tabu-sanctum and you'll see one on the main post in front of the door. Take that one for your home at Siale." "And what are its rules?" "Its rules are that when the house has rotted you must take it outside and blow a conch-shell for when you rebuild the roof, so that everyone around hears and shuts themselves inside their houses. Eventually, when the house is finished that day you take the ghost back inside and blow the conch-shell, everyone opens their houses and it's all clear."

Then this man Kwanangwailo brought the ghost to Siale and chased all his brothers away: "Go away, I've brought us peace. I don't want fighting." He kicked over the stones they had stood up all around Siale: "I don't want fighting, let's live in peace." Well, he put this ghost at Siale, and it was he who begot us, our four lineages of Siale.

The man called Korekorea [Scratcher] had a lot of scabies. He was the ghost who people came to Siale to worship for their food-crops to be good. His other name was Bili'a [Dirty]. His daughter was Rokisimae and she married Kwanangwailo of Siale. She came from Ma'efa'iara in marriage and saw the stream in the stone. She said "Make water-ducting like ours, for us at Siale to drink and wash."

So for this stream they took wild-banana stems and joined them up to it and the tabu-speaker would say "Hey, you come, your people have arrived ready to wash their bodies for worship." So then the water would come from within the stone and follow the wild-banana until it reached the place. While they were bathing, if people such as young boys joked at the water, because it was a woman, it would go back up, weigh down the banana, and it would all collapse. Then the boys would run away, and the tabu-speaker would know, and he'd say "Alright, I'll go again" and then he'd talk to it: "Oh, the boys were joking and you went back, come back", and the water would come back again. Eventually when the worship was finished they'd say "Oh, we're going back now, you go back too", and the water would roll back until it ended up in the stone.

Translated from Pijin and abridged

Eo nai kwa'i sulia ta'ena, nau ku 'ita ku tua na'a, nau ku oga nai sasia bubunga ne'e ke teoto'o. Ta ngwae 'okesi sū la'u 'uana. 'O ngwae Siale 'oko tuatua bore, ta kauburu ne'e go'o ne fa'ali kulu. 'Oko tafi go'o kwau ko 'uri, "Ae nau ku noa'a 'i Siale." . . . Ta ngwae tuatua ka leka go'o ka "Nau ku noa'a 'i Siale," ta ngwae ka tuatua 'i ne'e ka leka go'o kwau ka "Nau ku noa'a 'i Siale." Nau ku ogā nai labunga'inia ana Siale leleka ka sui, nau ku fi'i ūa 'ania. Nau ku 'engo 'uana rū nai'ari, nia nini'a nau ku ala'a sulia ta'ena fuana nai oli nau ku fasia na'a. Nai ta'ea kastomo, bubunga kulu ka teo nama 'ana sulia fulilana 'i na'o. Ta ngwae kesi rorā ano ta ngwae, ta ngwae kesi rorā futa'anga ta ngwae. Kira rora ka leleka kira ka maelia ka sui na'a. God nia dau nau 'ua fuana. Nia loko kastomo lo'oko ka nia 'i Kwasibu.

Yes, I'll deal with the present, I started out, I've lived and I want to make this island settle down. No man should dispute it any more. If you're a Siale man, wherever you live, it was only a gale which destroyed us. You fled away and you say "Eh, I'm not from Siale." . . . A man living somewhere goes and says "I'm not from Siale," a man living here goes away and says "I'm not from Siale." I want to stake out Siale and then eventually I'll stand it up. I persist in that, that's why I'm talking about it today, so I can return and plant it. I'll revive tradition, our island must remain according to its former foundation. A man shouldn't mistake another's land, a man shouldn't mistake another's genealogy. Those who were mistaken have eventually died from it. God still holds me to it. That's why tradition is over there at Kwasibu.[1]

Nia nini'a nau ku ala'a isi fafia ala'anga nau kī 'i ta'ena. Nau ku kwa'i sulia etangilana fanoa nai nini'ia. Sukulu ne'e etangia, ka leleka akalo ka rao 'uana, ka takaloa 'ania fanoa nau. Ta'ena god tala'u ma'i saena asi ka dao ka dadā na'a. Si fatalana god, nia fata 'uri "Ngwae fīto'oku kī, na fa'i ua loeri bore nai 'idua saena asi lo'oba. Nia fito'oku, afu asi lo'oko bore nai 'idua saena tolo lōri, nai dadā, nai 'idua." Noa'a ta kōgwata'a ta'ena kulu ka lafe. * * *

That's what I'm confirming as I end my talks today. I was relating the beginning of this country of mine. The mission began it, later on ghosts reached out for it and scattered my community. Today god has come over the sea and levelled it out. As the word of god says "If men have faith in me, I'll even move the mountain into the sea. If he has faith in me, I'll even move the sea inland, I'll level it, I'll move it." There's no pig-baking today and we're pleased. * * *

1 Kwasibu is the place in East Kwara'ae where community leaders or 'chiefs' have been meeting since the 1960s to discuss the re-establishment of traditional law and culture.

Kwara'ae histories

The kind of historical stories (*'a'emae*) referred to in Alasa'a's chronicle can be sung as epic chants (*kana*). These are usually performed at night, particularly for entertainment at festivals, to a rhythmic accompaniment beaten out on a plank or with rattles or sticks tapping in the bamboo lime-bottles used for betelnut chewing.

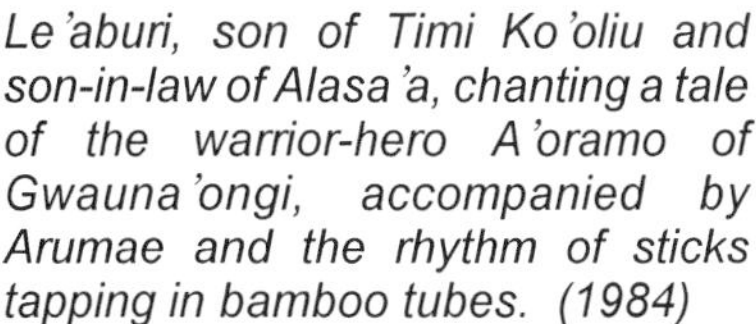

Le'aburi, son of Timi Ko'oliu and son-in-law of Alasa'a, chanting a tale of the warrior-hero A'oramo of Gwauna'ongi, accompanied by Arumae and the rhythm of sticks tapping in bamboo tubes. (1984)

A tale about killing

In 1984 Alasa'a dictated another story, in Pijin, which explains the origin of killing. It concerns a kinsman of Niufara, the warrior leader featured in Chapter 2, as well as Logomae of Rageto. Logomae was an ancestor of the 'Ailako group of clans in West Kwara'ae, a legendary supreme leader or 'lord' (*aofia*) whose title is a model for the position of 'paramount chief' in recent times.

As with many Kwara'ae stories of ancient times, famous ancestors are mentioned without much concern as to how long ago they lived. According to 'Ailako genealogies, Logomae lived about ten generations ago, but Alasa'a places this story much earlier. Of the places mentioned in the story, Kwaru is near Siale in the central inland (home of Niufara in the story on page 32) and Fiu is on the west coast. (Neither should be confused with places of the same name in Fairū in Chapter 3.)

The reference to Alasa'a's ancestral ghost Kwanamalefo hints at further stories which he did not record. Kwanamalefo was famous as a warrior and Alasa'a mentions later how he gained his wife Rokisimae as part of a reward for a killing.

Our big leaders prohibited killing, until it came to Logomae, the big leader we called a lord. He prohibited feuding and killing people. Later on a man in Kwaru, a kinsman of Niufara, Kona, lived near a big path at Merekeana, Faubaita, at a place with steep sides in a hill. There were two stones at the sides of the path and he put a spear on them to bar the path. When a man came past he would pull back his foreskin before he could go on, and if a woman or girl came along the path he'd say "Come here, I'll put my finger in your vagina before you go." If the woman said "That's tabu"; "Oh, in that case you can't come past, this spear bars the path."

Eventually there was a daughter of the lord Logomae, Ko'ongeo, who was still under-age, and her two brothers Fiulasi and Manoā. Well, their father treated his sores with salt water, he said "You all take bamboos and fill up with salt water at Fiu." They went before this man came to the path and when he came he said "I was still asleep, they've gone, that's too bad." When they came back the girl was carrying the bamboos on her back and asked her brothers "Where are you going?" Fiulasi said "We'll go up the path you came by." Then the girl said "Eh, I don't want this man to put his finger in my vagina," and Fiulasi said "Eh, he's your brother, he can't do anything even if we do go."

Then Kona barred the path, he saw the girl coming and said "Oh sister, come on, come on." Her two brothers came behind and the firstborn Fiulasi thought he'd kill him. She came near the spear and Kona said "Come, I'll hold your vagina." The girl Ko'ongio said "Eh, that's tabu man." "Even if it's tabu, I know you're tabu, come here." Fiulasi came and struck the spear, breaking it, and with an angle-club he killed him.

So fighting started with that girl. They killed him and threw him into a deep place and went to their house. Then Fiulasi said "Oh father, you prohibited fighting and I've killed a man over my sister." Then his father said "That's alright." Killing and fighting in Kwara'ae, in the central inland. Afterwards my ghost named Kwanamalefo killed ten men and just threw them into a gulley of the stream at Lasi'osi'o, in front of Siale. Then fighting began and went ahead until the government came.

Translated from Pijin and abridged

The festivals at Siale

Siale was once the centre for large and impressive sacrificial festivals, as Alasa'a's account implies. But as the Siale clans converted to Christianity a few families at a time from the 1910s onwards, these great events diminished and faded into memory. The last festival at Siale was held in the 1930s, under its last senior priest, Filo'isi of 'Aimomoko.

Aisah Osifera, a 'son' of Filo'isi, born about 1909, was old enough to remember Siale in it's heyday. In 1979 he dictated some recollections of the festivals he had witnessed there.

A panpipe dance of the kind once performed for festivals at Siale and elsewhere. (1979)

So, the festivals at Siale, there were four homelands, Siale, Fakula'e, 'Aenakwata and Tolinga. The four were born of one man, they covered Siale and got together to hold festivals at Siale.

When they brought the pigs, so, they left them there at Fuanaābu, also called 'Ainitolo. Siale is down there, 'Ainitolo is above. They made a path to the village, they cleared it and planted worship trees [*fo òka* / *Evodia*, valued for their smell]. At the village they planted many trees like that, like *dingale* [*Podocarpus*], many trees. It was place of origin, when they came from their origin in Asia they came and lived here. They put a big stone there which remains at present, a round one. Its body is unlike a stone; when the sun comes out it shines. So this was the place they put the pigs.

So next day they'd walk out from there. The pigs, they took them away. The ghost at Kwailafa would hear: "Kwailafa, take it away." So the ghost at Mānadari would hear of his pig: "Take it away." So the big ghost at Bobonaābu, Niuni is still [priest] there at present, would hear: "Take it away." So, this pig, the ghost at Saungwa would hear: "Take it away." So the ghost at Fauna'aibulu would hear: "Take it away." The ghost at Kwarui would hear: "Take it away." It was like an invocation, as they distributed them.

Eventually when it was finished, Filo'isi [the senior priest] was there alone, they'd gone out to Siale. Arriving at Siale, they put everything at Siale, all the pigs and taros, the bamboos and leaf [for cooking], until next morning when they'd cook them. That was the third day at Siale.

Now they'd call those who were staying there while they built the tabu-sanctum. So when it was finished they'd do things for it. During the tabu of Siale we would tabu coconuts, tabu pigs and fish, not eat them. Later when it was normal we could eat anything, but the festival they did now was tabu. The adult men could eat, the boys could eat too, because it was a festival. Only the sacrifices at 'Ainitolo were tabu for boys to eat. The women ate at another one, called the women's festival. It was only men and boys, it was tabu for girls and if girls ate it we would die.

Tabu covered the country while they were building the tabu-sanctum at Siale. Eventually, when the house was finished and they'd put everything inside it, when morning came they'd say "Oh, don't make a sound until we hear the gong." The tabu went on until they heard the signal, then they'd open the door and go out. The signal was a conch-trumpet, then the gong beat would reach there in 'Ere'ere, be heard all around, here in Latea, some gongs at the stones at Faureba would sound and be heard at the sea. Then they'd say "Oh, the tabu at Siale, it's the all clear, we can go outside, it's normal."

Now it was the women's festival. At the women's festival the women would eat, and the men too. They'd now go to the festival, arrive at Siale to eat. Everyone went, no-one stayed behind except a few women, a few old men. "Let's go and see Siale." Because they made the place like a town, they'd go not to eat but just to look; "Oh my word! It's no lie!" I saw it myself. Many men came. Sometimes I was frightened to approach them, frightened by the senior men with their crescent-pendants, spears and clubs. Eh, it was strange, the men looked special. When they made the water-supply down to the village it looked special too, they decorated it quite remarkably. That's why so many people came to see this water.

Translated from Pijin and abridged

The Siale shrine

The tabu-sanctum or shrine at Siale finally ceased to be used and maintained in the 1940s when its last priest, Filo'isi, joined the church after resisting Christianity for many years (see Burt 1994: 69-73, 158-9).

This plan of Siale was drawn by Adriel Rofate'e in the 1970s, from his earlier researches with Filo'isi and surveys of the site.

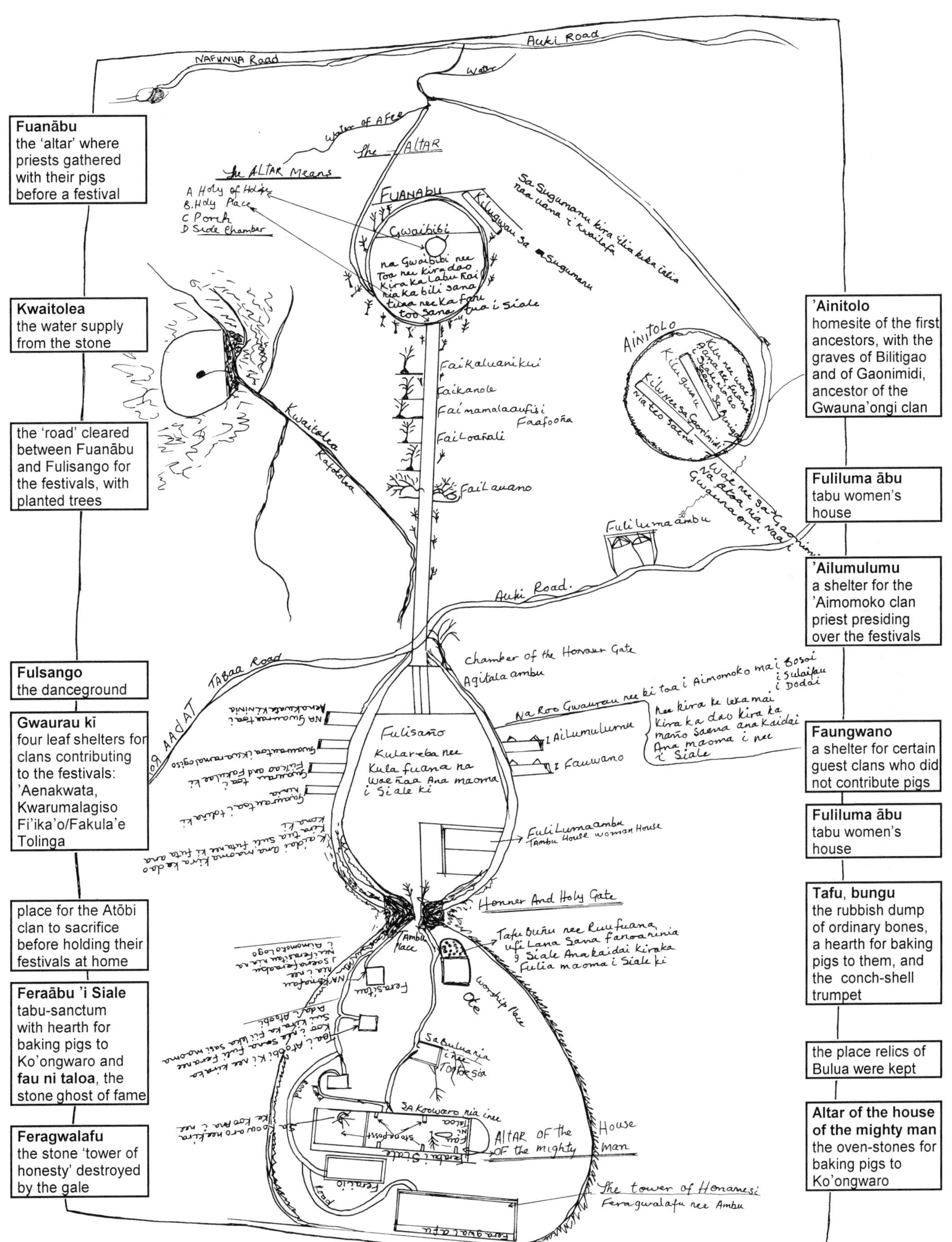

2

Na Fanoa 'i Tolinga

Nau ku oli la'u 'uana 'i Tolinga nini'a. Sa Biliate'e nai korea 'i Akabua, kini 'i Nabau, ka alua sa Asimaoma, ka alua sa Murara, ka alua sa Mumufilu, ka alua 'i Kelemaoma, ka alua 'i Angisirobo. Sa Asimaoma ne'e Tolinga na'a, sa Murara nini'a, atokale fū'ingwae sa Kwatefera, fū'ingwae sa Ngwaitingi, ne'e kira saka ana sa Felo. Nau kisi saea satada, kisi ōlobonobono la'u. Sa Murara, sa 'Ofadoe, sa 'Abuloga, sa Mumufilu, 'i Oreore'au, ma'e mae kira nari saka ana sa ngwane'e Murara. Sa Aburara nini'a sa Ngwaitingi. Sa 'Ofadoe nini'a, ngwae nini ki saea 'ania sa ngwane'e Felo, ma'e mae kira nai. Sa ngwane'e Filua, ma'e mae kira ne'e saka ana sa Murara ne'e oli na'a 'unari. Fa'i na'ona'o sa Asimaoma korea 'i Aralaua, ki saea 'ania Alisi, kini ana 'i Tufunigini. Ka alua sa Kauburu, ka alua sa ngwane'e Ko'ofo'e, ka alua sa Ra'ena, ka alua sa ngwane'e Tolimaoma, 'i Angisirobo. Sa Asimaoma ka fi'i alua sa Ko'o-fo'e, ka alua sa Ra'ena, ka alua sa Eromanu, ka alua sa Fiufanoa, nia nai. 'Unari sa Asimaoma, nia na'a 'i 'Efo, gwauna fanoa 'i Tolinga ne'e 'i 'Efo na'a, hetkwota ne'e 'i 'Efo na'a, Fi'ika'o, Ferafo'oka, 'Asifolota, Abutolingia. * * *

Nai kwa'i la'u sulia biru ne'e fonea fanoa nai 'i 'Efo. Biru ne'e fonea Otefarakau, nia to'o 'i Safunaki, ka koso ka liu 'i Kunufila, ka koso ka liu 'i Lolokale, ka koso 'i Kiluakalo, ka nia 'i saena, 'i Kunukunua ka nia 'i saena, ka saka ana fulibiru kira fasia fa'i liki ana ka dao 'i Ia'ania, ka fonea 'i Otefarakau. Nia koso sulia dodo 'i Darisingwa'u, leleka ka 'asi saena 'i Gwaro'a, na dodo ka donga toli 'i Gwaro'a, ka dao ana māna kafo ne'e ki saea 'ania 'i Mā'oro, ka ra'e 'i Nunu'ingali, ka saka 'i Faualubasi, ka ra'e lobo ana Gwarikaumanu, ka alafolo 'i nai'ari ka fonea sa Ula fa'ida. Ta bali nai, aia'a, 'a'erū, nia 'otofolo 'i nai'ari ka fonea. 'I Ususua ka nia 'i saena, 'i Gwaro'a ka nia 'i saena, 'i Kōngwae ka nia 'i saena 'aena fanoa nai nari. Ta ngwae kesi rao 'uana, nau ku kwauta ku uinimi ka sui na'a. Aia'a, biru ne'e fonea 'Aimomoko, nau ku 'iri ru'ufia 'ua. Māku nini'a ka rodo na'a, nau'a nini'a ku ngwaro na'a, ka no kutu ngela 'iri le'a fuana, ne'e nai leka 'i na'ona ma nai mae na'a ne nia ka boko na'a.

2

The Homeland of Tolinga

This is where I return again to Tolinga. Biliate'e married Akabua, a girl from Nabau, he begot Asimaoma, he begot Murara, he begot Mumufilu, he begot Kelemaoma, he begot Angisirobo. Asimaoma was Tolinga, it was Murara who begot the line of Kwatefera's clan, Ngwaitingi's clan, who emerged from Felo. I won't tell their names in ignorance. Murara, 'Ofadoe, 'Abuloga, Mumufilu, Oreore'au, that band of theirs emerged from that man Murara. It's Aburara who is Ngwaitingi's. It's 'Ofadoe who is the man we call Felo, it's their band. That man Filua, their band came from Murara and that's how it goes back. The first-born Asimaoma married Aralaua, who we call Alisi, a girl from Tufunigini. He begot Kauburu, he begot that man Ko'ofo'e, he begot Ra'ena, he begot that man Tolimaoma, and Angisirobo. Asimaoma then begot Ko'ofo'e, he begot Ra'ena, he begot Eromanu, he begot Fiuranoa, that's it. So then, Asimaoma, he was at 'Efo, the head of the Tolinga homeland was at 'Efo, the headquarters was at 'Efo, of Fi'ika'o, Ferafo'oka, 'Asifolota, Abutolingia. * * *

I'll relate more about the boundary closing off my homeland at 'Efo. The boundary closes off Otefarakau, it gets to Safunaki, descends past Kunufila, descends past Lolokale, descends to Kilakalo, it's inside, Kunukunua is inside, it emerges at the boundary-site they planted a *liki* tree at and arrives at Ia'ania, closing off Otefarakau. It goes down along the gulley at Darisingwa'u, eventually it falls into the Gwaro'a gulley, follows down the Gwaro'a and arrives at the water spout we call Mā'oro, climbs to Nunu'ingali and emerges at Faualu-basi, climbs up there to Gwarikaumanu, goes up across there and closes off Ula and the others. That's one side, the base, it crosses there and closes it off. Ususua is inside, Gwaro'a is inside, Kōngwae is inside the foot of my homeland there. No-one can reach out for them, I've already been to court and won. Well, the boundary closing off 'Aimomoko, I won't go into it yet. These eyes of mine are dark, I'm old now, if I don't have a son good enough, when I go before him and I'm dead, he's shut out.

The Tolinga clan

Chapter 2 tells the history of Alasa'a's clan of Tolinga, whose homeland near Siale their ancient ancestor settled about eight generations after the first arrival and fourteen generations before Alasa'a. Although most Tolinga people, like Alasa'a's family, have lived elsewhere in East and West Kwara'ae for many generations, they still identify with this original home and retain their claim to its lands. Formerly they maintained this connection by offering pigs to the ghosts of their ancestors who lived and died there.

But others also have ancient claims to some of these places, and the Tolinga people also have claims to lands elsewhere. Alasa'a tells the story of Tolinga and its focal 'headquarters' (*gwaunga 'i fanoa*) 'Efo to assert his seniority for this land, and then goes on to detail how certain lands in West Kwara'ae also came to be inherited by his Tolinga ancestors. (See page 35 for clarification of genealogies.)

A Kwara'ae settlement, probably the first ever photographed. Fote on the north-west coast was visited in 1906 by J.W. Beattie, a professional photographer from Hobart in Tasmania. He toured Vanuatu and Solomon Islands on the Melanesian Mission ship Southern Cross *and took over seventy photographs around the coasts of Malaita.*
From British Museum Ethnography Dept. pictorial collection

CAUTION

There are many disagreements and disputes about land histories and boundaries in Kwara'ae.

Although this book reports Alasa'a's words, it does not prove whether he is correct or not. Land boundaries are shown on the maps only to illustrate his stories and they should not be used in evidence.

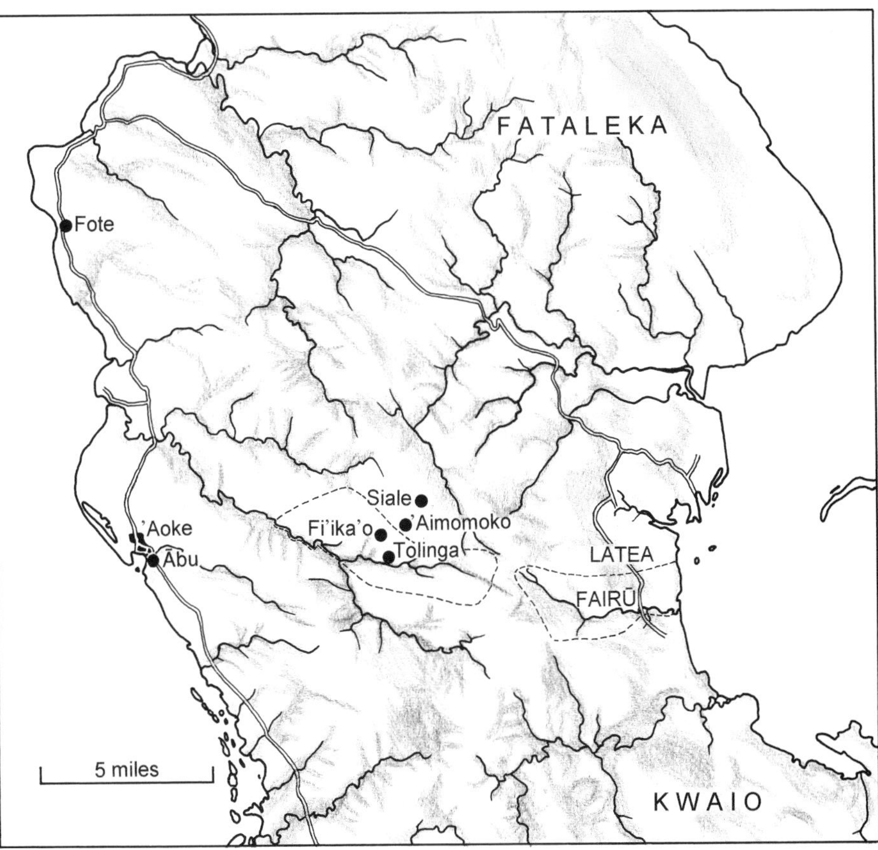

Kwara'ae, showing Alasa'a's clan lands of of Tolinga and Fairū, and some other places mentioned in this chapter. The road to East Kwara'ae was built in Alasa'a's last years, in the 1970s and 1980s.

Fanoa nai doedoe mala 'i na'o, fulimae'a sa Fo'e, fani to'a sa Kwaru, fani ngongo nia, nia 'oi 'aena fanoa nai nau ku kwatea ta bali. Biru na'o nia ra'e buira 'i 'Ainaasi, ka 'asia saena dodo 'i Gwaro'a, ka oli ka ra'e ka leleka ka saka 'i to'oba 'i Dingalelolo'a , ka alafo 'i nai'ari ka ra'e 'i Siale. Biru 'i na'o nai. Ka leleka sa Fo'e ka tua 'i Safunaki, ngongo nia ka laelae ka ra'e 'i 'Ako'ako, nia ka donga ka dao 'ofodangi, kira ka fu'usi ladea luana 'ania salu, kira ka ba'ea sulia kabara kini. 'Una'ari nia ka oli ka dao 'i Safunaki ka oli saena Kwaru mala, sa Niufarā, ka 'uri "Kwara'ae, nau ku isua gwata nai ka dao saena fanoa 'oe 'i 'Ako'ako ma kira ka taofi nau lala kwa! Kira ba'e nau sulia kabara kini kira ka saea ki ladea luaku 'ania salu." Sa Niufarā ka 'uri "'Oke olioli kwau, 'oko kwa'ia ta inamae noaima ta 'afe bore. Ko akoa 'ania ko du'ua ngongo 'oe."

Nia oli ka tolea mae nia ka kwa'ia musia fanoa 'i 'Ako'ako. 'Unari 'o'a ka angi, kira ka dao kira ka to'ea fanoa 'i Safunaki. Sa Niufarā koso ka lia ka noto na'a ka "Ō, nau ku alala go'o 'ania ta te'e 'afe, go'o te'e ngela ma ngwaefuta nau ka saungia fanoa nai ka sui, nia tolea ma'i mae." Nia ka dao ka saungidulu 'i Safunaki ka lalia to'a le'a ka tafi. Ka lala kini kī 'usia ta'i tala kī, ta ā ana ta bali tala, ta lima ana ta bali tala. Aia'a nia fi'i ūlunga 'ana nai, ka daudau ana 'o'a lōri laea dao go'o, kira ka kalifa'i saena ogana 'afe loko, lia go'o kira ka rafi saena masu'ua. Ka lalida 'i nai'ari, kira ka dudu na'a 'i Biangwa'a. Kira ka tua 'i nai'ari, ka lalida 'i nai'ari, akalo nai sa Asimaoma ka ra'e na'a. Ka lisida, ana ma'e mae le'a nini sa Ruale ma sa Lebekwao fa'ida, ka 'uri "Sē, ngwae kī logo funi re, moro oli ma'i fuaku," olita'inida 'uana 'i 'Efo. Kira ka dudu 'i 'Efo, mae ka fuli fafia sa Niufara. Sa Ko'obulu'a ka 'afia fani 'ai nai'ari lo ka to'osia gwa'i bibi lo ka teo go'o ana, olofana sulufau 'i 'Efo, buira luma sa Asimaoma.

My homeland was much bigger formerly, when Fo'e's feud with the people in Kwaru over his boar broke off the base of my home and I gave away one side. The former boundary climbed behind 'Ainaasi, fell into the Gwaro'a gully, came back climbing until it emerged up there at Dingalelolo'a, went up across there and climbed to Siale. That's the former boundary. Later on Fo'e was living at Safunaki and his boar ran off and climbed to 'Ako'ako, he followed and arrived in the morning and they threatened to stab his neck with a spear, they directed him to the women's latrine.[1] So then he went back to Safunaki and right into Kwaru, to Niufara, and said "Hey there, I pursued my pig and arrived at your home at 'Ako'ako but they cursed me! They directed me to the women's latrine and said they'd stab my neck with a spear." Niufara said "Go back and strike down an orphan or even a woman. Shout that you're paying back for your boar."

He returned bearing death and wiped out the community at 'Ako'ako. So then the gong cried and they came and carved up the community at Safunaki. Nuifarā came down and looked, dumbfounded: "Oh, I just allowed for a woman or a child, and my kinsman has killed my community off, he's carried death." He came and killed them at Safunaki and chased the fleeing survivors. He tied women to bar the paths, a foot on one side of the path, a hand on the other side of the path. Well, he stood them up, he sounded a gong and came running, they glanced into the woman's belly, looked and diverted into the forest. He chased them there and they retreated to Biangwa'a. They stayed there, he pursued them there, and my ghost Asimaoma came up. He looked at them, the band of survivors of Ruale, Lebekwao and the others,[2] and said "Hey, you men there, come back with me," and returned with them to 'Efo. They settled at 'Efo and a feud began with Niufara. Ko'obulu'a helped with magic and threw down the stabiliser which still lies under the stone wall at 'Efo, behind Asimaoma's house.

1 The 'Ako'ako people had already killed and eaten the pig, as Ko'ofoe could tell by the smell of meat.

2 Ruale and Lebekwao of Fakula'e are the survivors' descendants, Alasa'a's contemporaries, to whom this story is partly directed.

Ko'ofo'e and Asimaoma

Alasa'a tells the story of Ko'ofo'e's feud with Niufara of Kwaru to explain his claim to seniority for the land of Fi'ika'o. By his account, Fi'ika'o was first settled by his ancestor Kwanamalefodoe (see page 21) as part of the original country of Tolinga (more correctly known as 'Efo). (The Kwaru in this story, as on page 27, is a place in the central inland, not to be confused with the Kwaru near the east coast.)

Alasa'a's concern for Fi'ika'o stems from a disagreement with the Fakula'e clan, and he relates how their ancestor Ko'ofo'e was given refuge at Fi'ika'o by his own ancestor Asimoamadoe. Among other differences, Alasa'a says Ko'ofo'e was a son of Asimaomadoe, while a Fakula'e genealogy gives them as brothers.

In 1987 Michael Kwa'ioloa dictated further details of what his father Alasa'a told him about the story of Asimaoma and the refugees at Fi'ika'o. Like his father, Kwa'ioloa uses the story to explain their relationships with other people of the present day, in particular Aisah Osifera, descendant of Bulua and representative of the 'Aimomoko clan, who lived at Fi'ika'o for many years.

Because Asimaoma kept the enemies of Niufara, Niufara came and attacked them at 'Efo, my place. They came and really hurt my group at 'Efo, killed them too, and at present if you go into this tabu-sanctum of mine, my village, there lies a group of skulls and bones of people they killed, without regard to me. They've remained there until the present. For that Bulua, Osifera's ghost, took a stone we call a *bibi* [stabiliser] and he *bibi* upon it [stabilised it]. It means he cooled it down, quenched the anger, the fierce anger of that man Niufara, and he stopped killing that group of theirs.

This *bibi*, we call it a hog-stone [*fauboso*, as used for cooking pig in a stone oven], a black stone which you usually find in streams. And this hog-stone remains until today in the sanctum site at 'Efo. And when you see this *bibi* it means that there was the house of my ghost Asimaoma, it's behind it.

Gwaunakwata, the sanctum which Asimaoma cut out for them, was a very steep place which was not easy for people to get round. Any direction was difficult, because there was a river far below, the Fiu river, at Gwaro'a gulley, which is very steep. That's why he kept them there. But they couldn't stay there for ever, because it was not a convenient place for making feasts and festivals and weddings and things. Some of the Fakula'es stayed, but for most of them my ghost Asimaoma cut out some more sanctums nearby in Tolinga land at Fi'ika'o.

Before he made the new settlements he thought of something: "Eh, I must do something to defend them, so it won't be easy for people to come and attack them again." That's why he cleared the forest for a big pond, dug out the mud and made a very big pond at Fi'ika'o. When he cleared it he took the frogs we call *'iki'iki*, the small ones with long legs which make a noise like 'iki'iki'iki. This kind of frog cries and makes a lot of noise when happy, but if a man comes and it sees him or the ground shakes, all of them, even if there are hundreds or thousands of them, they all stop crying. From that, he thought it was one way to know that the enemies of Ko'ofo'e were coming to the sanctum. So he put the frogs there and they remain there until the present, at Fi'ika'o, where Osifera lives.

I was sorry for my people who were killed for the sake of these Fakula'e people, Ko'ofo'e and the others. Because with us, formerly, if people killed them like that, you must repay them. And Osifera's ghost, this man Bulua, he asked Asimaoma to compensate [*totoa*] them because, he said, "Oh, it was you who asked these people to come and live with you, and they killed my people as well as yours. So you must compensate me, because I helped you by fighting for you. And I won with you, so you must compensate for the lives of your people who died, and you must reward me too." So for this, some pieces of my land at Tolinga were also given by Asimaoma to the ghost of this man Osifera. So Osifera has some parts of Tolinga land, because they compensated him too.

Translated from Pijin and abridged.

Aia'a, Gwagwalukona ka 'afia nau'a ana sa Faneasi, leleka mae ka oifafia to'a nai'ari, nia ka aluda 'i 'Efo, ka koso ka 'ilia 'i Fi'ika'o, ka buringa'inida 'i Fi'ika'o, ka saungani fanoa 'i Gwaunkwata, ka fa'amaurida. Nia ne sa Lebekwao, sa Basia . . . nau ku fa'amaurida 'i saena fanoa nau. Kira'a ne'e Safunaki lala, kira'a ne'e Kunufila lala, kira'a ne'e Lolokale lala, kira'a ne'e Kunukunua lala, kira'a ne'e Biangwa'a lala, kira'a ne'e Kiluakalo lala. Fa'i bō nai'ari ka fone kaimili to'oto'o, nau'a ne'e 'i 'Efo na'a, nau ne'e 'i Fi'ika'o na'a, nau ne'e Fera'ere na'a, nau ne'e fanoa nini kira saea 'ania 'i Gwauna-kwata. Fanoa nau kī lala nai, 'i Tarafi, Ferafo'oka, 'i Tolinga, sa Bili'a teo na'a ana kira saea 'ania 'i Abutolingia. Du'ungana ne'e nia ngwaro na'a, ka 'idi'idila 'ania fata ma'udi'a, ka 'idi'idila 'ania kauburu, sa Asimaoma ka koso ka sasia fera fuada 'i nai'ari. 'I 'Asifolota go'o nari, no kisi tolingia go'o nini'a ki saea 'ania Abutolingia nini'a kamu ke saesaea 'ania Tolinga fasi nau 'i Tolinga, nau ngwae 'i 'Efo lala ne, gwauna fanoa nau ne'e 'i Efo, 'i Fi'ika'o nau ku gonia go'o to'a nai'ari ana.

Mae ka 'oi nau ku 'idua biru nai na 'Ainaoasi rū sa ngwane'e Osifera. Fūnangali rū sa Osifera, Gwa'inono'o rū sa Osifera, 'Aikini rū sa Osifera, sibialaen ka koso go'o sulia 'i Ata'ae, fonea na'a nai, nau ku toto 'ania bali nai'ari fuana. Anoābu nau ku toto 'ania rū sa Faneasi, nia dao ka lisia ka sui na'a ka keresia fuana ngela nia kī, nia ne ka fa'alia ta bali aku. Du'ungana sa Lebekwao fa'ida atokale'a kira ana sa Ko'ofo'e, nia ka kwate nau ku kwatea fanoa nai ka oli ka dokodoko. Tuatua kira kesi idu, Ata'ae ne'e rū nai go'o, Fuli'ere ne'e rū nai go'o, fanoa ne'e ki saea 'ania 'i Fo'a ne'e fanoa nai go'o. . . . Nau ku maemae, ma ngwa'i ngela nau kira ū na'a fuana 'i Fi'ika'o fa'inia 'i Efo saena ano 'i Tolinga. Nia nai nau ku ala'a kwau sulia ana rodo ne'e fuana ngela nau kī ma ko'o nau kī ke rongoa. . . .

Suli'ana nau'a go'o ne'e nau ku gonia Sirefe. Itana mae anai kira'a, sa Kalua sufia bebena ngwa'i kini 'i Rofa, mae ka fuli ana ka leka 'ania kaili 'i tolo. Leleka ka 'oi fa'asia, nau ku foneda. Aia'a, ruana sa Filua ka du'ua logo, ka sufia ngwa'i kini 'i Sirefe, mae ka fuli saea kira ka tafi logo fa'asia. Nau ku tua nama 'aku fuana, fulifanoa 'i Sirefe ne'e rū nau. Fataābu'a 'i Sirefe ne'e nau'a go'o.

Well, Gwagwalukona surrounds me, it's Faneasi's, eventually a feud enveloped those people, he put them at 'Efo, he went down and dug out Fi'ika'o and isolated them at Fi'ika'o, built a home at Gwaunakwata and saved them. That's how Lebekwao and Basia . . . I saved them in my home. They're from Safunaki, they're from Kunufilia, they're from Lolokale, they're from Kunukunua, they're from Biangawa'a, they're from Kiluakalo. That boundary closes off each of us, I am at 'Efo, I am at Fi'ika'o, I am at Fera'ere, I am that home they call Gwaunakwata. Those are my homes, Tarafi, Ferafo'oka, Tolinga, Bili'a lies at where they call Abutolingia. Because when he was old he was fed up with strong words, fed up with storms, Asimaoma went down and made a sanctum for them there. That was at 'Asifolota, they didn't distribute it so they called it Abutolingia [Undistributed], so you all call it Tolinga as if I was of Tolinga, but I'm a man of 'Efo, my headquarters is at 'Efo, and at Fi'ika'o I safeguarded those people.

When the feud broke off I moved my boundary, and 'Ainaoasi belongs to that man Osifera. Fūnangali belongs to Osifera, Gwa'inono'o belongs to Osifera, 'Aikini belongs to Osifera, the boundary goes along the Ata'ae, closing it off, and I compensated him with that side. Anoābu I compensated Faneasi with for something, he came and when he'd seen it he wrote it for his children, which damaged my interests. Because Lebekwao and the descendants of Ko'ofo'e made me give away my home, it was reduced. They stayed, wouldn't move, Ata'ae is mine, Fuli'ere belongs to me, the home we call Fo'a is my home. . . . When I'm dead my children will stand for Fi'ika'o and 'Efo in Tolinga land. That's why I'm speaking out about it tonight for my children and grandchildren to hear. . . .

Because it was I who safeguarded Sirefe. At the start of a feud with them, Kalua shaved the pubes of a group of girls at Rofa, a feud began and went on with us inland. Eventually it broke off, I stopped it. Well, secondly Filua repaid it and shaved a group of girls at Sirefe, a feud began and they fled from it too. I had to stay, I did, the home-site at Sirefe belonged to me. The tabu-speaking of Sirefe was mine.

Genealogy of Tolinga and Fakula'e
according to Samuel Alasa'a

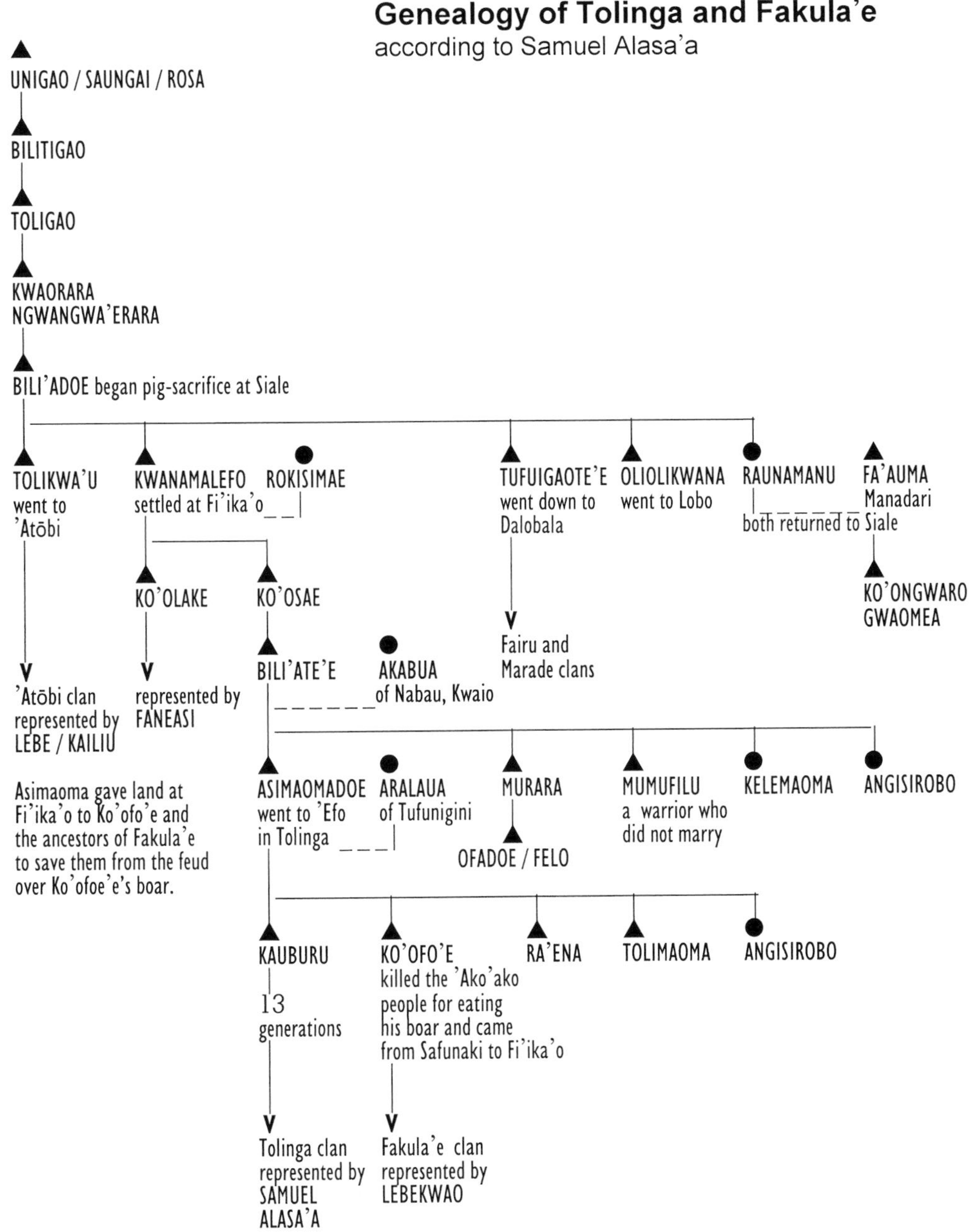

The feuds at Sirefe

Alasa'a refers briefly to two stories about Sirefe to assert his own ancient claim to the place, its home-site and priesthood, and hence its land.

According to the first story, when Kalua of Sirefe shaved the pubes of the Rofa girls they felt publicly shamed (as unmarried girls wore no pubic covering). So they killed themselves, leading their menfolk to seek vengeance.

Michael Kwa'ioloa tells the story of how this all began.

One time a man called Laumalefo, with Garī'a, arranged for a pudding-feast called a *suifa*. Then the man called Kalua also came to the *siufa*. So then, when they all fell to work on the mash in the bowl, Kalua pounded the ground with the pounder and also pounded with it in the mash. So someone saw him. So then, a man banged the pounder on Kalua's head. He stayed on and they watched the chanting in the night. Eventually when the chanting was most absorbing, Kalua burnt his dark-leaf [magical *Hedyotis* leaf] and sent all the men to sleep, and the women, then Kalua went into the girls' house and shaved the eight chosen girls who they'd invited to carry the coconuts and harvest the taro for the pudding-feast. So then day came and men, children and women arose and uncovered the stone-oven of cream-pudding. They uncovered it but the eight girls wouldn't come out because they were ashamed, they awoke and saw that Kalua had shaved one side of their vaginas. Then a women who saw them made it known. Then a feud began over what Kalua had done.
Translated from Kwara'ae

Aia'a, 'unari sa ngwane'e Fauala, sa Faurara, kira ka ragia fa'i mala'o ki saea 'ania fa'i kwalo, olofana 'i 'Aiketa. Kira ka bilia kira ka tafi fani, saka 'i Komenakinaki kira ka saka na'a to'ona, sa Bulu'a nia daudaro'o go'o nai. Kira ka tafi fani ka leleka kera'a ka ra'e fani 'i Sirefe,'una'ari kwaisufi'anga ra'e go'o sa Bulu'a ka "Rō fau kī ne kira ngalia bae kira ka tafi ka liu na'a toli." Kira dau ani 'ua kera'a ka koso saena 'i Gwaro'a kira ka ra'e to'oba 'i Sirefe, mae ka dao 'i nai'ari ka bubuta 'i nai'ari ka kwa'idulu 'i nai'ari.

Nau'a go'o, nau'a go'o, fuana 'i kira'a, noa'a kira kesi firi ana ta kula ana kula nau kī. Bali kira ne'e Sirefe na'a, bali kira ne'e Lofolofo na'a, bali kira ne'e Ferafila na'a, noa'a kira kesi rao la'u to'ona bali nau, biru fone kaili na'a. Fatalaku nai sulia fanoa nau . . . Nau ku 'aila 'ania kula ana fanoa nau, ngwae tua ana ke o'o go'o 'ana, ngwae ka tau ka tua fa'inau. Nau kusi fonea la'u fa'asia ta ngwae, fatalaku na'a nai. * * *

Ta'ena, nau'a nini'a nai ala'a, ngwae kira fu'usi soke ana, ki saea 'ania sa Alasa'a. Nau ngwae 'i Siale. Nai kwa'i sulia 'a'emae nai go'o nini'a, ka leleka ka dao ana nau'a. Ana saena agi rodo ne'e to'olana na'a ne'e nau ku tua nini'a, ka leka ngwae ka kaubarea fanoa 'i Tolinga, nau'a na'a ne'e nai kwauta ngela ne'e kī ka noa'a. Fatalaku na'a nari, ma nau ki 'īa na'a ne. Sa Bilitigao ne'e ngwae etangia na'a fanoa 'i Siale. Nia ka mae, ka nia 'i 'Ainitolo, kilu gwa'u nia teo, rō tafanga 'afu kī, ūla 'aba'aba ka teo go'o 'ana nini'ari. Ngwae ngenge nau ke leka lisia akalo nai ne'e fulia fanoa ne'e fuana nau'a. Ma nia ngwae sukulu lala, noa'a kira 'iri kō ana, ma nia teo fani gwa'i fau, na ma'e tōtō nai na'a nai saena fanoa 'i Siale. Aia'a, nau ki 'īa na'a nai.

Sa Bilitigao ne'e alua sa Toligao, sa Toligao ne'e alua sa Kwaorara, ne'e kira saea 'ania sa Ngwangwa'erara. Ka noa'a ta 'Umarara 'i Siale, 'Umarara kī rū sa Nakisi lala, nau'a ne'e sa Ngwangwa'erara lala, ma sa Tolikwao lala'u. Aia'a 'iniari, kōgwata'a etangia 'i nai'ari ana sa Ngwangwa'erara. Sa Bili'a ne'e sa Kwaorara alua, Kwaorara alua sa Bili'a, sa Bili'a ka lafua ma'a nia, ka etangia kōgwata'a na'i saena fu'a 'i Siale, nau ku saea fuana kaumulu ke rongoa. Nia ka kōgwata ka leleka ka dangulua, sa Bili'a ka alua sa Tolikwa'o, fa'i na'ona'o nia 'i Atōbi, sa [Gwa]Lebe ū fuana.

Well, so those men Fauala and Faurara, they stripped the bark of a *mala'o* tree, what we call a rope, below 'Aiketa. They stole it, fled with it, came out at Komenakinaki, they got there and Bulu'a caught them both. They fled with it and eventually climbed with it to Sirefe, and so the threat went up and Bulu'a said "Two of them took the bark and fled on down." They were still holding it as they went down into Gwaro'a and climbed up to Sirefe, the band arrived there, assembled there and struck them there.

It's me, it's me, so then, they can't claim any part of my places. Their side was Sirefe, their side was Lofolofo, their side was Ferafila, they can't reach out to my side, the boundary closes us off. That's my talk about my homeland . . . I don't want part of my home with a man living in it and gardening in it, a man from afar living with me. I haven't closed it off from anyone, that's what I'm saying. * * *

Today, it's me who's talking, the man they allege is lying, called Alasa'a. I'm a man of Siale. I'll relate this tale of mine, going on until it reaches myself. At this hour of the night, it's who it belongs to that I'm on about, and later if someone dispossesses the community of Tolinga, it's I who'll go to court, not the boys. That's what I say, and now I'll trace it out. Bilitigao was the man who began the country of Siale. He died and he's at 'Ainitolo, his empty grave lies there, two full fathoms and an arm-length long, it lies there at present. The man who argues this with me can go and see my ghost who founded this country for me. And he was a mission man, they didn't bake to him, and he lies with a stone, my marker in the country of Siale. Well, now I'll trace it out.

Bilitigao begot Toligao, Toligao begot Kwaorara, who they called Ngwangwa'erara. There's no 'Umarara at Siale, the 'Umararas belong to Nakisi, I have Ngwangwa'erara and Tolikwao instead. Well so then, pig-baking began there with Ngwangwa'erara. It's Bili'a who Kwaorara begot, Kwaorara begot Bili'a, Bili'a raised up his father and began pig-baking at the hearth at Siale, I'm saying it for you all to hear. He baked pigs until it was dropped, Bili'a begot Tolikwa'o, the senior one, he was at Atōbi, [Gwa]Lebe stands for him.

The feud over the stolen bark

The bark of the *malao* tree (*Trichospermum*) has many uses, including making rope from the saplings and boards from the full-grown tree. The story referred to by Alasa'a was narrated by Adriel Rofate'e of Gwauna'ongi in 1991, as an example of how formerly men would proclaim bans to protect resources such as this, and the consequences of disobeying them. Offences against such proclamations are a common cause of killing and feuds in Kwara'ae history.

This story involves the famous warrior ghost of Gwauna'ongi, 'Aramae (also known as 'Aoramo). The man at Okwala was Bulu'a, who put a stop to this feud as he did to Asimaomadoe's feud with Niufara.

Adriel Rofate'e Toemanu of Gwauna'ongi, Paramount Chief in the movement to reinstate Kwara'ae traditional culture, in his office in 1983. Rofate'e is an authority on Kwara'ae history and culture and a major source of information for the research on which this book is based.

This bark-tree was prohibited by 'Aramae, he told people "I'm prohibiting this bark-tree, it's for me to strip the bark off so I can make my shield from it." When he'd prohibited it everybody heard about it. So it was that two men from Sirefe heard about that prohibited bark-tree in the country of Gwauna'ongi, then they said "That man's a proud one; we'll go and see about that bark-tree of his." So they went and stripped it off and then they took the tree bark and went off with it, they went along past Sisigwata and Okwala and it got dark. They dragged it and a man living at Okwala heard the tree bark sliding and said "Hey, who's that?" He looked down and what his two men were doing was dragging the tree bark which they'd stripped and gone off with. He said "Oh, it's those two men from Sirefe, they're taking the tree bark which was dedicated in the community at Faureba" [in Gwauna'ongi]. But he didn't say anything to them and the two of them didn't see him.

Some time later the family living over at Lifulifula, which is in Faureba, saw that the bark-tree was wilted and fading. "Hey, what's that? That bark-tree's dead." Going down, they came and looked at it. "Oh, the tree bark you dedicated isn't there, they've stolen it, someone's stripped it." So then, the senior man at Okwala heard about it and said "Oh kinsmen, I saw those two men go past with it, they passed my home here in the evening." So he said "Who were they?" "Oh, it was the two men from Sirefe."

That was when the feud began. They went across to Sirefe, 'Aramae came along with his band, they arrived and attacked and fought over that bark-tree. They beat them up, a fight was fought, they struck them as they ran and 'Aramae and his band fought along after them. So eventually they arrived at Okwala and the man there said "Oh, let this feud rest." The man who finished the feud, stopped the Sirefes and stopped the people of Gwauna'ongi, was Bulu'a. So because he'd finished that feud, he took a bow and put it on the two rocks which they call the Bow-stopping [Fa'ifonelanabasi]. He said "On reaching here, you'll go back; I'm barring the place with this bow, you go back, you inland people go back." So that's where it came to; this kinsman of his of the 'Aimomoko family called Bulu'a stopped this feud and then it came to rest there.

Translated from Kwara'ae and abridged

Kwanamalefodoe nia ne'e korea 'i Rokisimae kini sa Niuni, kaimili ka ū fuana. Sa ngwane'e Tufu'igaote'e koso ka nia 'i Dalobala, nia 'aila 'ania bungu, ka alua kwalu Fiulasi kī, kwaula ne'e nia 'i Fairū. Aia'a sa Oliolikwana leka ka nia 'i Lobo, faina ngwae nari. Kini ne'e 'i Raunamanu ka 'afe toli 'i Mānadari fuana sa Fa'a'uma, ka olita'i ma'i ka nia 'i Siale, nia ka alua sa Gwauōmea, ki saea 'ania sa Ko'ongwaro, ka alua Kwanadoe Umalanga. Mango basi 'una'ari.

Kwanamalefodoe ne'e korea 'i Rokisimae, ka osia 'ania fo'oa 'i Maeru'a. Ma'a nia ka leka 'i sulia, ka mae ka nia saena tafu, kami ke kō ana 'etea na'iri'a. Ngwae nai'ari kira saea 'ania sa Ra'ena, ma'a 'i Rokisimae. 'I Rokisimae ka alua go'o sa Ko'olake, ka alua sa Ko'osae, go'o ka mae. Sa Ko'olake nini'a alua sa ko'o ne'e Ko'odangi, ka alua Gwagwalukwana, sa Faneasi ū fuana. Aia'a sa Ko'osae nini'a alua sa Bili'ate'e, ka alua sa Mūrarā, ka alua sa Mumufilu, ka alua 'i Oreore'au. Aia'a, fa'i na'ona'o ne'e sa Bili'ate'e ki fa'asata 'ania ko'o nia Bili'a lokoni'a, ki fa'asata 'ania sa ngwane'e sa Kwanamalefodoe futa ana. Aia'a, nia ne'e ka oli ma'i fuaimili 'i Fi'ika'o. Sa Mūrara korea kini sa Kwarui, sa Ruale ka ū fuana, ne'e alu ngwae'a sa Mūrarā nai, ka nini'a sa Dasa ka ū fuana. Kale'a sa Mūrarā nai, sa Fimanafelo ka ū fuana, kale'a sa Mūrarā lala nai, ai te'ete'e. 'I Oreore ne'e 'uru'uru ka mae go'o, ka 'iri 'afe. Sa Mumufilu ne'e ka ramoramo ka mae go'o, ka 'iri ara'i.

Sa Bili'a, kira dudu 'i 'Efo, 'i 'Efo ne'e rū nai na'a. Ka alua sa Asimaoma, ka alua sa Ko'ofoe, ka alua sa Ra'enate'e, ka alua sa Kwa'ilobo, ka alua sa ngwane'e Eromanudoe. Aia'a, sa Eromanu, sa Tolo'au kira ū fuana, kira ne'e kira saka ana. Nia fulia fanoa 'i Sirefe, ka kwatea fuana sa Alaba'e fa'ida. Ka koso ka nia na'a 'i Sigoria, nia noa'a fa'inau.

Kwanamalefodoe, he married Rokisimae, Niuni's girl,[1] we represent him. That man Tufu'igaote'e went down and he was at Dalobala, he rejected the conch,[2] he begot the eight Fiulasis, the eighth was in Fairū. Well, Oliolikwana went and he was at Lobo, that's the fourth man. The girl Raunamanu was married down at Mānadari to Fa'a'uma, she brought him back to Siale, he begot Gwauōmea, we call him Ko'ongwaro, he begot Kwanadoe Umalanga. Leave it at that.

Kwanamalefodoe married Rokisimae, he demolished the reward at Maeru'a.[3] Her father came along, he died and he's in the rubbish, we'd bake the exclusive one to him.[4] That man was called Ra'ena, the father of Rokisimae. Rokisimae just begot Ko'olake and begot Ko'osae, then she died. It was Ko'olake who begot the ancestor Ko'odangi and begot Gwagwalukwana, Faneasi stands for him. Well, it was Ko'osae who begot Bili'ate'e, he begot Mūrarā, he begot Mumufilu, he begot Oreore'au. Well, the senior one was Bili'ate'e, they named him for that ancestor of his Bili'a, they named him for the man Kwanamalefodoe was born of. Well, he returned to us at Fi'ika'o. Mūrarā married Kwarui's girl, Ruale stands for him, he begot Mūrarā's people, that's who Dasa stands for. Those born of Mūrarā, who Fimanafelo stands for, they're born of the other Mūrarā, the junior one. Oreore died single, she didn't marry. Mumufilu was a warrior until he died and didn't marry.[5]

Bili'a and the others settled at 'Efo, 'Efo which belongs to me. He begot Asimaoma, he begot Ko'ofo'e, he begot Ra'enate'e, he begot Kwa'ilobo, he begot that man Eromanudoe. Well, Eromanu, Tolo'au and them stand for him, they emerged from him. He founded the home at Sirefe and gave it to Alaba'e and them. He went down to be at Sigoria, not with me.

1 That is, Rokisimae was a girl of the clan now represented by Niuni.

2 'Rejecting the conch' probably means refusing to observe the tabu period at Siale which was signalled by blowing a conch-shell trumpet

3 Ra'ena had offered his daughter Rokisimae as part of the reward for a vengeance killing (as occurred in several old tales) and Kwanamalefodoe killed and collected the reward.

4 The 'rubbish' is the bone dump or ossuary (*tafurae*) of Siale, for the remains of the dead. An 'exclusive' sacrifice (*'etea*) was one too tabu to be eaten by any but direct male descendants of the ghost concerned.

5 The spiritual power of a warrior (*ramo*) required avoidance of women and was reduced if he married.

Funerals and ghosts

Alasa'a was brought up in the traditional religion and acted as tabu-speaker or priest for a time. Michael Kwa'ioloa questioned him shortly before he died in 1987 on the funeral procedures he had once taken part in, including depositing (*kwaiatoa*) the dead body and how a senior man came to be worshipped as a ghost by his descendants. Kwa'ioloa dictated this account soon afterwards.

I want to talk about when a man died, as I heard from my father Samuel Alasa'a. For example, if my father was ready to die and was sick, all of us brothers and sisters would come together and sit with him. And if we stayed with him until he died, then his daughters and daughters-in-law would sit around his body and cry with it, and the men would share in sympathy and mourn with the women. It was the women's work to cry continuously, because they were really sad. Then, when he had died, for all his sons it would be tabu to eat taro. Their wives could eat it, girls and children, but the men couldn't eat it. When a man died, his children couldn't bathe or walk to market or go anywhere that people gathered together.

Formerly, they didn't bury a man. When we had stayed and held the wake [*daurara*] with him for two or three days, then we took him and put him on a platform in a place we call tabu, where people don't usually go, a stony place with thick forest, not in the tabu sanctum but maybe near it. Then, my father said, each of his sons would try to pull off his eyebrow, one at a time, and if he couldn't pull off any hairs, he hadn't chosen that man and another would try. The son who pulled a lot of hair out very easily, that one would keep the man, he could call on him and offer sacrifices to him. That son would take it and wrap it in a cordyline leaf and put it in the smoke of the fire in the house.

Then they'd wait until the time they called normalisation [*mola'a*]. Normalisation means they'd gather the people and make pudding, get fish to eat with it, so that they'd be allowed to go around and work in the gardens. That was after the man had been on the platform on the rocks for about two months.

One more important thing; after the man had rotted, his sons went and the one he had chosen would take a collarbone, with his jaw and his skull. He'd take them and put them on a beam in the tabu-speaker's house in the village, in the private room where no-one could enter. It stayed there and the man looked at it from time to time, cooked some taro for him and did some things for his father, until he wanted a sacrifice to be offered to him of a pig. That was when someone was sick or had trouble in the family, the father would ask for a pig. He'd come and possess and shake the man he'd chosen, whom he let pull out his eyebrow, and he'd take a pig and say "Oh, we'll take this up to offer to our father, because he told me that if we do his grandchild will get better."

They didn't take the man's bones and skull to the tabu sanctum until the man he chose became sick. The man would be seriously ill and even if they offered pigs to other ancestors he would not be cured. That showed them "Oh, father wants us to take his bones to the tabu-sanctum," and they'd start to offer sacrifices to him. He was now an important ghost, to bless his family and defend them, to use men as warriors, use them to organise festivals and feasts with the co-operation of their relatives. The man was now a ghost.

Translated from Pijin and abridged

Aia'a, sa Ko'ofo'e oli ka nia 'i Safunaki, ka alua sa Basimamanu, kira ka saungia fasi sa 'i 'Okwala. Sa Fo'e kira ka sarea sa 'i Okwala, Fakula'e ne'e kira ka ru'u 'unari, ka nai 'i nai'ari. Aia'a, sa Ra'ena, gwa'i fau ka saungia, kira ka saea 'ania sa Ko'ofau, korea 'i Maeisi, kini 'i Kwalo, 'Aenakwata, ka alua sa Ko'omote, ka alua sa Gwaulumu. Ko'omote, sa 'Uikelema fa'ida ne'e ū fuana. Sa ngwane'e Ra'ena, Ra'ena sa Ko'orara ne'e ū fuana. Sa Kwa'ilogo leka ka nia 'i Na'ama, tua bali fu'uba, kira saea 'ania Alafena'ama nari. Aia'a, nau ku danga 'ania ai ne'e kī na'a kulu ka madako na'a, kaulu ka rongo'i na'a, bore ma nai ngalia lala ai nau.

Well, Ko'ofo'e returned and he was at Safunaki, he begot Basimamanu, they killed him out of 'Okwala. Fo'e was raised in Okwala, and the Fakula'es, that's where they come in.[1] Well, Ra'ena, a stone struck him, they called him Ko'ofau [Stone-ancestor], he married Mae'isi'isi, a girl from Kwalo, 'Aenakwata, he begot Ko'omote and begot Gwaulumu. Ko'omote, 'Uikelema and others stand for him. That man Ra'ena, Ko'orara stands for him. Kwa'ilogo went and was at Na'ama, living on the side down below which they call Alafena'ama. Well, I'm dropping these ones, you're clear now, you've heard them, but I'll take up my one instead.

Sa Bili'a nai korea kini Koio. Ka 'una'ari, sa Asimaoma ka alua sa Kauburu, Kauburu alua sa Ti'iti'i, Ti'iti'i ka alua sa Ko'obosi, Ko'obosi ka alua sa To'okona, To'okona ka alua sa 'Aida. 'Aida ka alua sa Asimaomate'e ne'e kira saea 'ania sa Maeorea ka fonea Tolinga ka sui, noa'a ta ngwae ka 'iri tua. Nia futa ana 'i Takanabulu, kini 'i Fa'alau. * * * Du'ungana tae? Kelema loni suia fanoa loeri, ka noa'a ta ngwae. Sa Kwai'ini, ngwae 'i Maelifua, alua sa 'Angiau, alua sa Angikona, alua sa Angifiu, 'i Bubuiasi, 'afe fuana ngwae nai'ari sa Kwa'i'au, ka ngalia ma'i kelema fu'uba 'i Gwa'idalo, fafona 'i Tautaumalefo, fafona 'i Kiluufi. Tafurae teo na'a lo kira saungia. Kira ka saungia sa Ko'okwalu, 'afe nia, fanoa nai tona 'ania gwa'i mae'a, kelema fu kira saungida, kira ka oli na'a ma'i 'i Tolinga. Go'o to'a fu 'i Tolinga kira ka 'uri "Saungida ka le'a go'o." Kira ka leka na'a 'i burida.

'Unari nia ka leka toli 'i sulida 'uana saena 'i 'Efo, kira ka 'i'ilala bore kesi to'otafa. Leleka kira ka ngalia lala gwauna sa ngwane'e Kwai'inidoe, ngwae kelema fuiri. Nia gwauna sulufaua lo 'i 'Efo, lumulumu'a na'a nini'ari, kira mangosia fa'alilana. Rū lōri ka 'itā, ta maoma ka olo, ta fanga'a ka leka, leleka maoma 'isi go'o, ka dao ka o'ea go'o sa To'okwana, sa 'Aida. "'Ofodangi ta'ena, 'o sa 'Aida 'oke saka 'oke kelemia ngwae, ke mae sa To'okwana ka oli ka a'ola. Maoma 'i buri, sa To'okwana ke saka 'ofodangi ke saungia ngwae, 'ae'o sa ngwane'e 'Aida 'oko oli ko a'ola."

Bili'a married a Kwaio girl. So then, Asimaoma begot Kauburu, Kauburu begot Ti'iti'i, Ti'iti'i begot Ko'obosi, Ko'obosi begot To'okona, To'okona begot 'Aida. 'Aida begot Asimaomate'e, who they called Maeorea, and closed Tolinga off, then no-one lived there. He was born of Takanabulu, a girl from Fa'alau. * * * What was the cause? Sorcery finished off that community, there was no-one left. Kwai'ini, a man from Maelifua, begot 'Angiau, begot Angikona, begot Angifiu, and Bubuiasi, wife of that man Kwa'i'au, he brought that sorcery from down at Gwa'idalo, above Tautaumalefo, above Kiluufi. An ossuary remains where they killed them. They killed Ko'okwalu and his wife, my community was shocked by the epidemic, the sorcery which killed them, they came back to Tolinga. Then the people at Tolinga said "It was alright to kill them." They came behind them.

So then it came down along with them into 'Efo, they divined but couldn't get an outcome. Eventually they took the head of Kwai'inidoe, the sorcerer, instead. It's at the head of the stone wall at 'Efo, now all mossy, they refrained from damaging it. That thing killed repeatedly, a festival fell due, a feast went on, eventually when the festival ended it came in a revelation to To'okwana and 'Aida. "This morning you, 'Aida, come out and sorcerise a person and when he dies To'okwana can return and triumph. At a later festival, To'okwana can come out in the morning to kill a person and you man, 'Aida, can return and triumph".

1 This is a reference to [Ko'o]Fo'e's feud over his boar and the refugees at Fi'ika'o, previously related.

Sorcery

Cases of sorcery (*kelema*) are not uncommon in Kwara'ae, and the destruction of Tolinga is the first of several in Alasa'a's history.

Under the traditional religion sickness may mean that ancestral ghosts are punishing or failing to protect their dependants because they have somehow been offended. Christians may suspect that God is treating them in the same way, or that they are suffering from disease. The obvious diagnoses or cures would be divination and sacrifice to the ghost or confession and prayer to God, herbal remedies or medical treatment. But if these fail, there is always the possibility that the person is suffering a malicious secret attack by sorcery.

The Kwara'ae translate sorcery as 'poison'. It may involve putting harmful substances in the victim's food or drink, mixing it with their leftover food or giving the food to a poisonous snake, throwing a magical object at them or leaving it for them to step over. But sorcerers also use the power of ghosts to make such methods work.

The sorcery epidemic at Tolinga

In this case it seems the sorcery epidemic followed the Tolinga people home from Gwa'idalo, and when divination failed to explain the sickness afflicting them, they unwisely tried to use the ghost of the original sorcerer Kwai'ini in the hope of stopping the epidemic. Sorcery ghosts demand to be used to kill, as this one did with To'okwana and his son 'Aida. The triumphal rejoicing (*kā'ola*) was intended to anger the victim's relatives and hence strengthen the sorcery. When they refused to use it, the sorcery ghost retaliated by killing off the Tolinga community.

The genealogical chart below takes the history of Tolinga through this period of devastation to the re-establishment of the clan by 'Aida's son Maeorea .

Genealogy of Tolinga

from Asimaomadoe to Asimaomate'e and his son Felega

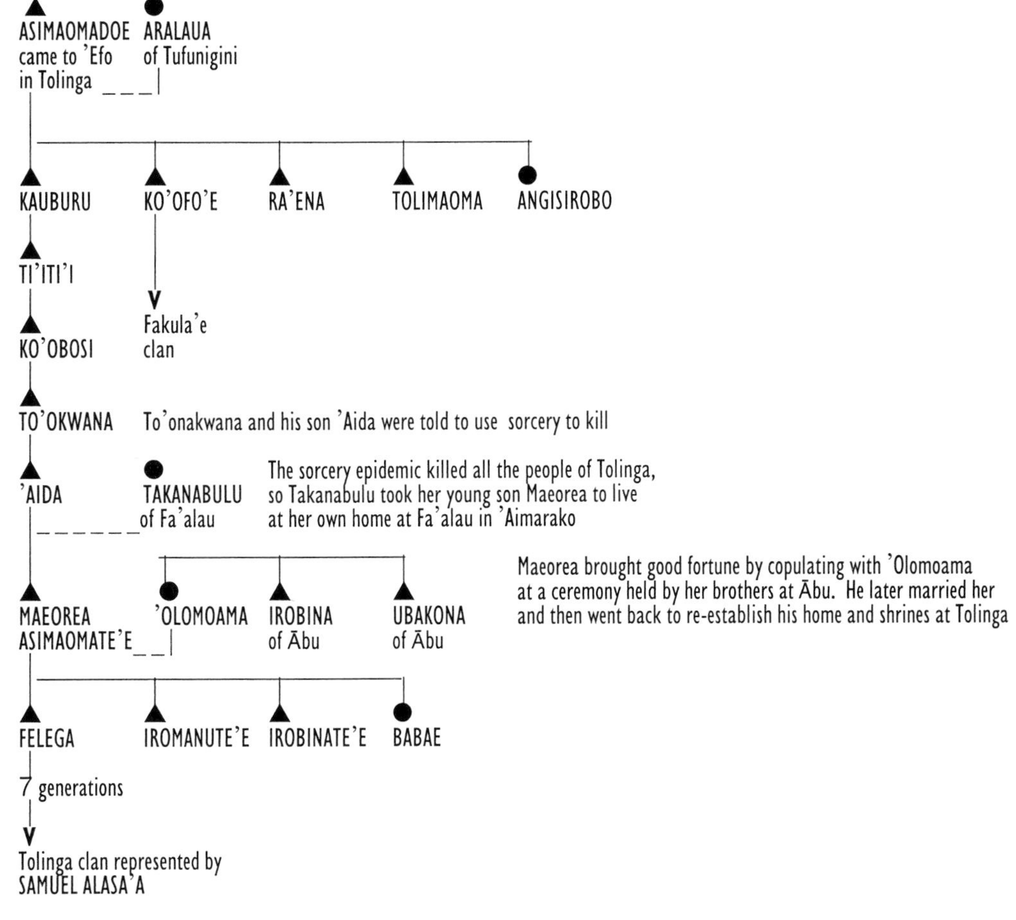

Kira ka 'aila go'o 'ania kelema loeri, ka oli go'o fanoa loeri ka sui na'a. Sa Maemaeorea na'a ne'e ka tua. Tua sulia fa'i bongi kī, fanoa lori ka moko na'a, 'i Takanabulu, ngela nia ka laua 'uana 'i Fa'alau, fanoa nia. Kira dao 'i Fa'alau, kira ka sarea sa Maeorea 'i lo'oko 'i 'Aimarako. Ano sa ngwane'e Maeorea ne'e 'i 'Aimarako na'a. Sarea ka leleka ka doe, buta mani lōri ka teo ana sa Gwaeni'a.

Akalo 'i Ābu, sasi 'uana fa'i alumā, sa Irobina, sa 'Ubakona, kera'a māmā adaada'a ka fa'atani. "'Oke oli kwau, kira furia na'a fa'i ka'o nai, na ngwaingwaena moro alu fafia, nia ke labungani māna keona ka bolo fani kwakwa fuiri, ka bakasia ka ngasi ka tua. Ngwae ke ra'e ma'i ke to'osia ta 'a fafona ta bali sasafa. Ta 'a ana ta sasafa ka durua toli duila saena fa'i ka'o nai'ari. Lekaleka nia foga na'ai, fanoa 'oe le'a na'a."

Nia go'o nai. Kira leka ka dao go'o 'i Ābu, kira ka ngalia na'a fa'i ka'o lo'oko ana ngwae adaada lo'oko, kira ka furia na'a ta fa'i 'ai sulia. Lo kira tufua na'a tafe lo'oko ki saea 'ania fa'i alumā, tatafe lo'oko na'a, fera na'a, kwakwa rō bali, noa'a kisi 'odoa. Go'o sa 'Obangwane ka lidi na'a, "Tai nini ke sasi fani rū ne'e, nini'a ngwae adaada ka saea ma'i? Fa'i ka'o ne'e ngwae dikoa na'a, fanoa nia le'a na'a, mae ka fuli ana. Nia nai." Ngwa'i kini fuiri kira fiku māna fera 'i Ābu'itolo nini'a ne'e kwā. Ābu'iasi funi'a 'i asi. 'Unari, 'i Falamaoma, fa'i na'ona'o, "Fuana tae nari?" Go'o kira ka ilia na'a, alua fa'i ka'o go'o, fa'i na'ona'o ka, "Ai, nau ku 'aila kisi sasia rū ne'ana, rū ta'a ne'ana." 'Una'ari, 'i Falakafa ka lisia ka 'aila, Falauru ka lisia ka 'aila. 'I 'Olomoama susuburi ka 'uri "Sai! ma ki 'ail'aila 'ania rū ne'e akalo sasi 'uana ma, tae ne'e ke sasi fanoa ne'e ke le'a? Nai sasia na'a 'aku."

Lo kira ka tufua tafe fuana. Nia ke ra'e ke tua, fingi kikiru ka dautoli na'a, kwalo 'ofa ka dautoli na'a, dao ka labungani fa'i ka'o fuiri ka bolo go'o fani kwakwa fu saena keona, ka bakasia ka ngiri go'o, sa Laubina ka ra'e na'a. Kabikabia kabi 'i kiriru fuiri, kabi 'i 'ofa fuiri, ka kwatea folo fuana ngwae lo'oko, ka kwatea ta kakabi ai fuana 'i 'Olomoama. Kira dami ka leleka ka sui go'o, "Koro ka leka na'a."

They rejected this sorcery, came back and the community was finished off. Maemaeorea it was who remained. After some days the home smelt and Takanabulu snatched her child off to Fa'alau, her home. They reached Fa'alau and they reared Maeorea over there, at 'Aimarako. The land of that man Maeorea was now at 'Aimarako. Reared him until he was big, and a package of money remained with Gwaeni'a.[1]

The ghost at Ābu was after a display, Irobina and 'Ubakona held a seance and revealed it. "When you return, they saw off a bamboo, a sister you decide on will thrust it into the opening of her vagina, fitting the hole, clamp it firm and sit. A man will climb up and throw a leg over her thigh. With a leg on her thigh, he inserts the penis down into the bamboo. Eventually when it cracks open, your home will have good fortune."

That was it. They went and arrived at Ābu, they took the bamboo from the seer and they sawed off a stick. They built a platform called a display, the platform was a sanctum open at both ends, they didn't wall it. Then 'Obangwane enquired "Who'll do this thing, which the seer told of? This bamboo a man splits open and his home has good fortune, a feud will come of it. That's what." A group of girls gathered in front of the sanctum at Ābu-inland, that's where. Ābu-on-sea is the one by the sea. So then, Falamaoma, the first-born: "What's it for?" They just tried it, putting in the bamboo, then the firstborn said "Hey, I don't like us doing this, it's bad." So then, Falakafa saw it and refused, Falauru saw it and refused. 'Olomoama, the last-born, said "Hey! if we refuse this thing the ghost is after, what will make our home have good fortune? I'll do it, I will."

Then they built the platform for her. She climbed and sat, a bunch of betelnut hung down, a vine of betel-leaf hung down, she came and thrust the bamboo to fit the hole in her vagina and clamped it tight, and Laubina climbed up. Taking a sprig of the betelnuts, a sprig of the betel-leaf, they gave them across to the man and gave a sprig to 'Olomoama. They chewed betel and then eventually, "Let's go."

1 This package of shell-money, evidently salvaged by Takanabulu from the deserted home at Tolinga and kept by her brother Gwaeni'a, was to be Maeorea's inheritance, as we see later.

Maeorea and the display at Ābu

Maeorea, also referred to as Maemaeorea and by his other name Asimaomate'e, was a child survivor of the sorcery epidemic at 'Efo. He later married 'Olomaoma from Ābu on the west coast (near the Malaita capital of 'Aoke) and re-established the Tolinga clan. The story of how he did so is important to Alasa'a because of the claim it gives him to the land of 'Olomaoma's clan, but it also has a certain curiosity value.

The sexual display ceremony held by the people of Ābu seems very strange by the standards of Kwara'ae culture of recent times. There are many tales of new cults arising from dreams or visions to bring people good fortune, but this one publicly breaks the very stong tabu on extra-marital sex (*usu'a*, which the Kwara'ae often translate as 'sin'). The whole episode is not only bizarre but scandalous. But then, historical tales often include strange or marvellous events which people would not expect to witness in their own time, and the Kwara'ae generally regard their ancient ancestors as having been somewhat larger than life.

A tale from Kwaio

Some Kwara'ae historical tales share incidents or themes with histories from other parts of Malaita. Whether this means that the tales originate in the same events or simply that they reflect the common culture of the island is not always easy to tell.

In 1996 Ma'aanamae, 'Aditalau and Bebea Animae, from 'Ai'eda in East Kwaio, dictated to the anthropologist David Akin the tale of a sexual ceremony similar to that practised at Ābu. The hero of this story, Lafusua, was a warrior of remarkable powers of whom many tales are told. As the story occurs in Kwara'ae and both Lafusua and his uncle Fee'ota were originally from Kwara'ae, it seems the stories have a common origin. But whether this means the ceremony was a Kwara'ae custom or merely a historical theme is another question.

The version of the tale given here is composed from accounts by all three of Akin's informants.

Lafusua visited a feast that was being held in Kwara'ae. At that feast they tied a woman up on a feasting platform with a piece of bamboo in her vagina. They challenged anyone to try to have sex with her up there, but warned that to do so would itself be taken as a challenge. "If anyone has sex with her, it's a fight!" But when all the warriors showed up at the feast and went up and looked at her, they were afraid to do anything because they didn't want to start a fight. Not one of them even got an erection. That night there was a big storm, with thunder thundering and lightning flashing, and the people all took shelter from the night in their houses. During the storm Lafusua climbed up on the platform and he had sex with that woman and shattered that bamboo, and then he took out his black flint blade and he cut her open, took out her liver, stuck it in his bag and left. When the weather cleared the people came out and they looked and, "Oh! Look at that girl over there!"

Lafusua ran away, with the girl's people in pursuit, and eventually they chased him into a place where he was up to his neck in mud, just standing on a timber under the mud. But when any warrior would walk out on that timber to attack him he would spin the timber with his feet and they would fall off and he would kill them. He would then stand on top of them there under the mud, and as he killed more and more he stood higher and higher and eventually he was standing on top of so many bodies that he was only up to his knees in the mud. His uncle Fee'ota heard about what was going on and said he was going to kill his nephew Lafusua himself, to head off the rewards that were sure to be offered to kill their group in vengeance for all of the killing Lafusua was doing.

"Here comes the man who will kill me" said Lafusua when he saw Fee'ota coming. The people told Fee'ota to stand safely at a distance and spear him from there. He did this and Lafusua was indeed speared. After, they cut off his head and took it back to cook it.

They had the head sitting by the cooking fire and a girl there was sniffling because the smoke from the fire was blowing in her eyes. Lafusua's head spoke, "What are you crying about?" She was afraid and she said, "I'm crying for you." He said, "When the lightning strikes next, close your eyes, and when the thunder sounds, open them again." She did what he said, and when she opened her eyes the head was gone, and that place of those people there crumbled and was destroyed.

Translated from Kwaio and edited by David Akin

Kira alumā ka leleka, sa Maeorea tua 'i 'Aimarako, ka leka ma'i so'olafi, leleka ka tua ka leleka fiku'a fuiri ka fiku, fiku ta'ifau, fuana alumā'a. Rodo ka rodo go'o ka tuatua go'o fuana 'i 'Olomoama, ta'e ka gunu ana 'i māna luma. 'Unari leleka 'i 'Olomoama māliu go'o, nia ka ta'e ka ra'efia go'o, nia go'o nai. 'I 'Olomoama ka 'uri "Sai! 'oko sasia rū ta'a 'aku." Tata'e ka liu go'o 'uana dangi.

Ka dangi go'o, kira ka lauma ka leleka go'o sa Maemaeorea ka alua sa Maomate'e ka ra'e, kwa'ia sulufaua ka ra'e bore ma 'i 'Olomoama lisia ka ta'a na'a ana. Ka 'eke na'a, labungani fa'i ka'o loeri, ka bakasia ka ngiri, sa Maeorea ka tua fafia ro 'a kī, ka tuafia sasana ka durungani toli ngwane-ngwanena, duila, ka kwatea kakabi 'i ofa lōri fuana, kakabi 'i malua lōri fuana. Nia ka sai nama ana ka 'urudua saena ngwa'i nia, te'e bota, te'e angoango go'o. Nia ka dikoa fa'i kikiru loeri, ka mū'ia kwailiu ka rata saena fena lōri ka lotofia. Ka'ika'ina lala go'o nai, lala go'o nai. Nia ka to'ongia go'o fena fuiri. Dolingani go'o, tata'e ka dikoa fa'i olomae lōri.

Go'o kika, akalo nai go'o ne'e dikoa fuana fanoa 'i Ābu, Ābu ne'e Dalobala logo. 'Unari, sa Irobina, sa Iliroba, sa 'Ubakona, nia tagā limana ka, "O, Ābu dudu fa'asia. Ābu dudu fa'asia, nia diko'a ka le'a na'a. Moro kata salosalonga." Kira dudu to'oto'o go'o. Faurodo lala, Sifiu lala, sa Lau'ofa lala, sa Lauri'i lala, ogada ta'a go'o nai, "Sai! kala ngwae sarea, leleka ka dikoa mala fa'i ka'o baera, rū fasi ta'i nama akulu." Tata'e kira ka oloolo go'o ana sa Asimaoma. Nia ka lofo ka to'o 'i ano, ka tarā na'a 'i 'Olomoama. Sikarani 'i nai'ari, kira ka ū fafia 'i nai'ari. Nia alifa'i go'o ka 'uri "'Io, moro tara kwau." Mae fuli nai kwa. Fa'alau ka dudu go'o, kira 'afia go'o sa ngwane'e Maeorea, Ābu ka dudu go'o, kira ka 'afia go'o sa Maeorea. Mae furi fuli, leleka kira ka fonea sa Maeorea ka tafi, ka noa'a ta rū. Sa Maeorea go'o ne'e fa'ale'ā fanoa 'i Ābu, 'ania fa'i alumā fuiri. Buri'ana kira fi'i tua saena le'anga'a.

They went on with the display and Maeorea, living at 'Aimarako, came in the evening, eventually he sat and eventually the group gathered, gathered every one, for the display. Night came and he stayed on for 'Olomoama, he got up and courted her in front of the house. So then eventually 'Olomoama slept and he got up and climbed onto her, he did. 'Olomoama said "Hey! you're doing something bad to me." She stayed up until day.

When day came they were careless and eventually Maemaeorea set Maomate'e to climb and make a stone platform, he climbed but 'Olomoama saw him and felt bad. She was ashamed, thrust in the bamboo and clamped it tight, Maeorea sat on both legs, he sat on her thigh and inserted his manhood, penis, and gave a sprig of betel-leaf to her, a sprig of betelnut. To make sure, he'd dropped into his bag a bit of leaf, a bit of creeper. He split open the betelnut, chewed it around and poked into the lime and sucked it. The stalk that is. He'd packaged that lime. After a pause he arose and split open the barrier.

Then they, it was my ghost who split it open, for the community at Ābu, Ābu which is also from Dalobala. So there were Irobina, Iliroba and 'Ubakona, and he held up his hand: "Oh, Ābu back off. Ābu back off, it's split open and all's well. You might shake it." They backed off one by one. However Faurodo, Sifiu, Lau'ofa and Lauri'i just felt angry, "Hey! the little boy we reared has actually gone and split open that bamboo, it should have been one of us." They got up and attacked Asimaoma. He jumped and hit the ground, and dragged 'Olomoama. Throwing her out, they stood over her there. He turned and said "Yes, drag her away." A feud began. The Fa'alaus stepped back and surrounded that man Maeorea, the Ābus stepped back and they surrounded Maeorea. The feud began and eventually they shielded Maeorea, he escaped and nothing happened. Maeorea had benefited the community at Ābu with that display. Afterwards they lived in good fortune.

Betelnut

Betelnut, the fruit of the Areca palm, is chewed with betel-pepper leaf and burnt coral-lime as a mild narcotic stimulant. It can be eaten by anyone at any time, but is also used in religious ritual and magic (as in the sacrificial ritual described on page 64). In the story of the display at Ābu it was evidently intended to act as an aphrodisiac, which Maeorea used to full effect.

Michael Kwa'ioloa writes about the importance of betelnut:

> Betelnut chewing is a means of uniting people to be kind to one another, in the past, present and future, for the great betelnut chewers shared it without paying for it. Sharing it with neigbours builds ties of friendship. People also use it when chewing medicines for curing. But on the other hand, it is also dangerous as a means to trap, trick and deceive enemies to kill them. People who have poison [*kelema* / sorcery] can put it in the betelnut and when their enemy bites it and eats it they die as if accidentally.
>
> Original English

This popular Solomon Islands t-shirt design from the 1990s satirises the effects of excessive betelnut chewing, as well as illustrating the betelnuts, the pepper-leaves and the lime in its bamboo container with spatula. Betelnut eaters habitually spit out red saliva.

From a design by Ken McArthur, with thanks to D.J. Graphics Ltd., Honiara

Ka teo 'unari ka leleka, sa Fautobe nia fu'uba 'i 'Aimarako, sa Gwaeli'a ka leka toli, kira ka fiku teo'a kira ka ala'a. 'I 'Olomoama kira saea 'ania diuri, kira 'aila 'ania du'ungana ne'e sa Maeorea karia fa'i ka'o ana. Tua 'i nai'ari, kira ala'a ka leleka ka "Rela, rū fuiri 'i 'Olomoama ne'e nia ke ngwaro na'a ma ta ngwae kesi ogā na'a." Sa Gwali'a kwai'ala 'uana fa'i fena ma nia tua saena 'isita'i ngwai nia fuiri. Ngwanengwanena sa Asimaoma ū takataka na'a, ka "Rela, kuke ala'a ana rū baera ma ne'e ngwanengwanena sa Asimaoma nini'a ū takataka na'a." "Sai moro leka gania ma'i re fuaku, 'i nai alua ta ngwae ke didifulia fanoa nau." Sa Gwaeli'a ka "Sai, ngwai, ma ke ta fita fafonai ta'u? Rorodo go'o ne'e koro ke ta'e, buta mani 'oe teo go'o 'ana."

Go'o nia ka gania go'o sa 'Ubakona fani sa Irobina kera'a ka ba'ea kwau rū nia. Kira ka kwatea fuana Maeorea. Kira kwatea 'i Fuku, Ratatatara fuana 'i 'Olomoama. Kira ka kwatea 'i Salu, 'i Makemāna, fuana 'i 'Olomoama na'i. 'Unari sa Maemaeorea ka tua ka tolea ma'i ta tafurae, nia 'i Fuku, ta tafurae nia 'i Salu, ano ana o'onga'a nia 'i Makemāna, fa'i ngali kī ni'i 'i Ratatatara, fa'i ngali kī ne'e 'i Makemāna, kira kwate'e fuana kini 'afe kira nai. Sa Maeorea ka oli ma'i ka tua 'i Ābu, ka alua sa Felega. Ngwai nia ka 'uri "Oli na'a, oli na'a, 'oko ara'i na'a. Tabua fanoa 'oe 'i Tolinga kwalitafu suli lokiri loko to'ene na'a ka sinafi'i na'a, 'oke goni'i na'a, ko alua na'a ngwae."

Nia oli ma'i ka tua na'a 'i Luli, 'i Gwaro'a, nia fu sa Maunu fa'ida tuafia go'o. Ka ra'e no'o na'a, ka nia na'a 'i bali lo'oko, nia ma'u 'ania fanoa nia, ra'e 'uana sa Sirefe, ra'e 'uana sa Fuluma, ra'e 'uana sa Likoa, ra'e 'uana sa Kwa'ala. Daua koko no'o fuiri, ka ra'e lo'oko 'i feraābu lo 'i Ebosatea, gwa'i ba'asi ma nia mū ka 'asi na'a. Sa Dau'ota tafi ka leka na'a 'uana 'i lo'oko saena 'i Ngwala, ka fataābu'a ana. Ra'e go'o 'i nai'ari ka ako na'a "Ō, 'oko mū ko 'asi'o na'a. Ka no na'a ta ngwae fuamu." Tua 'i nai'ari ka dangi ka "'Uri ma, akalo sa tai kī nini'a re?"

That's how it remained and eventually Fautobe was down at 'Aimarako, Gwaeli'a went down and they gathered to sleep and talk. They called 'Olomoama a whore, they rejected her on account of Maeorea splitting the bamboo. Sitting there, they talked and eventually said "Hey! this so-and-so 'Olomoama will get old and no man will want her." Gwaeli'a grabbed a lime-bottle and sat on his nephew's bed. Asimaoma's manhood stood erect: "Hey! when we talked about that, Asimaoma's manhood stood erect." "Eh, you two go and ask for her for me, so I can beget a son to replenish my community." Gwaeli'a said "Eh, nephew, how much longer shall we wait? Let's set out tomorrow, there's still your package of money."[1]

Then he asked 'Ubakona and Irobina and they sent her off to be his. They gave her to Maeorea. They gave Fuku and Ratatatara to 'Olomoama. They gave Salu, Makemāna, that is to 'Olomoama.[2] So then Maemaeorea stayed there and brought an ossuary, it's at Fuku, an ossuary is at Salu, the garden land is at Makemāna, the nut trees are at Ratatatara, there are nut trees at Makemāna, they gave them for their married woman. Maeorea came back and lived at Ābu, and begot Felega. His uncle said "Return, return, you're married now. Clear your home at Tolinga, there are bone-dumps lying out in the sun, you safeguard them, you've begotten a son."[3]

He came back and lived at Luli, at Gwaro'a, it's where Maunu and the others live. He was climbing for cuscus [possums] and was on the far side, he was afraid of his home and went up into Sirefe, into Fuluma, into Likoa, into Kwa'ala. Holding the bag of cuscus, he climbed over to the tabu-sanctum at Ebosatea: after a wasting-disease it had broken down and fallen. Dau'ota had fled and gone away over to Ngwala, he was tabu-speaker for it. Climbing there, he shouted "Oh, you're broken down and fallen. There's no-one for you." Staying there until next day, he said "So then, whose are these ghosts?"

1 Meaning "You already have the necessary shell-money for bridewealth."

2 These are the pieces of land, given to Olomaoma for the use of her husband and their descendants.

3 That is, "Go home and look after the bones of your ancestors for the sake of your son."

Marriage and bridewealth

A proper marriage is normally arranged by the couple's families and requires the husband's family to pay for his wife with a 'hanging up' (*daura'ia*) of shell-money as bridewealth. In the past the wife's family might demand a very large amount of high-value money strings which the husband could only provide by taking loans from many of his relatives. He would later have to return these as bridewealth contributions for the sons of the lenders' families or as distributions from bridewealth received for the marriage of his own family's daughters. These debts could be carried over from one generation to the next.

By inheriting the package of money from Tolinga, kept by his uncle Gwaeli'a, Maeorea found himself in the fortunate position of being able to choose a wife and marry without seeking loans from his relatives.

A girl from an old-fashioned community wearing the belt of red fibre which shows that she is still unmarried. When married she will wear a beaded belt and apron. (1984)

Giving land to a married woman

When a girl marries, especially if her husband comes to live with her family instead of taking her to live with him in the usual way, her father may give pieces of land and fruit trees for her and her husband to use. Their children will inherit this gift, which means that seniority for the land or trees passes from the wife's clan to her sons and their descendants in the male line, who form a section of her husband's clan.

As a result of this and other special gifts of land, all the major clan lands of Kwara'ae include an indefinite number of smaller pieces which are claimed by people of other clans, and everyone inherits claims in a number of lands. This makes Kwara'ae land tenure both very flexible and extremely complex, and claims depend on a detailed knowledge of local history.

In the story of Maeorea, Alasa'a explains his own claim to pieces of land which were given to Maeorea's wife 'Olomoama, eight generations before him.

A display of bride-wealth in the 1930s in north-west Kwara'ae. The presentation includes strings of shell-money, rolled pandanus mat-bags, cooked pig and a live pig (slung on a pole carried by two men on the right).

This is one of a series of photographs taken by the Revd. David Lloyd Francis of the Melanesian Mission in the hills above Fauābu, while stationed at Fauābu Hospital in 1932-3.

From British Museum Ethnography Dept. pictorial collection

Oli kira ka dao 'i Luli, gwa'i ba'asi lōri ka dao, nia ka kau saena luma lōri. 'Afe nia ka akwa, leleka ka dangi, ruana go'o, ba'eko lo 'i Fausasa ka dao ka 'uri "'Oko lisi nau na'a leka kō na'a aku." Dao go'o 'i nai'ari nia saka mamata lala nai. Sa Maemaeorea fi'i leka ka fi'i tabua gwa'i ba'asi lo'oko 'i Ebosatea, kedea mafula, do'ofia gwata ana, oli ka dao go'o, ba'asi lo'oko dao go'o ka "'Oke 'odoa kwalu luma kī fuaku, nau ki tua 'i saena." Nia sasia fuli luma lo'oko teo go'o 'ana 'i nini'ari 'i Nidi, Ote'age, Gwaro'a, Ususua. 'Aena Siale nari.

'Una'ari, fai tafulu kī 'asi'i saena kwalu luma fukiri nai. Fanoa lōri ka ngongora go'o ana gwata, alo ka suru ka teo go'o, ba'u ka ngeso ka teo go'o, ba'era ka taka go'o, ufu ka 'ere go'o, 'io. Sa Maeorea fi'i ra'e nai. Si'iria kwalu tafurae lokiri fiku'i na'a, saena 'i Ferafo'oka, lo ka 'uia tafurae lo'oko. Nau ku leka ku tala fa'ali'i go'o. Ma'a dao ka o'ea ka 'uri "Noa'a 'okesi ngalia orongaku, 'oko kōngia gwata 'oko 'ania ka sui na'a 'i ne'e." Kira saea 'ania suifuila, ka nia 'i 'Asifolota. Sa Bili'a, kilu gwa'u ana nia 'i Abutolingia. Tafanga ma fai malafunu. Nia na'a nai.

Aia, nau ku ala'a ka dao na'a ana gwalunga'irū nari, nai tolingia na'a nai. Nai tolingia na'a. Gwalunga'irū, sa Felega alua sa Faneadoe, sa Faneadoe alua sa Ko'obuna, sa Ko'obuna ka alua sa Kubu, ka alua sa Ngoraga, ka alua sa Fe'a, ka alua sa Arangali. Gwauna, fa'i na'ona'o 'i Tolinga nari. Ai sulia, sa Ko'o'aburu,'i Saku. Sa Ko'obuna nini'a alua sa Kubufo'oa ne'e ki saea 'ania sa Kauburu, sulia kauburu lo osia 'i Siale. Korea 'i 'Oifera ka alua sa Maena, ka alua 'i Fiunabulu, Maena 'iri alua go'o ta ngwae. 'Unari go'o, 'Oifera ka mae, sa Kubu ne'e ki saea 'ania sa Kauburu ka korea lala 'i Māsi, kini kira go'o. Ka alua 'i Urubata, Finokwaokwaola, nia nai, 'i Launangwala. Finokwaokwaola kira saungia. 'I Urubata nini kira saea 'ania 'i Maelefanga'a nini alua sa Abol. Ka nia 'i fu'uba Gwa'idalo, kula

On returning to Luli, the wasting-disease arrived, it hung inside the house. His wife shouted and eventually next day, the second, the deadly snake of Fausasa arrived and said "Now you've seen me, go and bake to me." It arrived there emerging separately. Maemaeorea then went and cleared the wasting-disease from Ebosatea, kindled a fire, cooked a pig on it, came back and the disease arrived: "Wall eight houses for me to live in." He made the house-sites which still remain there at Nidi, Ote'age, Gwaro'a, Ususua.[1] That's at the foot of Siale.

So then, forty pigs fell within these eight houses. The home was grunting with pigs, taro was ready to harvest, bananas were ripe, hibiscus-spinach was flowering, sugarcane was growing, yes.[2] Maeorea then climbed. Shifted the eight collected ossuaries into Ferafo'oka and set out the ossuary over there. I went myself and destroyed them.[3] His father came in a revelation and said "Don't take my food-remnants, when you bake a pig, eat it all here." They call it finish-on-site, it was at 'Asifolota. Bili'a, his empty grave is at Abutolingia. It's a fathom and four spans long. That's it.

Well, I've talked and come to the tree-top, now I'll throw down the fruit. I'll throw it down. At the top, Felega begot Faneadoe, Faneadoe begot Ko'obuna, Ko'obuna begot Kubu and begot Ngoraga and begot Fe'a and begot Arangali. That's the head, the first-born of Tolinga. The following one was Ko'o'aburu, and Saku. It was Ko'obuna who begot Kubufo'oa who they called Kauburu [Gale], after the gale which demolished Siale. Married 'Oifera and begot Maena, begot Fiunabulu, Maena didn't beget anyone. So then, 'Oifera died and Kubu who they called Kauburu married Māsi, their girl. He begot Urubata, Finokwaokwaola, that's who, and Launangwala. Finokwaokwaola they killed. It was Urubata, who they called Maelefanga'a, who begot Abel. He's down at Gwa'idalo, a place given to

1 This seems to be the story of a cult for the ghost which afflicted the people of Ebosatea with a wasting disease. It foreshadows cults of the colonial period which required houses to be built and pigs sacrificed (see Burt 1994: 136, 276) but the significance of the disease-ghost and the deadly snake is obscure.

2 This is a description of preparations for a festival, but for the disease-ghost rather than for the ancestors.

3 Maeorea, as sole survivor of his clan, moved the bones of his ancestors from several ('eight') tabu sites in order to care for and sacrifice to them more easily at one site, and Alasa'a destroyed them after he became a Christian, as a way of exorcising the ghosts.

kwatea fuana 'i 'Olomoama, tua go'o 'ana nini'ari, korea 'i I'alaua, ka 'aba'ato. Aia, 'i Launangwala nini'a 'afe fuana sa Gwere, Launangwala nia ka alua sa Bilimae'ate'e, kokorea 'i Kiniasi, futa ana 'i Usunga'i, ka futa ana sa Subua, ngwaingwena sa Nakisi. 'Unari ka fi'i alua 'i Dingasi, 'i Dingasi ka fi'i alua Mitilin, 'afe sa Kaumanu, ka alua ta ngela. Ka alua sa Bilimae'ate'e nau ku fa'afa'asata 'ania sa Arangeo ka leleka kira ka saea go'o 'ania ma'a nia, ka alua 'i Maefa'asia, nia nai. Rō kini kī na'a nai tata'e 'i nai'ari. Sa Bilimae'ate'e ara'i ka tua kwau 'i lo'oba saena faka, atokale'a nia ne'e ki 'iri sai na'a ana, ana fa'i na'ona'o. Nia oli na'a sulia te'a kira Maefa'asia ba alua rō ngela kī, nia na'a kwau 'i Matariu. * * * Sa ngwane'e Ko'okona alua sa ngwane'e Ngoraga, na atokale'a nia sa Maeanate'e fa'ida kira 'i Fiu, kira ne'e fa'i na'ona'o 'aimili, di'ia kira olioli ma'i kaili sulida. Kira'a ne'e kira ngalia fanoa 'i Fi'ika'o fuana kaimili.

Aia, ai kaimili sa 'Aburu nia korea 'i Ngidu'ofa, kini 'i Ferasagwali, ka alua sa Maelaua, ka alua 'i Ko'ogao. * * * 'I Saku [ngwaingwaena sa 'Aburu] nini'a ai kini 'afe fuana sa Folo'o'a, ka tua 'i Kori'ofenga. Sa 'Aburu korea 'i Ngidu'ofa, kini 'i Kwalo, sa Au lala ne'e kero'o futa sui. Ka oli ka tua gali Ferasagwali ne'e kira sasia fanoa lo'oko, kira ka tua 'i lo'oko. Ka mae ka nia 'i nai'ari, kōwata'a nai ka nia 'i Ferasagwali. Sa Au ne'e ke rao 'uana gwata nau, ngwaefuta ana ai ngwane sa Fanasia. Kera'a fi'i alua sa Maelaua, kera'a ka alua 'i Ko'ogau. Kera'a ka mae ta'ifau, sa tai ne'e gonida [rō ngela kī]? Rodo ne'e kira teofia māna luma, dangi kira saena tafu, 'anilana la'ena alo, korilana ta'e sode.

'Asi ka saka 'i Darikwasa, Folo'o'a ka liu 'i fanoa, kira ka "Reala ngela sa tai kī ne'e, liu go'o 'uana saungilada 'ufuni re!" Kera tua go'o 'i gwauna tafu fuana midilana ta'ena sode. "Aia'a fata 'amu īra, io, 'oko korea na'a 'a'ai kira Ko'osaku. Ngela futa ana sa ngwane'e Ko'o'aburu kī fu."

'Olomoama, lives there at present, married to I'alaua, and childless. Well, Launangwala was the wife of Gwere, Launangwala begot Bilimae'ate'e, married Kiniasi, born of Usunga'i, she was born of Subua and was the sister of Nakisi.[1] So then he begot Dingasi, Dingasi then begot Mitilin, wife of Kaumanu, and she bore a child. He begot Bilimae'ate'e, I gave him the name Arangeo but eventually they called him after his father, he begot Maefa'asia, that's it. There are two women there at present. Bilimae'ate'e married and lived away there abroad, his descendants we don't know, the first-born. It comes back to their mother Maefa'asia, who begot two children, she's now away at Matariu.[2] * * * That man Ko'okona begot that man Ngorage, his descendants are Maenate'e and the others at Fiu,[3] they are our senior ones, if they returned here we'd follow from them. They it was who brought the home at Fi'ika'o for us.

Well, our one 'Aburu married Ngidu'ofa, a girl from Ferasagwali, he begot Maelaua and begot Ko'ogao. * * * Saku ['Aburu's sister] was the woman married to Folo'o'a, she lived at Kori'ofenga. 'Aburu married Ngidu'ofa, a girl of Kwalo, Au and she were born together. He returned and lived around Ferasagwali where they made their home, they lived over there. He died and he's there, my pig-baking is at Ferasagwali. Au would reach for my pig, as kinsman of one on the male side, Fanasia.[4] They then begot Maelaua, they begot Ko'ogao. They both died and who was to keep them [the children]? By night they slept in front of the house, by day they were in the rubbish, eating taro peel, scraping out split cooking-bamboos.

A party came to Darikwasa, Folo'o'a passed the home and they said "Hey, whose are those children? they're going to get killed doing that!" They just sat on top of the rubbish to scavenge from the split bamboos. "Well you can talk, yes, you've married their aunt Ko'osaku. Those children are born of that man Ko'o'aburu."

1 Nakisi is the senior man of the Mānadari clan already mentioned on page 16.

2 Matariu is one of the Kwara'ae suburban villages of Honiara.

3 This is the Fiu in West Kwara'ae.

4 That is, Au's ghost, brother of Alasa'a's female ancestor Ngidu'ofa, would demand pig sacrifices from Alasa'a, as a kinsman of Fanasia, who was descended from him in the male line.

Nia ka leka kwau ka dao ka ngalia alo ka ngīa ka kwate fuadaro'o, kera'a ka 'ania. Kira ka saka ana asi, dao 'i Gwa'iu'ula, fuli fanga'a, sa Folo'o'a ka "O Saku, ngalia ma'i alo nau." Ngalia ka liu 'i fanoa ka ngīa buta ī'a fuiri, ka ngīa alo fūri ka sarea 'ania rō ngela lokiri. 'Asi buri, nia ka saka ana asi, dao 'i nai'ari 'i fuli fanga'a, Folo'o'a ka fata 'uri "Koro ke ū go'o 'akoro, ma koro ke leka go'o." 'I Saku la'umia 'okofa'u ka foea, kera liu na'a 'i Ferasagwali nai. Rō ngela fukiri ka lisia bore sa Folo'o'a ma kera lae na'a ma'i 'uana si kera'a 'ania na'a alo ana 'ofodangi, so'olafi. Ka dao, 'i Saku ka "'Oi! ngela ta'a sa tai kī nini?" Ara'i nia ka "O, ma fasi 'a'ai 'oe kī ne'e futa ana sa 'Aburu ne'ana, nia ka angi fa'inia 'a'ai nia kī." Kira ka ngali'i ka sareda 'i Kwari'ofenga.

Sa Tolosau nia gania 'i Ko'ogao fuana aiburina sa Raradoe nai, kira ka kwatea daura'ia doe 'uana kira ka ludangia kira ka oli la'u folo 'uana. Kira ngalia na'a nai, Ko'ogao fi'i alua sa Fulaniu, sa Firitalau. Fulaniu 'urungwae ka mae go'o. Firitalau nini'a alua sa Tōdoe, Tōdoe ka alua sa Ko'osara, Ko'osara ka alua sa Dikite'e, sa Dikite'e ka alua 'i Falenaramo, Falenaramo nini'a alua go'o sa Maeudua, sa Ka'i ka laua 'i Ri'ifa'asia ma nia korea na'a 'i Kwai. * * *

Sa Folo'o'a nia ka gania kini 'i Marade kira saea 'ania 'i 'Urukwai, kira kwatea fuana sa ngwane'e Maelaua, ka fi'i atokale faulu la'u, kaili fi'i tata'e la'u 'i nai'ari. Nia ka alua sa Fanea, ka alua sa Rongoa, ka alua sa Asaka, ka alua 'i Laguru. Fanea ne'e alua kaimili, sa Rongoa nai alua sa ngwane'e Bualimae fani ai te'ete'e kī. Sa Asaka nai alua sa Kwalea, Kwalea ka alua 'i Musia, Musia ka alua 'i Maesakoa, ka nia 'i fu'uba sa Gafana ū fuana, nia ngalia mae nia ka sui na'a aku. Aia'a, 'i Laguru 'afe lo'oko tolo, sa Ra'ate'e ka ū fuana, dao na'a 'unari. Iu, nai daro'ia na'a nai, nai daro'ia futa'anga kaili, nai kwatea to'oto'o na'a ana.

Sa Fanea, fa'i na'ona'o sa Maelaua, nia korea 'i Ko'ongidu, kini 'i Fairū. Sa Rongoa, ai sulia, nia alua sa Lolosau, sa Manufilu ne'e kira saungia go'o. Sa Manufilu noa'a ka 'iri alua ta ngwae. Aia'a, sa Lolosau alua sa Kamusute'e, ka alua 'i Kereomea. Kereomea nai 'afe fuana sa Kaobata, ka alua sa 'Una, ka alua sa 'Uae.

He went away and came bringing taro, broke it and gave to the two of them and they ate it. They came out to the sea, arrived at Gwa'iu'ula, the eating-place, and Folo'o'a said "Oh Saku, bring my taro." Taking it, he went to the home and broke open a packet of fish, broke taro and fed the two children with it. He came out to the sea after the others, arriving there at the eating-place, and Folo'o'a said "We're standing together, let's go." Saku folded up a burden-mat, loaded up, and they went to Ferasagwali. The two children saw Folo'o'a and ran to him, as they'd eaten taro morning and evening. Arriving, Saku said "Eh, whose are these nasty children?" Her husband said "Oh, it seems it's your nephew and niece born of 'Aburu, he's crying for his aunts." They took them and reared them at Kwari'ofenga.

Tolosau asked for Ko'ogao for his younger brother Raradoe, they gave a big bridewealth for her, they heaped it up and came back again for her. They took her, and Ko'ogao then begot Fulaniu and Firitalau. Fulaniu was single and died. It was Firitalau who begot Tōdoe, Tōdoe begot Ko'osara, Ko'osara begot Dikite'e, Dikite'e begot Falenaramo, it was Falenaramo who begot Maeudua, Ka'i abducted Ri'ifa'asia and he married her at Kwai. * * *

Folo'o'a asked for a girl at Marade called 'Urukwai,[1] they gave her for that man Maelaua, he then begot descendants anew, we'll set out again from here. He begot Fanea, he begot Rongoa, he begot Asaka, he begot Laguru. Fanea begot us, it was Rongoa who begot that man Bualimae and the junior ones. It was Asaka who begot Kwalea, Kwalea begot Musia, Musia begot Maesakoa, she's down there, Gafana stands for her, he's already taken his group from me. Well, Laguru was married over inland, Ra'ate'e stands for her, that's how it is. Yes, I'll set it out, I'll set out our family, I'll give out each one.

Fanea, the senior son of Maelaua, married Ko'ongidu, a girl from Fairū. Rongoa, the following one, he begot Lolosau and Manufilu whom they killed. Manufilu did not beget anyone. Well, Lolosau begot Kamusute'e, and begot Kereomea. Kereomea was married to Kaobata and begot 'Una and begot 'Uae.

1 Marade is in Latea and this marriage is important in giving Alasa'a a claim to Latea land.

The descendants of Felega

Having told the story of Maeorea Asimaomate'e and how he re-established the Tolinga clan and its shrines, Alasa'a goes on to trace his descendants to the present day, accounting for most of the Tolinga families of the 1980s.

From Maeorea's son Felega and his grandson Faneadoe, Alasa'a begins with the senior line descended from Faneadoe's first son Kubufo'oa Kauburu. But in the next generation this male line ends and their present day descendants are all 'born of women' of Tolinga.

It is the descendants of Faneadoe's second son Ko'o'aburu who are the present day senior members of the clan, 'born of men' of Ko'o'aburu's orphaned son Maelaua. Maelaua and his sons and grandsons married into the clans of Latea (Marade) and Fairū on the east coast and thus established the Tolinga people in these lands, where many of them live today.

Alasa'a gives only partial and rather selective genealogies, and the charts deal mainly with the relationships included in his narrative. He makes only passing mention of the senior branch of Tolinga, descendants of Ko'okona, who are based at Fiu in West Kwara'ae, and concentrates on relatives in his own neighbourhood in East Kwara'ae.

Alasa'a also knew a great deal more about the wives and junior descendants of the recent male ancestors than he mentions here. Michael Kwa'ioloa documented much of the old man's genealogical knowledge on other occasions, and this has helped to clarify his accounts for the charts on this and the following pages.

In the chart below the descendants of Maelaua's sons and grandsons are represented by those living men who 'stand for' them (*ū fuana*), and more details are given later. But the chart also traces some of their relatives 'born of women', whom Alasa'a includes in his genealogy as associates of the Tolinga clan.

Genealogy of Tolinga

The descendants of Felega

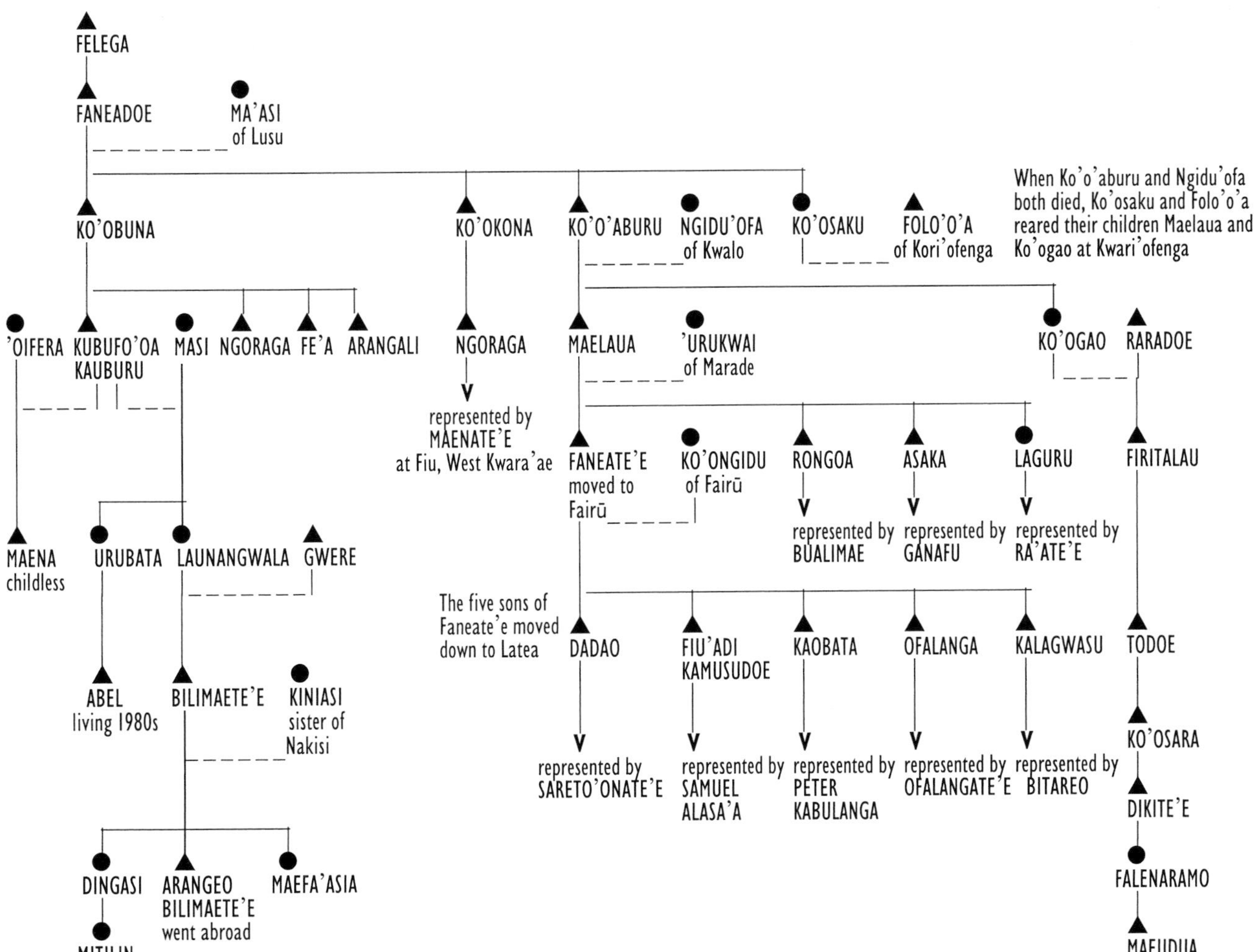

'Una na'a ne'e atokale, sa 'Uae 'iri alua na'a ta'a ngela, nia 'aba'ato. Aia'a, sa Samson ne'e ū 'i nai'ari fuana kale'a 'i Kereomea, fa'inia sa Kaobatate'ete'e.

Sa Rongoa, atokale'a nia nai kwa'ia 'i kaulu ke sai ana. Sa Kamusute'e korea 'i Maesakoa, ai nai'ari nau ku kina futa'anga nia. Di'ia nau ku 'ilia ta'ena ta rū lala nia ke teo 'ana, 'a'ai sa Filiga, ka fi'i alua sa Kumara, fa'i na'ona'o. Ka alua 'i Mae'usia ki saea 'ania 'i Masina, alua sa Manufioa, ka alua sa Fafaakalo, sa Manilu ū fuana. Ka alua sa Ma'uisae, sa Bualimae ka ū fuana. Ka alua sa ngwane'e Bualimaedoe, sa Manilofia ne'e ū fuana, Kalagwasu. Aia'a, 'i Ri'ite'e, sa Maunu ne'e ū fuana, futa ana 'i Musaria, 'A'emae, ngela ne'e sa Selo nari, kaulu ka rongoa. Atokalea sa Rongoa nari nau ku tolingia ka sui na'a kwau.

Atokalea sa Fanea fa'i na'ona'o. Nia alua sa Dadao, sa Dadao ka alua sa La'ugere, sa La'ugere ka alua sa ngwane'e Sareto'ona, sa Sareto'ona ka alua sa Kamusu, sa Sareto'onate'e ka ū fuana. Fa'i na'ona'o nai. Sa Fiu'adi, ne'e ki saea 'ania Kamusudoe, alua sa Maniramo, ka alu nau, nau ku ū fuana, sa Maesatana ne'e nia 'i māna. Sa Kaobata nia alua sa Kabulanga, sa Kabulanga ka alua sa Sele'au, sali sa Bita [Kabulanga] ne'e ū fuana, fa'ina'ona'o sa ngwane'e Sele'au. Aia'a, sa Ofalanga alua logo sa Gwaorara, sa Gwaorara ka alua sa Ofalangate'e. Sa Ofalanga 'aba'ato, nia loko tua ka lia go'o 'ana nini'ari nia ū 'i nai'ari. Sa Fanea ka alua sa Kalagwasu, sa Kalagwasu ka alua sa Kwa'ioloa, ka alua sa Di'au Bonemae, sa Ilito'ona ne'e didifuila sa Di'au. Sa Bitareo ne'e ū fuana, ne'e nia alua sa Manilofia, ka alua sa Bitareo. Kala 'a'emae kaimili ana 'i Ko'ongidu nai, fa'i na'ona'o sa Fanea nai.

Aia'a, 'i Gwalafea ne'e 'afe 'i tolo, nia 'afe fuana sa Sango, ka alua sa Ngwasa'elo, ka alua sa Osi'au. Sa Osi'au korea 'i Lalite'e, ka alu ngwae ka nia 'i Fauābu. Sa Ngwasa'elo ka korea kini 'i Kwakwarea, ka alua sa Funusui, ka nia logo 'i Fauābu.

Una has descendants, 'Uae didn't beget anyone, he's childless. Well, Samson[1] there stands for those born of Kereomea and Kaobatate'ete'e.

Rongoa, I'll relate his descendants so you'll know them. Kamusute'e married Maesakoa, that's one I don't know the lineage of. If I try it today it will become something else, Filiga's aunt,[2] he then begot Kumara, the senior one. He begot Mae'usia who we called Masina, begot Manufioa, and begot Fafaakalo, Manilu stands for him. He begot Ma'uisae, Bualimae stands for him. He begot that man Bualimaedoe, Manilofia stands for him, Kalagwasu. Well, Ri'ite'e, Manu stands for her, born of Musaria, 'A'emae, that's Selo's daughter, you've heard of her. That's the descendants of Rongoa I've finished setting out for you.

The descendants of Fanea are senior. He begot Dadao, Dadao begot La'ugere, La'ugere begot that man Sareto'ona, Sareto'ona begot Kamusu, and Sareto'onate'e stands for him. That's the senior one. Fiu'adi, who they called Kamusudoe, begot Maniramo and he begot me, I stand for him, Maesatana is out in front.[3] Kaobata begot Kabulanga, Kabulanga begot Sele'au, perhaps Peter [Kabulanga] stands for him, the senior son of that man Sele'au. Well, Ofalanga also begot Gwaorara, Gwaorara begot Ofalangate'e. Ofalangate'e is childless, he's still alive at present, he stands there. Fanea begot Kalagwasu, Kalagwasu begot Kwa'ioloa and begot Joe Bonemae, Ilito'ona replaced Joe. Bitareo stands for him, as he begot Manilofia and begot Bitareo. That's our little tale of Ko'ongidu and the senior one, Fanea.

Well, Gwalafea was married inland, she was married to Sango, she begot Ngwasa'elo, and begot Osi'au. Osi'au married Lalite'e and begot someone who's at Fauābu. Ngwasa'elo married a girl from Kwakwarea and begot Funusui, he's also at Fauābu.

1 Samson Una Folotate'e is the husband of Alasa'a's youngest daughter Arana.

2 Maesakoa was actually the sister of Filiga of Latea, who was the father of Alasa's's brother-in-law Ramo'itolo (see genealogy page 91.)

3 That is, Alasa'a's eldest son John Maesatana is senior in the next generation.

The descendants of Maelaua

With Maelaua and his descendants, Alasa'a is dealing with his closest Tolinga relatives, down to the senior living men of the 1980s. Several of their grandfathers and fathers appear again in the history of the colonial period of Alasa'a's youth (Chapter 4) and some of his own Tolinga ancestors also play a part in the history of his mother's clan of Fairū (Chapter 3).

Alasa'a's grandfather Fiu'adi Kamusudoe was an old man in 1919 and he died about 1932. He and his brothers may have been born in the 1840s, and their grandfather Maelaua perhaps in the 1780s or 1790s.

A look at where recent generations of Tolinga men have lived illustrates the dispersed nature of Kwara'ae clans. Although they inherit a clan identity and land of origin in the central inland through many generations of ancestors in the male line, they all live in the homelands of various female ancestors towards the coasts, in east or west. In East Kwara'ae, Alasa'a, Sareto'ona and the family of Marcus Bualimae (pictured page 17) all live in neigbouring settlements in the land of Latea, while Alasa'a's son Maniramo lives in Fairū. Many have also moved to Honiara or further abroad for employment.

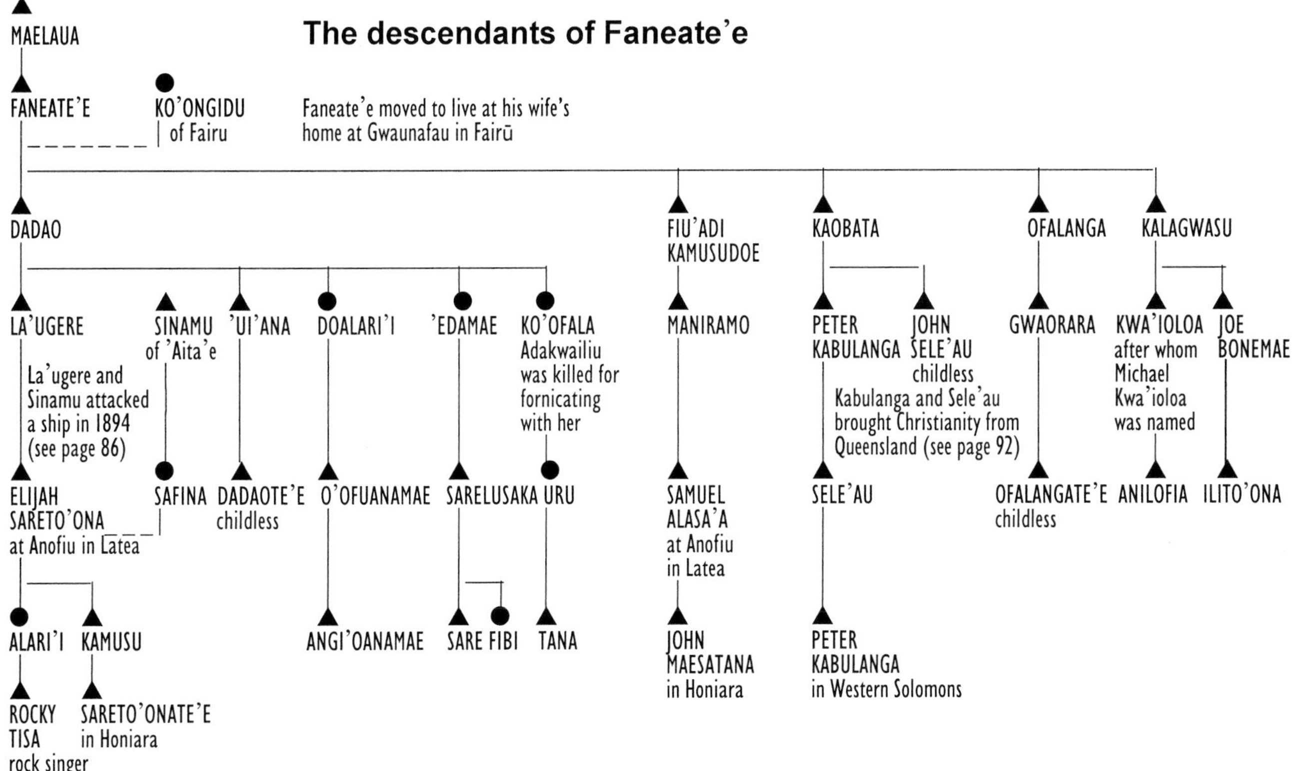

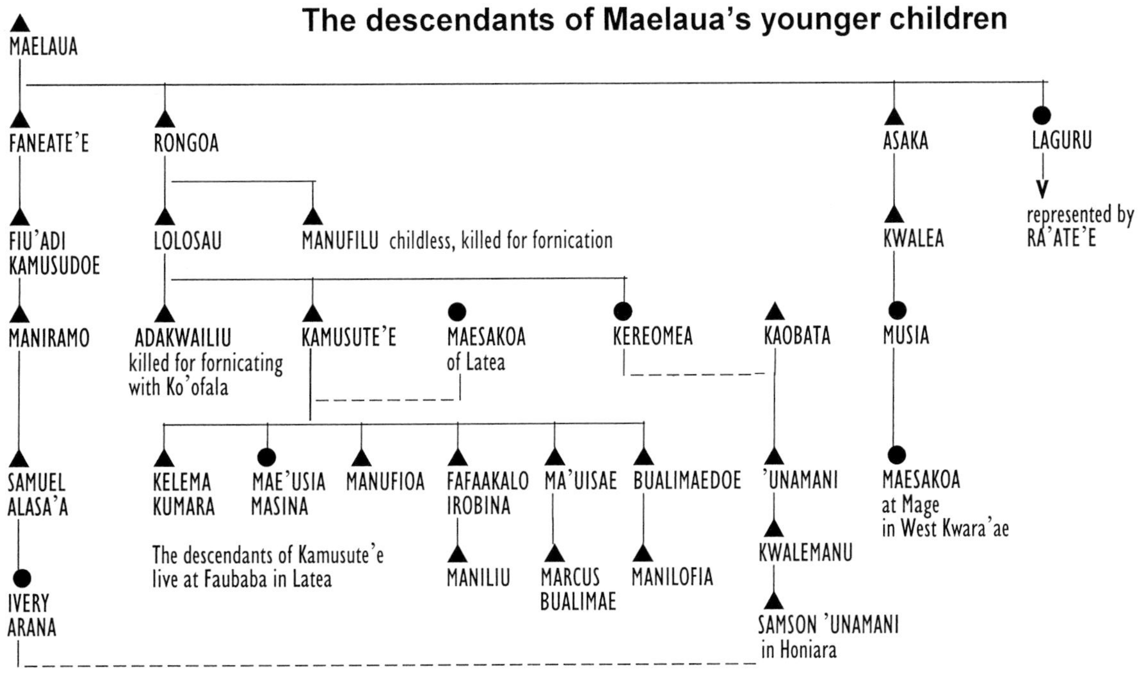

Kale'a fa'i na'ona'o sa Dadao nai tolingia la'u. Sa Dadao ne'e alua sa La'ugere, La'ugere alua sa Sare, sa 'Ui'ania, sa Sare ka alua sa Kamu, sa Kamu ne'e ka alua sa Sarete'ete'e ka ū fuana. Sa'Ui'ania ne'e alua sa Dadaote'e, ka 'iri alua go'o ta ngwae. Aia'a, 'i Doalari'i, kini, nia 'afe fuana sa To'ani'i'a , ngwae 'i Ubasi, ka alua sa O'ofuanamae, sa O'ofuanamae ka alua sa Angi'oanamae, ka nia 'i Matariu. Aia'a, 'i 'Edamae 'afe fuana sa Misimanu, ka alua sa Sare, ka alua 'i Fibi, sa Misimanute'e ne'e ka ū fuana ai nai'ari. Kale'a sa Dadao nai, dao 'i nai'ari ka sui.

Sa Kaobata alua sa Kabulanga, ka alua 'i Aruanamae, 'i Aruanamae ne'e alua sa ngwane'e Sele'audoe, fa'asata Sele'au lokoni'a 'i Kobito. Sa Angi'oanamae ne'e nia kwau 'i fa'i bani, ne'e ū fuana. Atokale'a sa Kaobata nai. Sa Ofalanga ka alua sa ngwane'e Gwaorara, sa Gwaorara ka alua sa Ofalanga, ka 'iri alua ta ngwae. Ai kini Dingana 'afe fuana sa Kwalemanu, ka alua sa ngwane'e Danisi, ka alua sa Tomekara, ka alua sa Ngisia, sa Ngisia ne'e alua 'i Ko'okwalu.

Ta ngela kini ana sa Dadao ne'e 'i Ko'ofala. Sa Adakwailau ne'e fa'ainā, aina'ona sa Kamusu, ka laua ka ngalia sa rodo ka laua ka leka teo fa'inia saena Faodamokota'a. 'Unari, ma'a sa Kwasiomea ogana ka ta'a, sa Kwasiomea fa'ida ka saungia. Kira saungia fa'asia 'i Ko'ofala. Ko'ofala kira ka fa'amauria ka tafi, ka 'afe fuana sa ngwane'e I'alifu, ka alua 'i Uru, Uru ka 'afe fuana sa Kwatefera, ka alua sa Tana, nia 'i 'Ako'ako.

Aia'a, atokale'a nai la'u. Sa Fiu'adi ne'e ki saea 'ania sa Kamudoe, ka alua sa Maniramo, ka alua 'i Akabua. 'I Akabua ne'e 'afe fuana sa Gere'a, ka alua sa Arangeo, sa Arangeo ka alua sa Gere'a. Aia'a, ma'a nau ne'e sa Maniramo alua 'i Siumalefo, Siumalefo ka alua sa So'ai, ka ū fuana. Ka alua 'i Sefo,'i Sefo ka 'afe fuana sa Mauta'i, ngwae 'Ere'ere, ka alua sa Kwalafaga ne'e ū fuana. Atokalea nai na'iri'a, nau'a ne'e te'e ngwae go'o te'e ngwangwane, nini'a nau ku alu ngwae go'o, sui na'a.

The senior line born of Dadao, I'll set it out too. Dadao begot La'ugere, La'ugere begot Sare, 'Ui'ania, Sare begot Kamu, Kamu begot Sarete'ete'e who stands for him. 'Ui'ania begot Dadaote'e and he didn't beget anyone. Well, Doalari'i, a girl, she was married to To'ani'i'a, a man of Ubasi, and begot O'ofuanamae, O'ofuanamae begot Angi'oanamae and he's at Matariu [Honiara]. Well, 'Edamae was married to Misimanu and begot Sare, and begot Fibi, Misimanute'e stands for that one. That's those born of Dadao, right up to the present.

Kaobata begot Kabulanga, and begot Aruanamae, Aruanamae who begot the man who Sele'audoe named Sele'au, the one at Kobito [Honiara]. Angi'oanamae, wherever he is, stands for him. That's the descendants of Kaobata. Ofalanga begot that man Gwaorara, Gwaorara begot Ofalanga and didn't beget anyone else. The girl Dingana married Kwalemanu and begot that man Danisi, and begot Tomekara and begot Ngisia, Ngisia begot Ko'okwalu.

A daughter of Dadao was Ko'ofala. Adakwailau made her pregnant, the elder brother of Kamusu, he seized and took her in the night, seized and went and lay with her in Mokota'a [Bad-smelling] Cave. So then, the father of Kwasiomea was angry and Kwasiomea and others killed him. They killed him from Ko'ofala. Ko'ofala they saved, she escaped and was married to that man I'alifu, and begot Uru, Uru was married to Kwatefera, she begot Tana, he's at 'Ako'ako.

Well, more of my descent. Fiu'adi who they called Kamudoe, begot Maniramo, and begot Akabua. Akabua was married to Gere'a, and begot Arangeo, Arangeo begot Gere'a. Well, my father Maniramo begot Siumalefo,[1] Siumalefo begot So'ai, he stands for her. He begot Sefo, Sefo was married to Mauta'i, an 'Ere'ere man, and begot Kwalafaga who stands for her. That's my descent, I'm a man of the male line, who has begotten people, and that's the end.

1 Siumalefo was the wife of Ramo'itolo of Latea: see pages 81 and 91.

The Tolingas move to Fairū and Latea

When Faneate'e of Tolinga, son of Maelaua, married Ko'ongidu he began the Tolinga presence in her land of Fairū. As Alasa'a mentions in the next chapter, Faneate'e lived and died at Gwaunafau in Fairū, where his son Fiu'adi Kamusudoe, Alasa'a's grandfather, also lived.

From this time, Tolinga people were also settling in the land of Latea to the north of Fairū, home of their ancestor 'Urukwai from the Marade area of Latea who married Maelaua. Fiu'adi Kamusudoe and his four brothers probably moved from their father's home at Gwaunafau. His namesake Kamusute'e, grandson of his father Fanea's brother Rongoa, also married a Marade woman and their descendants also live in Latea.

In 1968 Elijah Sareto'ona, a grandson of Fiu'adi Kamusudoe's eldest brother Dadao, living at Anofiu in Latea, told the story of how his and Alasa'a's grandfathers came to Latea, as evidence for a court hearing on the leadership for Latea land. The court case did not involve the Tolinga people directly, but Sareto'ona's statement shows how they were welcomed to live in Latea by their distant kinsmen. The question at issue in his evidence is whose ancestors demonstrated their leadership for Latea land by giving the Tolinga new arrivals permission to live and work there.

Sareto'ona's statement provides another example of the detailed knowledge of genealogical history which underpins Kwara'ae land tenure and local politics. Although disagreeing with Alasa'a's account in some details, it also adds further information on the complex relationships between the clans of Tolinga, Fairū and Latea.

If Fiu'adi and his brothers were born in the 1840s, they may have moved to Fairū and Latea as young married men in the 1860s.

<u>6th Witness Saretoona Sworn</u> State

Said:- Today I come to court not to say what I heard of some man, but what I know from my grandfather, when my grandfather came from Toliña there was no man in here. There are 5 brothers who came first in Latea land here are names. Dadao, Fiuadi, Ofalaña, Kaobata, Kalagwasu. They came first to Fulibae, then down to Andakoa and they asked a man Mautai said where is a man Buñia, Mautai said he was at Talakali. They ask Mautai to go and ask Buñia to come and see them. So Buñia came and see this brothers at Fulibae. Yes when they come there no man in the land of Latea, a man Udali was at Gwaiketekete he went and bring food for their brothers at Fulibae. These 5 brothers said to Buñia and Udali we see this land and it was a forest land and we want to start and cut down and work the village. Buñia and Udali said we only two men and we cannot do any thing to this forest, not because they want to work the land only but they are of Marade land. The 5 brothers and Buñia they born of two women, here are their names Kooñidu and Meana, this two women born of one woman Urufikwai of Marade. Urufikwai her father was Alafamae and she married to Niulafa of Fairu. Then this woman Kooñidu married to a man Fanea of Toliña. Then Kooñidu born that 5 brothers mention above. So these 5 brothers came from Toliña to their brothers Buñia and talk together and start this place of Latea. They also want their brother Udali because he feed them when they just came and he also know how to block the wild devil in this land. Buñia & Udali they born of woman but still they of Marade land.

Civil land case No 29/68, Solomon Islands National Archives.
Original English

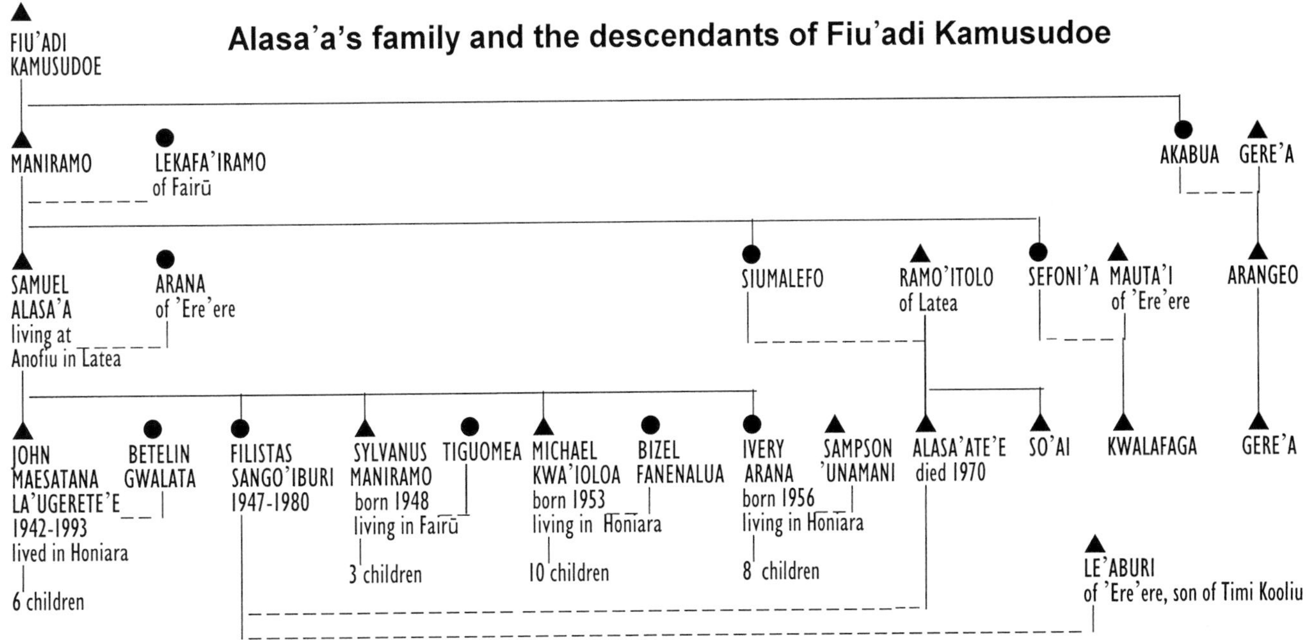

3
Na Fanoa 'i Fairū

Iu, nau'a nini'a, nau ku ala'a sulia Fairū nau ku firi ana. Nau'a sa Alasa'a. Si nia ta'e saena feraābu nau 'i Siale. Sa Bili'adoe alua sa Kwanamalefo, ka alua sa Tolikwao, ka alua sa Tufuigaote'e. Ka koso ka nia 'i Dalobala. Ka alua sa Ngwa'erobo, sa Ngwa'erobo ka alua sa Fiulasi, sa Fiulasi ka alua sa Maefolosia. Na akalo na'a ne'e sa Maefolosia. 'Unari, sa Maefolosia ka alua sa Niurara. Ka alua sa Niurara, ka leka, leka ka tua 'i 'Abui, ka koso ka nia 'i Ūa. Ka to'ofolo, ka nia 'i Sisilo, ka olioli ka ngalia ma'a nia sa Maefolosia, sū'asia, ka alua ana fa'i 'ako ābu, ka ābu. Kauburu ka osida, kira ka leka, kira ka tua 'i Totongwala. Nia ka ngalia ka alua ana fa'i ngara, ka ābu ka leleka ta'ena, nia mae kira ka alua fi'i tatali 'i fuila. Nia ka tua 'i nai'ari, kauburu ka osida. Sa 'Oifanoa ne'e koso, ka nia 'i Uka. Sa Elamalefo ne'e ka koso, ka nia 'i Uka: ma'a nia, aiburina sa Niurara. Kira ka mae ta'ifau 'i Uka, sa Rauna'au ka fulia 'i Fuliba'e. Na isufuta'a na'a nai'ari, sa Nongwae lala ne'e ū fuana. Sa 'Oifanoa ka alua sa Te'ekwa'u, ka koso ka nia 'i Marade, ne'e nau ku firi ana Latea fani.

'Aia'a. Sa Niurara ka ta'e ka 'oia 'i Malakwalo. Sa Akafo'oa ka leka ka nia saena Kwaru, 'i 'Aimela, ne'e nau ku firi ana Kwaru 'i sulia. 'Unari kauburu ka osida, kira ka tata'e, kira ka tua 'i Gwaunafau, ne'e nau ku firi ana Gwaunafau 'i sulia, si akalo nau na'iri'a fulia fanoa nai'ari kī. Kira ka koso, kira ka tua 'i 'Eda'eda, ka alua sa Maelongasi, ruana sata ana sa Ba'ulau. Nau ku ō'i gwata 'ania ana feraābu ne'e nau ku leka fa'asia, sukulu ka fa'alia na'a. Ka alua sa Suli'ioko, ka leka, ka nia 'i 'Ai'ako. 'Unari, sa Niurara ka ngalia ma'a nia, su'asia nai'ari sa Maefolosia, ka alua 'i gwauna fau angwa'i, fau ni ma'a nia sa angwa'i nia fū 'i bae, nia 'i Kula'ikwai, ka ābu ka dao 'i ta'ena. 'Unari, sa Ba'ulau ka ngalia ka alua 'i 'aena 'ai 'ako, kira ka fa'asatā fanoa nai'ari 'ania 'i 'Ai'ako.

3
The Homeland of Fairū

Yes, it's me, I'm talking about Fairū and my claim to it. Me, Alasa'a. As it arises from my tabu-sanctum at Siale. Bili'adoe begot Kwanamalefo, he begot Tolikwao, he begot Tufuigaote'e. He went down and was at Dalobala. He begot Ngwa'erobo, Ngwa'erobo begot Fiulasi, Fiulasi begot Maefolosia. He was the ghost, Maefolosia. So then, Maefolosia begot Niurara. He begot Niurara and went, went to live at 'Abui, he went down and was at Ūa. He crossed over and was at Sisilo, returned and took his father Maefolosia, the consuming ghost,[1] and put him in a tabu *'ako* tree, it's tabu. A gale demolished them, they went and lived at Totongwala. He took him and put him in a *ngara* tree, it's tabu until today, and when he died they put a hibiscus clump at the site. He lived there and a gale demolished them. 'Oifanoa went down and was at Uka. Elamelefo went down and was at Uka: his father was the younger brother of Niurara. They all died at Uka and Rauna'au founded Fuliba'e. That's the genealogy, but Nongwae stands for them. 'Oifanoa begot Te'ekwa'u, he went down and was at Marade, so I have a claim to Latea from that.

Well. Niurara set out and settled Malakwalo. Akafo'oa went and was in Kwaru, at 'Aimela, so I have a claim to Kwaru because of that. So then, a gale demolished them, they set off and lived at Gwaunafau, so I have a claim to Gwaunafau because of that, as it was my ghosts who founded those homes. They went down and lived at 'Eda'eda and he begot Maelongasi, whose second name was Ba'ulau. I offered pigs through him at a tabu-sanctum which I've left, the mission has destroyed it. He begot Suli'ioko and went and was at 'Ai'ako. So then, Niurara took his father, the consuming ghost Maefolosia, and put him at the head of an overhanging rock, his father's rock in the overhang is the base of the shrine, it's at Kula'ikwai, it's tabu until today. So then, Ba'ulau took him and put him at the foot of an *'ako* tree and they called that home 'Ai'ako [*'Ako*-tree].

1 As a 'consuming ghost' (*sū'asia*) Maefolosia was particularly tabu. His relics were kept apart from other ghosts and he received burnt offerings of a piglet rather than sacrifices eaten by men of the congregation.

Alasa'a's claim to Fairū

Chapter 3 is the history of the homeland of Fairū, where Alasa'a's Tolinga clan ancestors came to live three generations before him. He inherited his claims to this land through his mother, grandmother and great-grandmother, all women of Fairū who married Tolinga men.

To demonstrate these claims, Alasa'a recounts the history of the Fairū people and their neighbours of Kwaru from their arrival fourteen generations before him to a series of damaging feuds which continued up to his youth. As the strongest claims to seniority or leadership for land pass through the male line, such detailed history is particularly important in claims on the female side. There are people who dispute Alasa'a's claim to Fairū, and there may be differences of opinion about the land boundary. This book does not make a judgement as to whose versions are correct.

In the 1980s, when Alasa'a was recounting this history, more than 500 people were living on Fairū land in about 20 settlements. The map shows East Kwara'ae at this time, with recently built roads, larger settlements as clusters of small dots, and some of the places mentioned in this and later chapters.

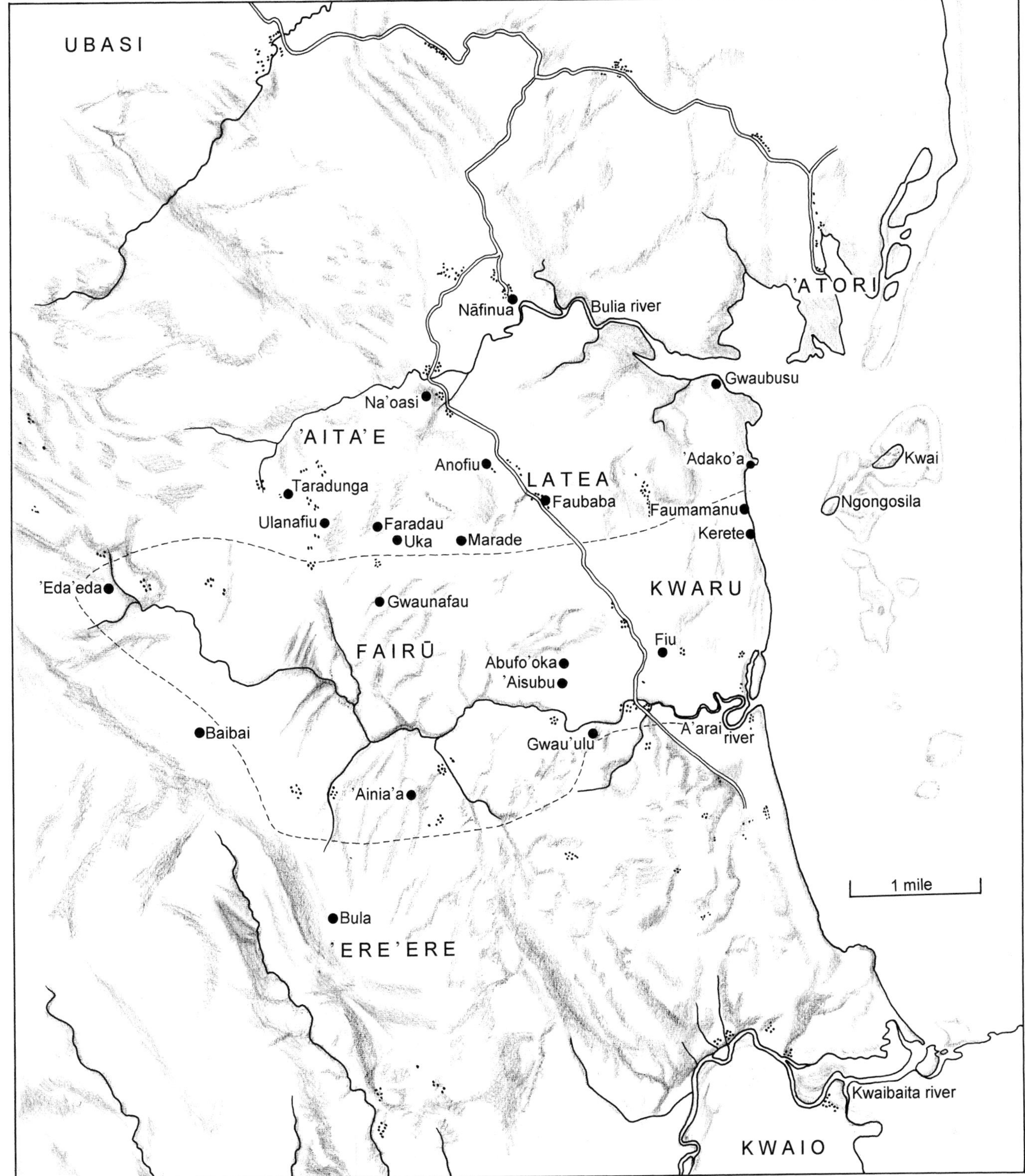

Ka alua sa Maluarara ka koso ka nia 'i Faradau. Ka ngalia su'asia nai'ari ka alua 'i Faradau. 'Unari, nia ka 'asia na'a 'i Faradau, gwauna fanoa nau kī na'iri'a ne'e nau ku firi ani nari.

'Unari, ka alua sa Niufara ka koso ka 'oia 'i Fairū. Fairū noa'a la'u bali nini'a 'i 'Eda'eda, Fairū nia lala 'i bali lo'oko. 'Unari, sa Niufara ka alua sa Bulinimae. Nau ku 'isi 'ania feraābu 'i Fairū, kira koso fa'asia, kira fa'alia. 'Unari sa Bulinimae ka alua sa Muniga, nia ka tata'e ka 'oia 'i Lā'i, 'i Lā'i ne'e ngela nau sa Kwa'ioloa fa'asatā go'o 'ania 'i Anobala. Ka fi'i alua sa Kwasufanoa, nia ka ra'e ka nia 'i 'Aisubu, ruana sata ana nia ke keresia buli kī, kira ka saea 'ania sa Kerebuli. Nau ku 'isia 'ania feraābu 'i Fairū. 'Unari ka fi'i alua sa Ko'obaita, sa Ko'obaita ka fi'i alua sa Būfanoa, ka leka ka nia saena Kwaru 'i Fiu: rō Fiu kī nai'ari nia atokale fuana. 'Unari nia ka fi'i alua sa Mao'a fa'inia sa Ko'obula. Ai te'ete'e nai'ari, nia alua go'o rō ngwae kī. Sa Mao'a nia alua sa Ko'ola'a, ruana sata ana sa Ko'odangi, ka alua sa Biraome'a, ka alua 'i Mangona. Sa Biraome'a ne'e nau ku futa logo ana, sulia 'i Lekafa'iramo ne'e futa ana sa Folifanoa, sulia futa'anga nau 'i Fairū, sa Di'iakalo ne'e ka nia ana. Aia'a, 'unari, sa Ko'ola'a ka alua sa Mudi'a, sa Mudi'a ka alua sa Maeisua, ka alua 'i Ko'ongidu, nia'a nini nau ku firi ana kula ne'e kī sulia. * * *

Kira fa'ali dangulua ta'ena. Kira tofe nau fa'asia, kira ka ngalia gaua na'a, fanoa 'i Fairū, ta kafo ka 'iri teo na'a, ta 'ai ka 'iri teo na'a, ta ano ka 'iri teo na'a, kira ngali'i kira ka nau na'a 'ani'i fuada, fanoa 'i Fairū nia lofo na'a. Nai ala'a sulia saena rekwauta ne'e, ngela nai sa Kwa'oloa Michael ke ngalingali aka'u, nia ne nau ku ala'a sulia ta'ena. Aia, nau ki etangia go'o ala'anga nai.

Sa Fikiramo nini, nia rora ka ra'e saena Kwaru, ka korea 'i Gwauketa, kini 'i Kwakwali, ka alua sa ngwane'e Foli'a, ka alua sa Ī'adoe, ka alua sa Ī'agura, ka alua sa Ī'ate'ete'e, go'o 'afe nia kera'a ka mae ta'ifau na'a saena Kwaru. Fai ngwae ne'e kī kira oli, kira'a 'i 'Aisubu. Kira tua na'a 'i nai'ari fani to'a Fairū.

He begot Maluarara and went down and was at Faradau. He took that consuming ghost and put him at Faradau. So then, it's now fallen from use at Faradau, which is head of my homes which I have a claim to.

So then, he begot Niufara and went down and settled Fairū. Fairū is not on the 'Eda'eda side, Fairū is on the far side. So then, Niufara begot Bulinimae. I've finished with the Fairū tabu-sanctum, they've left it and destroyed it. Well then, Bulinimae begot Muniga and he set out and settled Lā'i, the Lā'i which my son Kwa'ioloa named Anobala.[1] He then begot Kwasufanoa, he went up and was at 'Aisubu and had a second name, he'd scrape tree resin and they called him Kerebuli [Scrape-resin].[2] I've finished with the Fairū tabu-sanctums. So then he begot Ko'obaita, Ko'obaita then begot Būfanoa, he went and he was in Kwaru at Fiu; the two Fius are descended from him. So he then begot Mao'a and Ko'obula. That younger brother just begot two men. Mao'a begot Ko'ola'a, [Ancestor-dawn] whose second name was Ko'odangi [Ancestor-day], and begot Biraome'a, and begot Mangona. Biraome'a I'm descended from too, because Lekafa'iramo was born of Folifanoa, through my lineage at Fairū, which Di'iakalo belongs to. Well, so then, Ko'ola'a begot Mudi'a, Mudi'a begot Maeisua and begot Ko'ongidu, and it's through her I claim those places. * * *

They're completely ruining it today. They're denying it to me, they've misappropriated the country of Fairū, not a stream remains, not a tree remains, no land remains, they've said it's theirs and the community of Fairū has flown off. I'll talk about it into this recorder, my son Kwa'ioloa Michael can take it and hang on, that's why I'm talking about it today. Well, I'll begin my talk.

It was Fikiramo, he strayed off and climbed to Kwaru, he married Gwauketa, a girl of Kwakwali and begot the man Foli'a, and begot Ī'adoe, and begot 'Ī'agura, and begot Ī'ate'e, then he and his wife both died in Kwaru. These four men returned and they were at 'Aisubu. They stayed there with the Fairū people.

1 Michael Kwa'ioloa gave the name Anobala to the home he built at Lā'i in 1973.

2 Resin scraped from nut (*ngali* / *Canarium*) trees is used for torches and for caulking cracks in canoes.

The priests of Fairū

Michael Kwa'ioloa took some notes from his father which help to clarify the early history of Fairū and the succession of tabu-speakers or priests, and tabu-sanctums or shrines. This history follows a common pattern in which the senior son of each generation (who is remembered even if his brothers are not) becomes priest for his father and earlier ancestors, adding another name to the genealogical invocation (*fiki'a*) which he used when baking pigs to them.

Mudi'a, the last priest in this list, was Alasa'a's great-great-grandfather. Alasa'a's detailed history of events in Fairū begins with a quarrel between Mudi'a and his in-laws, the sons of Fikiramo.

Taken from Samuel Alasa'a 23-2-84
The headquarters of Fairū is at 'Eda'eda. The ghost who my father and the others baked to was Maefolosia, the consuming ghost. No man could eat the leftovers [from the sacrifice]. The tabu-speaker Niurara (1st tabu-speaker) would invoke thus with the pig: "You, Maefolosia, take hold of *your* pig." When Niurara died, his son Maelongasi was tabu-speaker (2nd tabu-speaker), his second name was Baula'u. He would invoke thus: "Maefolosia, Niurara, take hold of *your* pig." When Maelongasi died Suluioko was tabu-speaker (3rd tabu-speaker). Maelongasi died at 'Ai'ako. When Suluioko died Malurara was the next tabu-speaker (4th tabu-speaker), he baked in the tabu-sanctum at 'Ai'ako. When Malurara died Niufarate'e was the next tabu-speaker (5th tabu-speaker). He baked in the tabu-sanctums at 'Ai'ako, at Faradau and at Kekeke. When Niufarate'e died, Bulinimae was the next tabu-speaker (6th tabu-speaker), when he died Muniga was the next tabu-speaker (7th tabu-speaker). When Muniga died, Kwasufanoa was the next tabu-speaker (8th tabu-speaker). He baked in the sanctum-site at 'Aisubu. When Kwasufanoa died, Ko'obaita was the next tabu-speaker (9th tabu-speaker). When Ko'obaita died Būfanoa was the next tabu-speaker (10th tabu-speaker), he baked at Fiu. When Būfanoa died Maoa was the next tabu-speaker (11th tabu-speaker). When Maoa died Mudi'a was the next tabu-speaker (12th tabu-speaker), he baked at 'Ai'ako. Then 'Ai'ako and Faradau and Kekeke and even Gwau'ulu were closed down.
Translated from Kwara'ae manuscript

The story of Fikiramo

Fikiramo was a fugitive from the neighbouring language group of Kwaio to the south who was taken in by his mother's relatives of Fairū. He lived at Kwaru, an area between Fairū and the neighbouring land of Latea which his descendants still claim.

The opening comments with which Alasa'a's introduces this branch of the clan are a complaint against their claim to leadership for Fairū land, and he gives his version of who the present-day inhabitants of Fairū really are. Because of this dispute, Fikiramo's story has been documented several times.

Adriel Rofate'e of Gwauna'ongi, as a leading local historian, wrote:

Rorakona he come from Gwaunaasi Koio he come to Kwara'ae and he married long Kwara'ae Fairū and he went back to his home and he begat son. And his son came back to Kwara'ae and he married girl from Latea and he live to Latea and they give the land for him.

Rorakona married Koeimae who was a girl from Fairū. Rorakona begot Fikiramo and Fikiramo came from his home and he lived in Latea, he lived at Kwaru. Because they rejected him as a man-eater, he ate children and they rejected him and he returned to his mother's side, he married and after that he lived in his mother's home at Fairū and he produced the Fairūs.
From manuscript, part English, part translated from Kwara'ae

Michael Kwa'iola noted his father's version of the story as follows:

Fikiramo from Nuina Sinaragu District Koio has eaten one of his mother the 8th wife of Baeloa. His father reject him and he travel the coast and arrived at Kwaru. He was kept by Būfanoa. Būfanoa stopped him not to go but he stayed there and Būfanoa educated him how to live a good life. Fikiramo was not killed but Basuau from Fa'i'ako was killed by Alimango and Baubau from 'Airade above Lama'a village.

Būfanoa also asked for him a girl from Kwakwali, Nongwae's girl, her name Rauketa, her father is Ko'oofo.

Fikiramo begot the following:
(1) Folia (2) I'adoe (3) I'agura'a (4) I'ate'e.
From English manuscript, grammar and spelling edited

Tuatua 'i nai'ari, fa'i na'ona'o sa Foli'a korea 'i Kō'imae, ngwaingaena sa Mao'a. Fanoa 'i Fairū kira ka miting, ala'a kira ka 'uri "Ki daro'ia. To'a nini kira futa ana sa ngwane'e Fikiramo, kaulu oli na'a 'i to'oba fani sa Biraomea, ngela nia sa Basila, To'ofoloa 'O'ota, mulu ka alu ngwae na'a, mulu ka alu gwata na'a fuana feraābu 'i Gwau'ulu. Kaili ke tua na'a 'i ne'e, mili ka alu gwata na'a fuana 'i 'Aisubu." Kira daro'ia 'unari ana. Go'o Ī'adoe ka leka na'a, Ī'agura ka leka na'a, Ī'ate'e ka leka na'a. Dao kira ka tua na'a fani sa Basila, dao kira ka tua fani sa Biraomea, dao kira ka tua na'a fani To'ofoloa 'O'ota, kira fi'i 'uia fanoa lo 'i 'Ainia'a, sulufaua loko ofo na'a. Kira ka 'uia sulufaua ka leleka ka sui, kira ka tata'e kira ka tua na'a 'i nai'ari.

Kira ka alu gwata na'a fuana 'i Gwau'ulu, sa To'ofoloa fi'i saea ka'o lo'oko, Ka'o sa 'O'ota. Nia ka lu'ia ka'o ne'e fuana maoma ne'e ke ōlo, kira 'oia fuana dodongilana 'ania saena gwata ne'e, ka'o lo'oko lo teo go'o 'ana. Kira sarea ngwa'i gwata lo'oko leleka, kira ka to'osia fera'abu lo 'i Gwau'ulu, kira ka 'oia ka'o lo'oko, kira ka dodoa 'ania. Ruana maoma la'u, kira ka alua la'u, 'unari sa Ko'otaba'a, futa ana sa Kereto'o, ka 'iri dau sulia su'asia kira re, ka 'iri ngalia ta gwata fuana. 'Uia naki go'o folo saena limana, ubuubu go'o ka mae. Ka alua sa Taba'a, sa Taba'a alu go'o nai, ka fa'asatā 'ania 'ai. Sa Kwalaioa, ngwae 'i Gwau'ulu ka leka ma'i ka dao, ka fatarorā to'a lo'oko, kira ka maemae ka sui, ka noa'a ta ngwae 'i Gwau'ulu, feraāabu na'a.

Ruana maoma nai, kira sasia ka sui kira ka sasia sango ana feraābu i Gwau'ulu nai. Kira ka 'ania ka sui, sa Taba'a dao go'o ka 'isia buta taba'a lo'oko. 'O ū sulia kula ka langa, moka koria buta taba'a, moka lalia, moka taka 'ania saena kula langa nai'ari, ko ngīa fa'a'asia saena falisi, ko fi'i kilua 'ania alo loere, ko ngīa fa'a'asia rū ne'e kira saea 'ania. To'a lo'oko kira sasia go'o 'i 'Ainia'a, falisi lo'oko ka doe go'o, alo lo'oko ka doe go'o, rū lo'oko kī teo go'o nai. 'Unari fanoa lo 'i 'Ainia'a ne'e kira to'ifolo na'a ana alo, kai fani fana.

Staying on there, the first-born Foli'a married Kō'imae, the sister of Mao'a. The community of Fairū had a meeting, talked and said "We'll divide it up. The people born of the man Fikiramo, you all go back over there with Biraomea and his son Basila and To'ofoloa 'O'ota, you beget sons and produce pigs for the tabu-sanctum at Gwau'ulu. We'll stay here and we'll produce pigs for 'Aisubu." They divided it up like that. Then Ī'adoe went off, Ī'agura went off, Ī'ate'e went off. They came and stayed with Basila, came and stayed with Biraomea, came and stayed with To'ofoloa 'O'ota, they then laid out a home at 'Ainia'a, where the stone wall has now collapsed. They laid out the stone wall then eventually they set out and stayed there.

They produced pigs for Gwau'ulu, and To'ofoloa called the bamboo over there 'O'ota's Bamboo. He prohibited the bamboo for when a festival fell due, they broke it off for flask-cooking the pigs' innards,[1] and that bamboo is still there. They fed a herd of pigs over there and eventually, when they thatched the tabu-sanctum at Gwau'ulu, they broke off that bamboo and cooked in it. At a second festival they did it again, so then Ko'otaba'a, born of Kereto'o, didn't uphold their consuming ghost and didn't bring a pig for him. Broke a flint, cut his hand, swelled up and died.[2] He begot Taba'a, when Taba'a was born he was named for the [*taba'a*] tree. Kwalaioa, a man of Gwau'ulu, arrived and misdirected those people, they all died and then there was no-one at Gwau'ulu, it was a tabu-sanctum.

The second festival, they did it and then did the dance at the tabu-sanctum at Gwau'ulu. They ate and then Taba'a came and completed the *taba'a* parcel. You stand on the unburnt [garden] area, you scrape a parcel of *taba'a*-bark, you invoke and scatter it on that unburnt area, you break and drop it on the yam garden, you plant taro with it, you break and drop this thing they speak of. Those people did it at 'Ainia'a and the yams were big, the taros were big, that's how things were. So the community of 'Ainia'a was rich in taro, yam and pana-yam.

1 For quick cooking, flasks of green bamboo are stuffed with food and laid on the fire.

2 That is, he cut his hand while chipping a flint blade and died of blood poisoning, punished by the ghost.

'Aisubu and 'Ainia'a

The story of Fikiramo introduces a series of disasters which afflicted the people of Fairū from about four generations before Alasa'a's time. When the Fairū people decided that Fikiramo's sons should move from the main settlement at 'Aisubu to live with a junior branch of the clan at 'Ainia'a, this probably means there were already tensions within the family. Before long there was serious ill-feeling, with disastrous consequences.

Alasa'a traces the conflict between the two communities to the prosperity of the 'Ainia'a group, based on *taba'a* garden-magic performed at a festival for the rebuilding of the shrine at Gwau'ulu.

Gardening and wealth

Formerly the main foods, for both people and their pigs, were taro and yam (including pana or 'lesser yam'), grown in temporary gardens cleared from the forest. A secure livelihood depended on working hard in the gardens and feeding many pigs as sacrifices to the ghosts for spiritual support. Holding sacrificial festivals also brought high social standing through generosity to the living.

To ensure good harvests, people prayed to ghosts when making gardens, prepared the ground with herbal substances and grew protective plants among the crops. For *taba'a* magic, a parcel of scrapings of *taba'a* tree *(Alstonia scholaris)* bark are scattered in a new garden to promote the growth of the crops.

Gardening: Aisah Osifera weeding his garden of taro in 1984.

The festival dance at Gwau'ulu might have looked rather like this photograph taken by the Revd. David Lloyd Francis in north-west Kwara'ae in 1932-3.

The dancers, men and boys only, wear ornaments of shell, shell-beads and dolphin teeth and nut-shell leg-rattles. They carry seed hand-rattles, hornbill-batons and leafy branches and dance around a group of singers seated on a wooden frame.

From British Museum Ethnography Dept. pictorial collection

Sa Mudi'a tua 'i 'Aisubu ka liufia go'o mae, gwata bili'a. Noa'a nia kesi o'o go'o talana, 'afe nia, 'i Uruuru leka ana asi, nia garasia alo fuiri, ka dodoa bi'i gala fuana 'anilana ana fuli fanga'a. Kala gala nia kī go'o, nia liu sulia ta'itala, fifinga'i 'age go'o, fifinga'i salu go'o, fingi kikiru kwasi go'o, dao ka usi na'a 'ani'i. Usi 'ania kira ka oli ka tua 'i Fautangi, logea buta ko'a nia, ka alua sulia 'aena, ta afu gala go'o nia 'ania, ngīa ta afu ko'a. Ngwa'i 'afe loko 'i 'Ainia'a kira ka lisia,"'Oi, kwate ana saulaka." Ta 'afe tata'e fani ta afu alo go'o fani ta buta ī'a ka "Uruuru, afu 'ao 'oe ne sata, ngwae 'oke 'ania mala afu liu'a ana sa Mudi'a. 'Ae'o mala loko, nau'a, kui to'ifolo ana alo lo'oko." Tona bore tai ka dao fani ta afu kai ka "O Uruuru, afu kai 'oe kwau sata, 'oke 'ania afu liu'a ana sa Mudi'a. 'Ae'o mala loko 'i 'Ainia'a ki to'ifolo mala ana afu kai loko." Tai ka ta'e go'o fani ta afu fana ne'e kōngia ka du'a go'o ka "O Uruuru, buta ī'a 'oe, fana 'oe. 'Ae'o mala loko nau'a nai to'ifolo ana fana doe lo'oko kī."

Mudi'a lived at 'Aisubu and excelled merely at feuding and pig theft. He wouldn't garden himself, and when his wife Uruuru went to the sea [to market] she scraped taro and flask-cooked taro stocks to eat at the eating place. With just her taro stocks, she passed along the path, taking a bundle of ginger-leaf, a bundle of vine-leaf, a bunch of wild betelnut, arrived and marketed them. They marketed, returned and sat at Fautangi and, undoing her mangrove-pudding, she hid it by her leg, ate a piece of taro stock and broke off a piece of mangrove. The group of women from 'Ainia'a saw her: "Oh, give to our sister-in-law." A woman got up with some taro and a parcel of fish: "Uruuru, some taro for you, namesake,[1] the person who eats the wandering of Mudi'a. That's you; me, I'm rich in this taro." She was startled but someone came with some yam: "Oh Uruuru, some yam for you, namesake, you who eat the wandering of Mudi'a. That's you, at 'Ainia'a we're really rich in this yam." Someone got up with some pana-yam, baked and cooked: "Oh Uruuru, a parcel of fish for you, pana for you. That's you; me, I'm rich in these big panas."

'I Uruuru rongoa na'a ka rao 'uani ka to'ongi'i saena ngwa'i, ka ra'e 'i 'Aisubu, didifuila 'ania afu gala nia kī. Go'o sa Mudi'a ka leleka ka dao, ka kanusua fo'osae ka daura'inia 'i māna fera loni'a, ngwa'i nia fani subi, ka ru'u ka "Uruuru, ai ufela, ta kalarū kī te'e 'ania." 'I Uruuru ma'u, kesi fata fuana. 'I Uruuru ta'e go'o ka ngalia 'okorū lo'oko ka kwatea na'a, ngwa'i ī'a lo'oko ka kwate'e na'a. "'Ania afu falisi 'i 'Ainia'a ne, afu 'ao 'i 'Ainia'a ne, afu kai 'i 'Ainia'a. Kira kwatea kira ka saea nau ki 'ania mala afu liu'a amu. Okesi o'o talaku." Sa Mudi'a rongo ka "Haē, nia le'a, ki'a ka 'ania na'a 'aka." Na'i nia ogata'a na'a nai.

Uruuru heard and reached for them and put them away in her bag, she climbed to 'Aisubu and switched it with her pieces of taro stock. Then Mudi'a arrived, took off his girdle and hung it over in front of the sanctum with his bag and angle-club and came in: "Uruuru, hey there, how about a little something to eat." Uruuru was afraid and didn't speak to him. Uruuru got up and took the bundle and gave it to him, and gave him the bag of fish. "Eat some yam from 'Ainia'a, some taro from 'Ainia'a, some yam from 'Ainia'a. They gave them and said I had to eat your wandering. You don't work, only me." Mudi'a listened: "Ha, that's good, now we can eat." So now he was angry.

Tuatua ka 'uri "Nai leka dao 'i lo'oko 'i Feralalo." Feralalo lo ki saea 'ania 'i Luluga, lulunga'i ī'a, 'i 'Auridi. Nia ka leka ka dao 'i lo'oko fuana sa Buamae. Leleka ka dao 'i lo'oko ma ana kaisa'i ana kōgwata'anga 'i Folokwa'e, ana akalo kini 'i Folokwa'e.

Later on he said "I'm going over to Feralalo." Feralalo is where we call Luluga [Parcel], parcel of baked fish, at 'Auridi. He went over there for Buamae. When he arrived there it was the time of a pig-baking at Folokwa'e, to the woman ghost at Folokwa'e.

1 'Namesake' (*sata*, 'name', implying 'my name') is a joking form of address between friends, in this case used with a little mockery.

Marketing

The trouble between 'Aisubu and 'Ainia'a began at market, the occasion which brings neighbours together to talk, exchange news and socialise.

As an inland people, the Kwara'ae exchange surplus crops for fish supplied by the sea people who live mainly on offshore islands, at markets on the coast. The women do the marketing, formerly exchanging standard portions of produce, nowadays selling them for cash. In East Kwara'ae the sea people live on the islands of Kwai, Ngongosila and Leili. Formerly markets could be tense occasions , the women accompanied by armed men, ready for trouble between enemy clans and particularly between inland and sea people.

The market-place where the Fairū women went in Alasa'a's story would probably have been at Faumamanu, on the coast of Fairū. Here his ancestor Uruuru revealed her poverty by marketing only wild produce gathered along the way; leaf for wrapping and serving food and inferior wild betelnut. When the Fairū women stopped to eat on the way home she had only her taro stocks (immature plants which had not yet produced tubers), and mangrove-seed pudding from the market, another inferior wild product. Her prosperous in-laws had fish as well as their home-grown foods, and mocked her for her husband's idle wandering.

Sea people from the offshore islands attending a market near Faumamanu in 1983.

Women and girls from the inland on the beach at Fote in West Kwara'ae, probably on the way home from market. This is another of J. W. Beattie's photographs from 1906.
From British Museum Ethnography Dept pictorial collection

Kira ka daua gwata kira dao kira ka lalā na'a, kira ka saka na'a saena rodo fani. Ofodangi kira tata'e go'o sa Mudi'a ka leka na'a fa'inida. Leleka ka dao 'i Folokwa'e, kira ka li'oa gwata fuiri, sa Buamae ka ngalia na fa'i kikiru fuiri ka alua ka tarā gwata fuiri ka unuunulia. Sa Mudi'a dumulia go'o fa'i kikiru fuiri ka dangulua saena fo'osae 'i alana. Unuunulia gwata lo'oba, ngali kira ka saungia ka sui, ngali kira ka gwa'abi fafia, oli kira ke lulului na'a: "Reala, fa'i kikiru baera fasi ki mola ana kōgwata'a ne'e." Lululua ka noa'a go'o, ka mola na'a ana afu 'ao fani afu gwata. Aia'a, to'a ne'e ka "Tai ngalia, ke fa'alia 'ania ta fanoa nini."

Kwa'ia gwata fuiri ka sui kira ka oli ma'i, kira dao 'i Aulanabasi, ka "'Oke koso toli 'uri?" Sa Mudi'a ka "Ae, mulu kwatea kwau." Leka'a leka nai. Dao 'i Tafe'ai, "'Oke koso toli 'uri?" "Ae, moro kwatea kwau." Dao 'i Fulifata'a kira ka "'Oke koso toli 'uri?" "Ae, moro kwatea kwau." Dao go'o 'i 'Ui'ui nia ka "Aia'a, mulu leka na'a kwau 'aumulu. Nai afeo na'a 'i ne'e kwa." Go'o sa Buamae ka "O, ngwae ne'e ke fa'alia ta fanoa 'i ne'e. Fa'i kikiru baera nia ngalia, go'o ka afeo na'a."

Ka ra'e 'i 'Ainia'a, fanoa 'i 'Ainia'a gafu ana sau'a ma kwalelana falisi, saungi kata. "'Ae tua tau." Nia ra'e go'o ka dudu 'i māna sulufaua lo'oko. Kira ka "Sē ara'i kwa, leka ma'i ko tua le'a 'i fuiri kwa. Ngwa'i ngela ne'e kira rada bi'i ngali kira kī fuana kira ke kwaea 'ania ngwae fu kira fasia fi'i fana kira kī." Nia ka "Eo, nia le'a, nau ku kwaikwai'akofi." Mānunu'ia to'a fuiri, kira akau ana rao'a fuiri, nia ka rao 'uana fa'i kikiru ka durua saena sulufaua fuiri, māna sinamā ma'e tafā, ka ta'ea subi ka tata'e. "Sē, 'oke leka na'a ma sau'a ne'e ke suisui, 'oke ngalia ta kata kwa." "Ae, nau ku 'aila kisi 'ania kata gwari kī. Nau ku dao bore 'i 'Aisubu nai saungia go'o kata 'ako'ako nai ki 'ania logo."

'Una'ari ka sui nia ka ra'e 'i Gwa'itaba'a, ka dao fuana sa ngwane'e Biraomea, ngela nia sa Basila, sa Ko'oroko, sa Dadao, sa Nongwae, sa ngwane'e Barea, To'ofoloa. Ra'e ka "Rela, moro sasia sau'a ki 'ania re," kira ka "Nia nini'a, 'oko dao ka le'a."

They'd caught the pig, they arrived pulling it, they came in with it at night. In the morning they set out and Mudi'a went with them. Going on to Folokwa'e, they strangled the pig, Buamae took the betelnut, put it down and dragged the pig and singed it. Mudi'a just grabbed the betelnut and dropped it inside the girdle at his waist. Singeing the pig over there, they'd brought it and killed it, then they put the oven over it and they returned to search: "Hey, that betelnut was to normalise the pig-baking." Searched in vain and normalised the taro and pig-meat. Well, the people said "Whoever took it will damage some community with it."[1]

Having dealt with the pig, they came back and arrived at Aulanabasi: "Are you going down this way?" Mudi'a said "Oh, you go on." The party went on. Arriving at Tafe'ai: "Are you going down this way?" "Oh, you two go on." Arriving at Fulifata'a, they said "Are you going down this way?" "Oh, you two go on." Arriving at 'Ui'ui, he said "Well, all of you, on you go. I'll turn off here." Then Buamae said "Oh, this man will damage a community here. That betelnut, he took it, now he's turning off."

He climbed to 'Ainia'a and the home at 'Ainia'a was astir with pounding, shifting piles of yams, pounding nut-pudding. "You're far from home." He climbed and squatted over in front of the stone wall. They said "Eh, sir, come and sit properly down here. This bunch of children are pounding their bamboos of nuts to repay the men who planted their clumps of pana-yam." He said "Oh, it's alright, I'm feeling the heat." Eyeing those people absorbed in the work, he reached for the betelnut and inserted it into the stone wall, at the threshold of an exit, raised his angle-club and got up. "Hey, you're going already, but when the pounding finishes you can take some pudding." "Oh, I don't want to eat cold pudding. When I reach 'Aisubu I'll pound a hot pudding and I'll eat."

Well then, after that he climbed to Gwa'i-taba'a and came to that man Biraomea, his son Basila, Ko'oroko, Dadao, Nongwae, that man Barea and To'ofoloa. Climbing he said "Hey, you're making pudding, let's eat it," they said "Here it is, you're welcome."

1 This betelnut was tabu and potentially dangerous, as it was for the tabu-speaker to chew and spit over the tabu sacrificial meat and taro, making it 'normal' (*mola*) for the men to eat without offending the ghost.

The revenge of Mudi'a

Mudi'a was Alasa'a's great-great-grandfather, and his quarrel with his relatives at 'Ainia'a began a series of disasters for the community of Fairū.

Having planned his revenge for the 'Ainia'a women mocking his wife, Mudi'a visited their home and experienced the same patronising sarcasm. The 'Ainia'a people were evidently preparing a big feast, a prestigious give-away for relatives and neighbours, with great puddings of nuts (*ngali*, canarium almonds) and taro pounded in wooden bowls. But to exaggerate their own prosperity and mock Mudi'a for his laziness and poverty, they told him it was just children pounding nuts in bamboo flasks, as if to make a small pudding.

Mudi'a planned revenge on the 'Ainia'a people by hiding the consecrated betelnut from the sacrifice at their home and then swearing at them. His intention was for the ghost to react against the community where her betelnut had been thus defiled.

Gwa'itaba'a, home of Biraomea, was close by 'Ainia'a and part of the same community. But Biraomea was Mudi'a's close 'father' (his father's brother) and his sons and grandsons his close brothers and sons. The 'Ainia'a people were their in-laws, descendants of Fikiramo, whose eldest son Foli'a had married Mudi'a's grandfather's sister. This explains why Mudi'a warned Biraomea's family when he cursed 'Ainia'a, allowing them to escape the impending disaster. Foli'a's family were not involved since they were living at 'Aisubu with Mudi'a. Their descendants formed the Kwaru clan of Fairū in Alasa'a's time. (For clarification of these relationships, see the genealogy on page 67.)

At twenty-five to thirty years per generation, we can estimate this event to have occurred between about 1800 and 1820.

Hammering nuts for pudding in the 1930s. Under a temporary leaf shelter the people sit amidst piles of nuts and nut husks, the women lined up on one side, the men on the other. As they carefully crack open each nut with a stone hammer and anvil, they put the kernels into bamboo containers.
From photo at Bitama, 1937, by Alexander Waddell, British Museum Ethnography Dept. pictorial collection

A household's wooden bowls, used as mortars for pounding puddings of taro and nuts or coconut. Some of them have handles shaped like the heads of birds such as eagles and hornbills. Formerly much larger bowls were made for pudding feasts (siufa), but these have not been held in Kwara'ae in recent generations.

Ra'e ka dao 'i lōri, "Ngwa'i ngela kira kosida kira ka saungia bi'i ngali kira, kira kata dao ana saena sau'a doe loeri kwa!" Sau ka leleka kira ka daro'ia sau'a lōri. Kira ngalia kata ka kwatea go'o fuana. Tata'e go'o ka ūria sa 'O'ota, lae ka oli go'o ka "Mulu tafitafi na'a, mulu tafitafi na'a. Nau ku nau ku 'oni na'a 'i 'Ainia'a. Mulu tafitafi na'a. Ma asoa go'o nari." Tafa'a tafa na'a 'i 'Aisubu nai. Sa Biraomea ka tafi, sa Basila ka tafi, sa Dadao ka tafi, sa Roko ka tafi. 'I Mamadiliolofa kira fiku kira ka sasi gwaurau na'a 'i to'oba, kira tua 'i nai'ari kira ka lia na'a.

Rodo rodo go'o, akalo kini 'i Folokwa'e dao ka mango na'a ana sulufaua lo'oko, tata'e ka ofo go'o nai. 'Arange'enge'e koe ka liu na'a, kaura ka koe ka liu na'a, a'asae ka koe ka liu na'a. Mangofia go'o fanoa lo'oko nai, nia ka tua 'i to'oba, māna ka ōla 'i 'Ainia'a. Ta 'afe 'ani'ania kata fuiri, sirana ka fī ka ngelongelosia, teo na'a saena luma nia. Ta ngwae kwalasae saungia, lae galogalo go'o, ngwafila alea 'elo'elota'i ka ego na'a. Ta kini lada rodo'a, ba'eko ka saungia, nia mae ka teo na'a. Fanoa lo'oba alanga'i gwau go'o ana rodo lo'oko nai kwa. Leleka ka dangi ka noa'a na'a ta gwagwarongorongoa, ka noa'a na'a ta mafula, fanoa lo'oko aroaro na'a. Kira mae sulia rodo leleka ka dangi na'a.

Sa Biraomea ka "Rela, kisi ma'uma'u ki leka dao ki sai ana saena fanoa fuiri, ta mafula 'iri du'a na'a. 'O'ota lae ka ra'e lo'oba 'i Mamadili, koso ka lia saena fanoa fuiri ma kira mae ta'ifau na'a. Kira mae sulia asoa fuiri leleka ka rodo, leleka ka dangi go'o 'Ainia'a ka sui. Nia go'o nai, kira ka dao go'o 'i lo'oko, kira ka tata'e kira ka o'omae 'i 'aena ngali nai'ari kira saea 'ania Gwa'io'omae. Tai ne'e dao 'i lo'oko, 'afe lo'oko o'omae na'a, gwangwalu o'omae'a ka leleka ka dangi, o'omae sulia asoa lo'oko leleka ka rodo. Fanoa lo'oko sui go'o nai.

'Unari, sa Biraomea, sa Basila, sa Roko, sa ngwane'e Barea, koso ma'i kira 'i Fi'itatali. Kira koso ma'i 'uana 'i Anobū, go'o sa Biraomea ka mae, kira ka kwaiatoa 'i nai'ari olofana 'i 'Aingwa'a, fafona fi'i lumu. Kira fasia fi'i rodo ana. Sa Roko tata'e, ka fulia na'a 'i Luma'ofa, nia go'o nai, tua na'a 'i nai'ari.

Climbing up there, "The children are being kept occupied pounding their bamboos of nuts, lest they get into that big pudding-feast!" The pounding went on until they shared out the pudding. They took some nut-pudding and gave it to him. Getting up, he stood over 'O'ota, came back and said "All of you flee, all of you flee. I, I shit on 'Ainia'a. All of you flee. This very day." He fled and escaped to 'Aisubu. Biraomea fled, Basila fled, Dadao fled, Roko fled. At Mamadiliolofa they gathered and made a leaf-shelter up there, they stayed there and watched.

In the dark of night the woman ghost of Folokwa'e came and paused at that stone wall, arose and attacked. An *'arange'enge'e* bird shrieked past, a *kaura* bird shrieked past, an *a'asae* bird shrieked past.[1] Breathing on that home, she sat up there, on account of being defiled at 'Ainia'a. A woman had eaten the nut-pudding, her belly wrung with pain, she lay in her house. A man was struck by diarrhoea, went berserk, a centipede bit him, he struggled and flopped. A woman rushed out into the night [to the latrine], a snake struck her, she lay dead. That community just bowed its head that night. When day came there was not a sound to be heard, there was no fire, the home was silent. They died through the night until day.

Biraomea said "Hey, let's not be afraid, let's go and learn what's in that home, there's no fire burning." 'O'ota went climbing over to Mamadili, came down and looked into the home and they were all dead. They died during that day and on until night, and by next day 'Ainia'a was finished. That was it, they arrived there, they got up and lamented at the foot of the nut-tree they call Gwa'io'omae [Lamentation]. Whoever arrived there, the women lamented, the lamentation went on until day, lamenting during that day on until night. That community was finished off.

Well, Biraomea, Basila, Roko and the man Barea came down and were at Fi'itatali. They came down to Anobū, then Biraomea died, they deposited him there below 'Aingwa'a, on a clump of moss. They planted a clump of dark croton on it. Roko set out and founded Luma'ofa, he did, and lived there.

1 These are birds of ill-omen, but it has not been possible to identify them by English or scientific names.

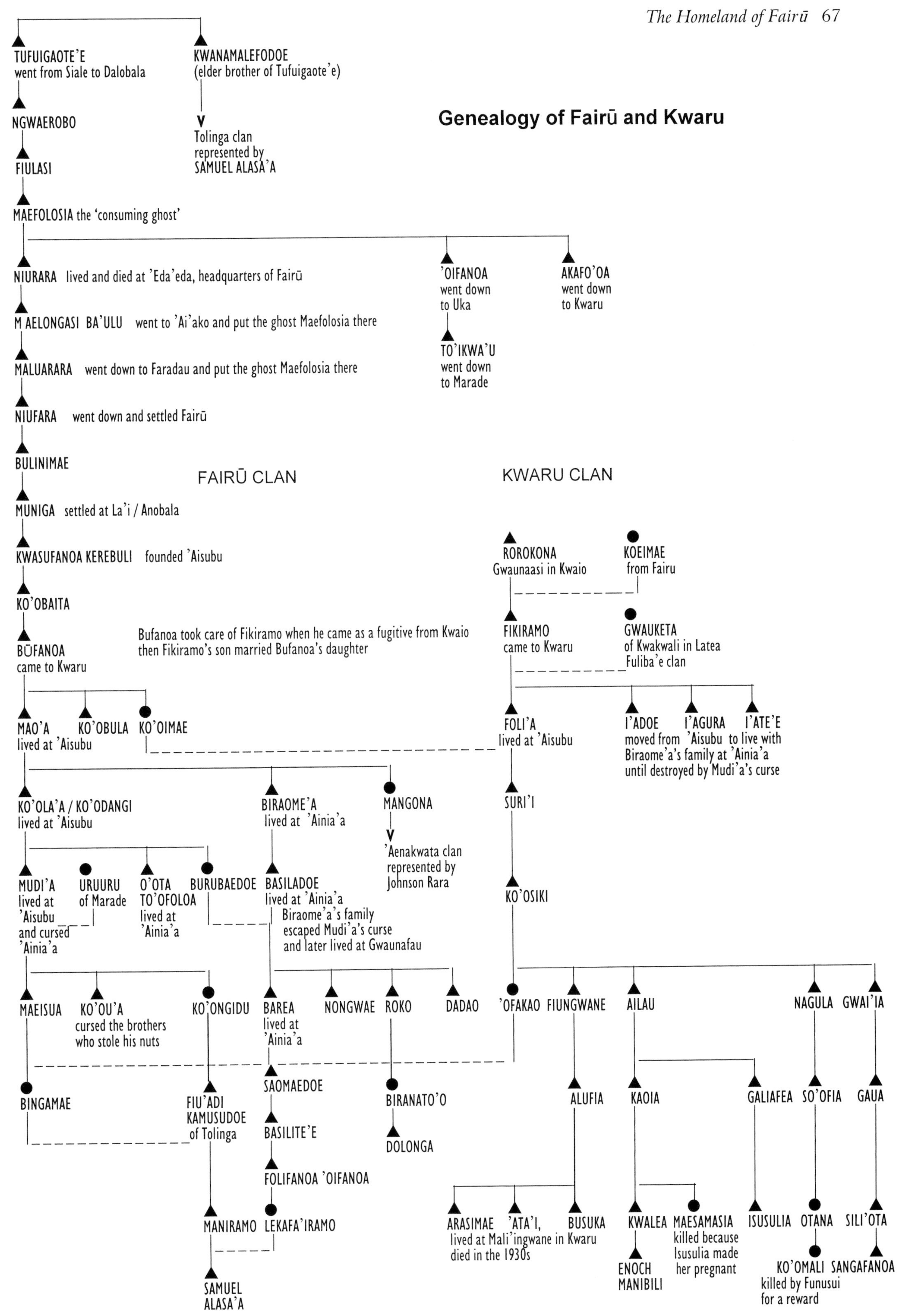
Genealogy of Fairū and Kwaru
TUFUIGAOTE'E went from Siale to Dalobala
KWANAMALEFODOE (elder brother of Tufuigaote'e)
Tolinga clan represented by SAMUEL ALASA'A
NGWAEROBO
FIULASI
MAEFOLOSIA the 'consuming ghost'
NIURARA lived and died at 'Eda'eda, headquarters of Fairū
'OIFANOA went down to Uka
AKAFO'OA went down to Kwaru
TO'IKWA'U went down to Marade
M AELONGASI BA'ULU went to 'Ai'ako and put the ghost Maefolosia there
MALUARARA went down to Faradau and put the ghost Maefolosia there
NIUFARA went down and settled Fairū
BULINIMAE
FAIRŪ CLAN
KWARU CLAN
MUNIGA settled at La'i / Anobala
KWASUFANOA KEREBULI founded 'Aisubu
KO'OBAITA
BŪFANOA came to Kwaru
Bufanoa took care of Fikiramo when he came as a fugitive from Kwaio then Fikiramo's son married Bufanoa's daughter
ROROKONA Gwaunaasi in Kwaio
KOEIMAE from Fairu
FIKIRAMO came to Kwaru
GWAUKETA of Kwakwali in Latea Fuliba'e clan
MAO'A lived at 'Aisubu
KO'OBULA
KO'OIMAE
FOLI'A lived at 'Aisubu
I'ADOE
I'AGURA
I'ATE'E
moved from 'Aisubu to live with Biraome'a's family at 'Ainia'a until destroyed by Mudi'a's curse
KO'OLA'A / KO'ODANGI lived at 'Aisubu
BIRAOME'A lived at 'Ainia'a
MANGONA
'Aenakwata clan represented by Johnson Rara
SURI'I
MUDI'A lived at 'Aisubu and cursed 'Ainia'a
URUURU of Marade
O'OTA TO'OFOLOA lived at 'Ainia'a
BURUBAEDOE
BASILADOE lived at 'Ainia'a
Biraome'a's family escaped Mudi'a's curse and later lived at Gwaunafau
KO'OSIKI
MAEISUA
KO'OU'A cursed the brothers who stole his nuts
KO'ONGIDU
BAREA lived at 'Ainia'a
NONGWAE
ROKO
DADAO
'OFAKAO
FIUNGWANE
AILAU
NAGULA
GWAI'IA
BINGAMAE
FIU'ADI KAMUSUDOE of Tolinga
SAOMAEDOE
BIRANATO'O
ALUFIA
KAOIA
GALIAFEA
SO'OFIA
GAUA
BASILITE'E
DOLONGA
FOLIFANOA 'OIFANOA
MANIRAMO
LEKAFA'IRAMO
ARASIMAE
'ATA'I, lived at Mali'ingwane in Kwaru died in the 1930s
BUSUKA
KWALEA
MAESAMASIA killed because Isusulia made her pregnant
ISUSULIA
OTANA
SILI'OTA
SAMUEL ALASA'A
ENOCH MANIBILI
KO'OMALI killed by Funusui for a reward
SANGAFANOA

Nia ka alua 'i Biranato'o, ngela kini go'o, ka 'afe 'i Kunubulu fuana sa ngwane'e Ko'odeke, ka alua sa Biraomea, alua sa Dolonga, alua sa Fa'atolo, alua sa Totolo, nai atokale'a nia nai. 'I Burinato'o ka gania ma'a nia, ngwae 'urungwae ka koso ma'i ka tua fani 'i Luma'ofa. Rongoa sa Dadao sa Roko kwatea luma'a fuana ngela kini nia 'i Burinato'o. Burinato'o nini ka alua go'o sa Dolonga. Sa Dolonga ka alua go'o - nau ku matafirua na'a, nau ku kwa'ia go'o ma sa Diosi ka ngali ka kwatea fuana sa Futai. Kula sa Sulute'e lala, kula sa Sia lala. . . .

He begot Biranato'o, just a girl, she was married at Kunubulu to the man Ko'odeke, and begot Biramoea, begot Dolonga, begot Fa'atolo, begot Totola, those are her descendants. Burinato'o asked for her father, a widower, and came down and lived with him at Luma'ofa. Listening to Dadao, Roko gave housing for his daughter Burinato'o. It was Burinato'o who begot Dolonga. Dolonga just begot - I've too much on my mind, I related it and Diosi took it and gave it to Futai. It's actually Sulate'e's part, Sia's part. . . .

'Unari, to'a nai'ari kira tua 'i 'Aisubu kira ka lia dao na'a ana sa Mudi'a, kira ka 'uri "Rela'ae ki tua fani malimae, nia fa'alia logo fanoa ne'e, kulu tafi, kulu oli 'uana 'i Bula, bali te'a kulu." Rō akwala kī oli 'ala'a kira ka tuafia 'i Bula. To'a 'i Ulanafiu, di'i kira ka tata'e ma'i kira ka daro'ia rū lo'ori kira 'odo 'i tofungana. Ta rō akwala oli, ta rō akwala ka oli.

So then, the people living at 'Aisubu looked at Mudi'a and said "Hey, we're living with an enemy, he's destroyed this community, let's flee, let's return to Bula, on our mother's side." A score went back up and lived at Bula. The people of Ulanafiu, their cousins, came and divided their things down the middle and separated them. A score went back, and the other score went back.

Kira ka tua 'i nai'ari ka leleka, sa Rokomeso'i, sa Isusulia, di'i kira sa Ko'obula, ngwae 'i Ulanafiu, kira liu kira ka siu 'i māna 'i Faubaba nai. Sa Roko fani sa Ko'obula kera'a olisu'usu'u, kera'a ka 'oidorele sa Bula tata'e go'o ka "Roko, fanasia 'oniku." Sa Roko ka "Ta'ena nai fanasia," ka ra'e 'ala'a ka botā 'onina ka "Fanasia 'oniku ne Roko." Ngwae nia taringani sima 'i māna dadalo, ka "Ta'ena nai fanasi'o nena." Ruana nia ka ra'e 'ala'a ka "Fanasia 'oniku ne Roko." Nia botafolo 'onina, ūla go'o sa Roko ka dangulua sima fuiri. Donga tata'e merona ka tafa olofana satena. Ridi ka to'o go'o, kira ka ngalia ka to'osia saena tafu 'age, nangatani sima ka to'osia, nia ka anokwalo ka tata'e tafa 'i fanoa.

They lived there until Rokomeso'i, Isusulia and their cousin Ko'obula, a man from Ulanafiu, went and bathed at the spout on the Faubaba. Roko and Ko'obula were arguing, they were joking and Bula got up and said "Roko, shoot my arse." Roko said "I'll shoot it right now," he climbed upwards and stuck out his arse: "Shoot my arse Roko." The man set an arrow to the string; "I'll shoot you right now." A second time he climbed upwards: "Shoot my arse Roko." He bent and stuck out his arse and the third time, Roko let off the arrow. Following up his anus, it came out under his chin. He slid and fell, they took him and threw him into the ginger-leaf litter,[1] tugged out the arrow and threw it away, he vanished and set off home.

Mae loko fuli go'o nai. Ngwa'i 'afe kira ufi ka'o na'a, kira ka liu kika lisia sa Ko'obula kira ka fai'are'are na'a,"Ō, ngwae saungia sa Ko'obula." Kira tata'e kira ka folo saena fanoa lokiri ka leleka kira kesi folo go'o to'ona. Kira ka "Rela ngwae nini saungia sa Ko'obula nia 'i fa'i?" Na rū mae teo go'o 'ana saena fera. Kira angi, ka makalokalo'a, sa Roko ka "'Ai rela, kulu tafitafi na'a, nau'a fu nau ku saungia sa Ko'o-bula, na'i kwa!" Rō akwala kī tafi go'o nai. Ka fi'i dangi ma'i, kira 'i 'Aisubu, teo ka dangi kira ka faia 'i Abufo'oka, kira fi'i faia fanoa fuiri kira ka teo na'a 'i nai'ari.

The feud now began. A group of women filling bamboo bottles passed by and saw Ko'obula and had a fright: "Oh, someone's killed Ko'obula." They set out and investigated those homes and they couldn't detect him. They said "Hey, the man who killed Ko'obula, where is he?" The corpse just lay in the sanctum. They cried and at dusk Roko said "Hey there, let's flee, it was I who killed Ko'obula, that's what!" A score just fled. As day came they were at 'Aisubu and when it was day they cleared Abufo'oka, they cleared a home there and they stayed there.

1 The ginger-leaf was left from making coiled spouts for bamboo water bottles filled at the water spout.

The first feud to damage Fairū

After the destruction of 'Ainia'a, when one family of 'Aisubu people decided to move to their mother's home at Bula in the central inland, their cousins of Ulanafiu (also in Fairū) mediated the split by coming between them to prevent a fight. But before long a feud began when one of the men at Bula, Rokomeso'i, killed an Ulanafiu man, Ko'obula, over an offensive joke.

The Faubaba stream, where this occurred, runs past the settlement of that name in Latea, where the Tolinga descendants of Kamusute'e later came to live (see pages 52-3). To escape retaliation, Roko's people fled back to Fairū and built a new home at Abufo'oka, near their former home at 'Aisubu.

Weapons

Kwara'e men fought with spears, bows and arrows, and several kinds of clubs. Formerly they carried such weapons with them whenever they left home, to guard against attack in the feuds which regularly threatened one community or another.

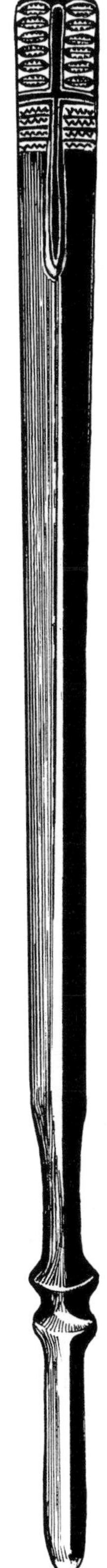

Kwara'ae clubs.
*The lozenge-shaped 'angle-club' (*subi*) is an ancestral relic of the Ubasi clan. The longer 'deflector' (*alafolo*), with projections to hook aside spears, belonged to the 'Ere'ere warrior Arumae Bakate'e, Alasa'a's father-in-law.*

*In 1979 Clement Maletege O'ogau of Mānadodo demonstrated the fighting gear he used in his unruly youth. The spears, blessed by a tabu-speaker with the power to find their mark, were used as a pair, one to be thrown and one kept for defence until the first was recovered. The girdle (*fo'osae*) of split rattan gave strength, and the tusk pendants came from the pigs he stole. As a Christian, O'ogau kept these things in his church to neutralise their ghostly power.*

Atokale'a nini sa Di'iakalo fa'ida, kira oli kwau, sa Barea tuafia na'a 'i Gwa'irufa loko. Kilu gwa'u nai'ari lo kira fasia go'o 'ai ba ke nunufia kaukau kī, kira ka tua na'a 'i nai'ari.

Kira tata'e kira ka tua 'i nai'ari, kira ka alua fo'oa ka teo na'a 'i Ulunafiu, kira ka 'engoda 'ania, Sasadili nama nai, sa Bulufaka oli 'uana 'i Fauboso, ka alua Fauboso. Leleka ki lisia fo'oa lo ka dao 'i Kunubulu, "Rela, to'a baera kira saungia sa Ko'obula." Kira oli ma'i kira "'I fa'i kwa?" Sasadili ka "Kira oli ma'i kira ka tua 'i Abufo'oka, Lulungwasa. Ū, ki saungwae 'uana fo'oa lori ki 'oka na'a." Fikua go'o mae, kwa'iamusia go'o to'a 'i Abufo'oka ma 'i Lulungwasa, rō akwala kī teo go'o nai. 'Ata lo tafi go'o sulia oli'a kini, Isusulia ka lada ka ago safitana dako kī. Sa Di'iakalo fa'ida kira ra'e kira 'i Gwa'irufa, gwauna fa'i niu sa Bita. Kira tua 'ada 'i nai'ari. Mae lo'oko kwa'i kira ka tafi ka tau na'a, 'i 'Ata lo fi'i dao ka o'omae, 'Ata lo 'afe fuana sa Ramosui, ka alua go'o sa Keta'i. Nau ku do'ofia go'o gwata nai ana, go'o ku leka sukulu. Rela o'omae'a ne'e leka na'a. Bo'obo'o kira ka lae ka dao bore ma 'abu 'i ngwae ke langa na'a.

Rō loba kī nai, kira to'osia fuana 'i Fairū. Ka teo ka leleka, sa Kwalu'i ka o'o 'i lōri 'i Likonabasi, kula ki kwatea fuana sa Lili'a fani 'i Kwa'ito'o, kira ka kwatea fuana su'asia suifuila sa Ale. Sada gwari ana tala 'i gwa'i ere fuiri, ka leka sulia rarana fai lo'oko. Ka busu ka dao 'i Kwari'ai, leleka ka dao 'i Gwale, ka fi'i ngalia ma'e akalo, sa 'O'ota 'isia fuana sa Sa'engwane, nia nai ne'e korea Ko'omangonate'e, alua sa Sangafanoa fa'ida, oli go'o ka alua Anoanokona. Saungia sa Kwalu'i ka mae go'o 'i Baibai, kira rikida ma'i 'i Lidi'a, sa Mamanu ka ta'e go'o, na'ona aiburina kī kira ta'e kira ka 'erea go'o 'i 'Asai. Go'o sa 'O'otate'e rao go'o 'uana sa Geso aiburina, kwatea go'o sa Ōdoe ka ngalia. Saungia kira ka oli kira ka kwaiatoa sa Kwalu'i, ngwae to'ofolo ma'i Fairū nai.

Their descendants Di'iakalo and others went back and Barea lived over at Gwa'irufa. That empty pit where they planted that tree which shades cacao trees, they now lived there.

When they set out to live there, they put down a reward at Ulanafiu, they pursued them with it, that was the Sasadilis, Bulufaka who returned to Fauboso and begot the Faubosos. Eventually the reward came within sight of Kunubulu, "Hey, it's for those people who killed Ko'obula." They came back and said "But where?" The Sasadilis said "They came back and live at Abufo'oka, Lulungwasa. Yes, let's kill someone for the reward and feel pleased." Gathering a band, they struck out the people of Abufo'oka and Lulungwasa, a score fell there. 'Ata fled through the women's toilet, Isusulia rushed to hide among the bowls. Di'iakalo and others climbed to Gwa'irufa, at the head of Peter's coconut grove. They stayed there. When the feud struck they fled far away, 'Ata then came and lamented, 'Ata who married Ramosui and bore Keta'i. I cooked my pigs to her, then went to the mission. What a lamentation went on! Their need continued even when the blood had dried.

There were two massacres they inflicted on Fairū. It lay until Kwalu'i gardened over at Likonabasi, the place we gave to Lili'a and Kwa'ito'o, they gave it for Ale's consuming ghost of burnt offerings. Setting up a fire to burn, it went along a *fai*-tree branch. Explosions [of burning bamboo] reached Kwari'ai, he arrived at Gwale and then took the magic 'O'ota conferred on Sa'engwane, he who married Ko'omangonate'e, begot Sangafanoa and them, returned and begot Anoanokona. It struck Kwalu'i and he died at Baibai, they enquired at Lidi'a and Mamanu set out, leading his younger brothers, they set out and encircled 'Asai. Then 'O'otate'e reached for Geso, his younger brother, and gave him for Ōdoe to take. Killing him, they returned and deposited Kwalu'i, the man who had crossed over to Fairū.

The first feud (continued)

The Ulanafiu people offered a reward to avenge the death of Ko'obula and the Sasadili people of 'Ere'ere (ancestors of Timi Ko'oliu) massacred the people of Abufo'oka to collect it.

The second feud to damage Fairū

This complex incident also involved the Sasadili clan of 'Ere'ere, who had killed the Fairū people of Abufo'oka. Kwalu'i, a Sasadili man from Baibai in 'Ere'ere, came into Fairū to clear a garden on land which had been given to Lili'a of Lidi'a in 'Ere'ere, his father or grandfather. The noise of bamboos exploding in his garden fire apparently angered Kwari'ai, which somehow led to Kwalu'i dying from magic which O'ota of Fairū (brother of Mudi'a) had given to Sa'engwae, an in-law of the Kwaru clan of Fairū. The people of Lidi'a came to O'ota's home at 'Asai for revenge and O'ota gave a younger brother for them to kill in compensation.

Timi Ko'oliu demonstrates the dance of a warrior coming to collect a reward, waving his bow as he comes stamping forward, exclaiming 'He!' with each step. (1984)

Vengeance and rewards

An important principle of Kwara'ae law is restitution, showing respect for the injured party by 'making him tabu' again (*fa'aābua*) to 'make him feel better' (*fa'aogale'ā*). For a serious offence, one way to achieve this was to kill someone. On the principle that a family or community shares responsibility for its members' actions, the person held to account need not be the one who caused the offence. Victims were often easy targets, as in some of the later incidents in this chapter.

People who wanted to 'pay back' (*du'ua māna*) an offence without having to kill for themselves might announce a reward (*fo'oa*) of shell-money, with pigs and gardens of food for a feast, for whoever would kill for them. When a reward was on offer it threatened many people, and women or children often paid for offences caused by men.

In 1984 Timi Ko'oliu told the story of a reward he witnessed as a child. In 1911 Gwangalu of 'Ere'ere sent his sons to attack the ship *Ruby*, anchored off the coast to recruit plantation workers. They were repulsed and Lusumani swam to Kwai island, where he was killed by one of the sea people, Sigili.

> Well, Gwangalu heard: "Well, they've killed my son, here are the pigs, from my sons. Those at home won't cut their hair." Gwangalu said "Anyone who kills Sigili, the man who killed my son, can come and take these pigs to eat, take these moneys, and we'll cut our hair."

Some time later, Ko'oliu's 'fathers' Nunute'e and Bakete (father of Alasa'a's wife Arana) lured Sigili to the beach near Faumamanu on pretence of going on a fishing trip. Nunute'e struck him in the neck with an axe and they killed him.

> At the time I was about the size of this boy [about 10 years old]. Me and another boy were standing at the place we came to today [in 'Ere'ere]. They came and beat the gong. I heard: "What's that?" "Oh, they've killed Sigili, and that man Gwangalu will lose his pigs and his red money." Well, Gwangalu heard it at his home and came running, reaching my grandfather and me: "Why this gong?" "Why, my sons have killed the man who killed your son." "Well, they can eat my pigs, I'll give the moneys to them." Well, after that they set five days and and everyone, with my two fathers who killed Sigili, went to Gwangalu's home, sounded the gong, shouted, and built the houses. So Gwangalu said "Well, after ten days you all come." Well, after ten days they caught the pigs, twenty pigs. No one man could carry them, they carried them on litters and brought them all there. Oh, I saw them, they were first rate! Pigs for a reward formerly were extraordinarily big, almost like cattle. When it was time to take them they did as I showed it, "He! he! he!" waving their bows, "He! he! he!" I went to it, I ate the pigs, when I was like this child.
> Translated from Pijin and abridged

In 1983 Aisah Osifera recalled the last collection of a reward in Kwara'ae, resulting from the killing of three men by colonial police at Lama in 1919.

> When they came up for the reward, they danced and came up and reached for the moneys. This was the reward with which they avenged the two boys they'd killed. They decorated their bags, they held their bows, and they held red cordylines, they picked them and held them with their bows, and they stepped up for the reward. When they did this it was more like a dance, and they reached out for the moneys on the platform, they climbed up by a ladder and they reached for it and came down. To look at, rewards really looked like dances. They looked really good, because they were decorated with pattern-armbands, crescent-pendants, and shell-disks, they were decorated. The first men would hold red cordylines. Then they'd collect the reward.
> Translated from Kwara'ae

Ka teo ka leleka, ngali ragia loko nai go'o, sa Ko'ou'a ka lu'ia, alua ūli 'ai fuana. Sa Oforodo aiburina nairi, Saubilia, Tadili, tua 'i Lulungwasa Abufo'oka, "O rorodo kulu leka 'uia ngali fuiri re!" "Ae, sa Ko'ou'a kata saea ta rū akulu." Nia ka "Ae ma aina'oku go'o lokoni'a. Si 'uri ma kira ke leka fa'arongoa, kulu ka noa'a logo. Kira tata'e kira ka 'uia ngali fuiri leleka kira ka ngalia fofo bī fuiri, kira saungia saena rodo kira ka 'ania 'i Abufo'oka. 'Ofodangi sa Ko'ou'a leka o'o lo'oko 'i Ano'o'a, dao go'o na'a, tafuta'e ka langolango'a na'a. Go'o nia ka ragia ngali lo kira saea 'ania Ngaliragia go'o nai. Oli ka ra'e go'o saena Kwaru ngalia 'o'a ka taofia 'ania to'a lo'oko. * * * Leleka ka dangi, kira ka ta'ea mae kira ka saungia 'i Laubisi, ngwaingwaena sa Fina'i. * * *

Sa Lulufanoa saungia 'i Laubisia, sa Filiga tua fani fo'oa ka bubungida 'ania. Leleka kira ka ma'u ka 'ato ana kula lo'oko. 'I Ko'omali ne futa go'o ana sa ngwane'e So'ofia. So'ofia alua go'o 'i Otana, Otana alua go' o sa Taemana. Ngwaingwaena nia go'o ne'e. Sa Funusui ū 'uana 'i Ano'oa ka fa'ata'i ana, ka gunu ana ka sokea, leka fani ka ra'e 'i Ano'afe'o. Kira ka saungia, kira ka kōngia, kira ka 'ania, sulu'ia fo'oa nai'ari ka to'o fuana Fairū na'i. Ūla mae nai kwa, nini kira fa'alia 'ania fanoa 'i Fairū.

Ka teo ka leleka, sa Ra'efemae oli sa Kwaru, ta'e ka 'uia 'i Robona lo'oko 'i Ma'easi, na gwa'i 'uru, * * * ka ra'e 'ala'a ka bu saena fo'oa 'i Karudaudau ana sa Ngaute'e. * * * Ka oli ma'i, kika to'ea saena Kwaru. Sa Olita'imae futa ana 'i Ko'ofaneta, sa Aini ne'e korea ka alua sa Olita'imae. Sa Olita'imae ne'e alua go'o sa Diosi.

Rodo kira ka dao kira ka iroa, Kwaru ka 'ato, oli kwau ka nia 'i Ulanafiu, teo ka māliu 'ana. Ofodangi go'o sa Ra'efemae ka 'aga kwanga 'uia 'ania 'i Robona, ka māla na'a, Gwaunafau na'a, 'Eda'eda na'a, ngwa'i 'afe furi lisia, tata'e kira ka o'omae kira ka ra'e na'a ma'i, "'Oko saungia 'afe kami." Sa Dionga mala, sa 'Oiramo mala, sa Kuba mala, kira ka "Sai, sasi la'u īra ana ngela kaimili, nia ke liu mo 'i fa'i? Ta ngwae kata saungia, nia liu ka ego aimili ka le'a nena." Ra'e 'i Talakwata, dao ka to'ea gwata sa Ngaute'e loni'a saungwae 'uana, nia ka alu daudau ka teo na'a 'i nai'ari.

It lay until there was the pollarded nut-tree, Ko'ou'a prohibited it, putting a tree-frond on it. Oforodo, who was his younger brother, Saubilia and Tadili lived at Lulungwasa Abufo'oka: "Oh tomorrow let's go and crack those nuts!" "Eh, Ko'ou'a might have some-thing to say to us." He said "Oh, he's my elder brother. So others should go and inform him, not us." They set out and cracked the nuts until they'd taken a bundle of bamboos-full, they pounded them at night and ate them at Abufo'oka. Next morning Ko'ou'a went to garden over at Ano'o'a and on arrival the husks were already fly-ridden. Then he pollarded the nut-tree they call Ngaliragia [Pollarded-nut]. Climbing back to Kwaru, he took a gong and cursed those people with it. * * * Later when day came they raised a band and killed Laubisia, sister of Fina'i. * * *

Lulufanoa killed Laubisia, Filiga stood by with a reward and observed them. Eventually they were afraid to approach the place. Ko'o-mali was born of that man So'ofia. So'ofia begot Otana, Otana begot Taemana. She was his [Taemana's] sister. Funusui stood by for her at Ano'oa and signed to her, he courted her, deceived her and climbed with her to Ano'afe'o. They killed her, they baked her, they ate her, and picked up that reward aimed at Fairū. That was the third feud in which they damaged the community of Fairū.

It lay until Ra'efemae returned to Kwaru, set out and shot Robona over at Ma'easi, a widow, * * * and climbed up and stamped his foot for the reward at Karudaudau, from Ngaute'e. * * * He returned and they ambushed him in Kwaru. Olita'imae was born of Ko'ofaneta, Aini married her and begot Olita'imae. It was Olita'imae who begot Diosi.

One night they came and spied, Kwaru was difficult and they went back to Ulanafiu, lay down and slept. In the morning Ra'efemae shouldered a gun and shot Robona with it, she was wounded and at Gwaunafau, at 'Eda'eda, the women who saw her set out and lamented, they came climbing: "You struck our woman." There was Dionga, there was 'Oiramo, there was Kuba, they said "Hey, he can't do that to our daughter, where can he go? If someone kills him, it's fine, he relies on us." Climbing to Talakwata, he came and captured Ngaute'e's pig, the one he'd killed for, and set a trap there.

The third feud to damage Fairū

This feud involved Ko'o'ua, a son of Mudi'a and brother of Alasa'a's great-grandmother Ko'ongidu (see genealogy page 67). Ko'ou'a put a leafy branch on a nut tree as a public sign that he was reserving the nuts for his own use. Oforodo of Abufo'oka, who stole the nuts, would have been a son of one of the families who left 'Aisubu to get away from Ko'ou'a's father Mudi'a. When Ko'o'ua found the nuts were gone he pollarded the tree in anger to stop it bearing and cursed whoever had stolen them. (Pollarding, *ragia*, is usually done by ring-barking, to encourage new growth).

Finding themselves cursed, the culprits sought restitution by killing a girl called Laubisia, and this again brought in the people of 'Ere'ere. To avenge Laubisia and at the same time collect a reward already on offer for the killing of someone from Fairū, Funusui of 'Ere'ere killed another unsuspecting girl, Ko'omali of Kwaru (her mother Otana was descended in the male line from Fikiramo, the Kwaio founder of the Kwaru clan). This feud may have occurred in the 1850s.

The fourth feud to damage Fairū

Once again a woman was attacked, although apparently not killed, for a reward. This time the culprit was a Kwaru man, Ra'efemae, so rather than kill a member of their own community, the Fairū people arranged for the Fakula'es to kill Ra'efemae by using the reward to lure him into an ambush. It was understood they would not seek reprisals for his death.

This is the earliest mention of guns in Alasa'a's stories, so we are now in the colonial period, perhaps during the 1880s.

Cursing with the slit-gong or 'drum' used to signal messages means sounding it to punctuate a spoken curse, broadcasting it so that neither the living or the dead could ignore it. In 1983 Aisah Osifera gave this demonstration of the gong, now used mostly to announce church services.

Curses

Swearing by saying something defiling about a man is not only insulting but, in the past, also acted as a curse by offending his ancestral ghosts, who would abandon or afflict him. He was obliged to seek restitution and often only bloodshed would satisfy him or his ghosts.

In 1928 Norman Deck of the South Sea Evangelical Mission wrote a report on this subject for the colonial government, describing practices which had ceased only about ten years before. As this extract shows, Deck had a detailed understanding of the Kwara'ae and north Malaita culture he was dedicated to reforming.

Being defiled he cannot go inside the man's house (biu or fera), but can only sleep in the house where his wife dwells (luma), he is too ashamed to join in with the other men in going to market or any other community business, he knows that everyone will be thinking of that swear, he is miserable, his eye is "deabi".

He then goes out to "lulu fa'abu" lit. seek for propitiation or justification, he will kill anyone he falls in with, man, woman or child even of his own line (waefuta nia), upon doing this his name is cleared from shame, he is no longer defiled, human blood has been shed.

He adorns himself with branches of trees about his body ferns or ornamental leaves in his hair, comes back to biu, the man's house, makes a big noise, he rejoices aloud. Everyone takes notice and they start to make a big noise with him, sometimes one of the elder men becomes "possessed" (akalo ta'o), and the spirit of his line expresses approval of the "fa'abua" through this man.

The man now goes behind the man's house (biu, fera) and bites a betel nut in two, at the same time praying to his family akalo, saying "this is your betel nut" and telling him that he has cleansed himself, he then returns to the front of the house, and everyone shouts out approval, and they ring the drum to announce the kill far and wide that all may know that his name is now cleared.

From Public Record Office CO225/225/54/22A, with thanks to David Akin

Kwatea ala'anga ka lalili ka leleka, ra'e 'i Suli'ua: "O'ofodangi kaulu na'a 'i sulufaua 'i Fauboso. Sa Ra'efemae koso 'i ne'ana, ka 'uri kaulu saungia na'a 'uana fo'oa."

Fakula'e kira ladefu'a na'a ne'e ana Malanga'idodo, nia liu na'a ana dikoa na'a, 'uana fo'oa māna 'i Robonadoe. "Nia koso ma'i 'i ne'e, ma kaili nini'a na'a." Lae kira ka saea fuana sa Olita'imae, mae fūri dao go'o, kira ka ladefu'a na'a 'i lo'oko 'i gwauna 'i Talakwata ma 'i Busui. Sa Bō'ingū korea 'i Gwamanu, alua sa Laungi'au; asoa na'a ka fi'i koso ma'i na'ona sa Ra'efemae. 'Unari kira ka "O nia lo koso na'a ma'i, ki lia 'ala'a na'a ana nai kwa." Tala fu 'i Talakwata ne'e nia 'ato, dau mala 'ania lali 'ai ma 'oke koso. Leleka sa Olita'imae ka dao, ma'a sa Maeladoe sa Raungasi ka koso saena kafo kira ka ra'e kira ka tua saena faoda lo'oko, ta'i tala lae ka liu go'o 'i ninimana. Kira ka dao 'i nai'ari, sa Bō'ingū ka "Kwarae, ngwae nini'a ra'e 'aena ka isila go'o ne'e." Sa Ra'efemae lo dau a'oa'o ana kwanga ke mānunu'ia go'o. Sa Raungasi ma sa Olita'imae ka abirani rō fa'i bolo kī, lafua 'ania nia ka leleka ka rurū go'o saena kafo lo'oko. Lalia sa ngwane'e Bō'ingū tafi ka leka na'a 'uana 'i Suli'ua. Kira ka folosia sa Ra'efemae, kōngia kira ka 'ania logo, to'o fuana fanoa 'i Fairū.

Teo 'una'ari, sa Maebiri nini ka mae 'i Baibai, to'ofolo fanoa lō 'i Ta'efa'i 'i Rodobusu. 'Agania 'o'a fuiri leleka ka sui ki dangulua. Ara'i fuiri mae fafalegolego ka teo na'a. Rongoa go'o ana 'o'a fuiri, ka la'ungani limana ka danga 'ania. Ruana nia ka rao 'uana 'o'a fuiri, ka la'ungani limana ka danga 'ania. To'a lo'oko ka rongoa rao go'o 'uana subi ka "Sai, ngwae lo'oko 'iri rongo la'u 'o'a nini nau ku 'uia ana maelana ngwaingwaena nau." Sa Alumae laefolo ka dao, sa Alumae alua go'o sa Kwasiomea, sa Kwasiomea alua go'o sa Ba'eakalo. Lae ma'i kira ka dao 'i Dariba'era, ka ra'e go'o 'i Rodoi. Go'o sa Tolosau ka "No 'o'iri rongo la'u ta rū kwa?" Nia ka rao su ka kamea fofo sua ka falia ta'i ai, ka "Sai, 'oto'asi'o ko leka fani rū 'oe kwa! Sa tai ne'e rongorongo rū 'oe?" Go'o ka rao 'uana ifuna ka "Etana, ruana, ūla," nia dikoa go'o gwauna nai. Oli kira ka kwaiatoa nama 'ana ana mae fuiri teo nama 'ana fuana fanoa 'i Fairū nai. Teo ka leleka nau ku doe, saungia 'i Maesamasia kira ka taka na'a 'ania kafo 'i Lu'ata. * * *

Sent word speeding up to Suli'ua: "In the morning be at the stone platform at Fauboso. When Ra'efemae comes down there, you can kill him for the reward."

The Fakula'es waited patiently at Malanga-'idodo and he went to destruction, for the reward in return for Robonadoe. "When he comes down here, here we are." They went and told Olita'imae, the band arrived, they waited patiently over at the head of Talakwata and Busui. Bō'ingū married Gwamanu and begot Laungi'au; when it was day he came down in front of Ra'efemae. So then they said "Oh, when he comes down, we'll be looking up at him." The path to Talakwata is difficult, you must hold on to tree roots as you go down. Eventually Olita'imae arrived and the father of Maeladoe, Raungasi, came down into the stream, they climbed and stayed inside a cave, the path went past alongside it. They arrived there and Bō'ingū said "Hey, that's a man who climbed and his foot slipped." Ra'efemae held his gun aloft to stare at it. Raungasi and Olita-'imae let off two bullets, lifting him, and he just went on and into the stream. Chasing that man Bō'ingū, he escaped and went for Suli'ua. They carved up Ra'efemae, baked him and ate him, a strike for the community of Fairū.

So it lay, and Maebiri died at Baibai, across from the home of Ta'efa'i at Rodobusu. The beating of the gong went on and then ceased. The man who died was laid out. On hearing the gong, an arm was bent and let drop. The second one reached for the gong, bent his arm and let it drop. The people over there heard and reached for angle-clubs, "Hey, someone over there still can't hear the gong I'm beating for the death of my sister." Alumae went across, Alumae begot Kwasiomea, Kwasiomea begot Ba'eakalo. They came and arrived at Dariba'era and climbed to Rodoi. Then Tolosau said "Can't you hear anything then?" He reached out and grabbed a bundle of spears and took one out, "Eh, drop what you're doing and go! Who's listening to yours?" Then he reached for his hair and "One, two, three," he cracked his head. Returning they had to deposit him, in the feud which lay with the community of Fairū. It lay until I was big and they killed Maesamasia and scattered her in the stream at Lu'ata. * * *

The killing over the gong

The Fairū people and the'Ere'ere people of Baibai seem to have quarrelled over the simultaneous announcement by gong signals of deaths in their communities, each accusing the other of disrespect. Exactly who killed who is unclear, but Alasa'a seems to imply that the Kwaru girl Maesamasia was later killed in retaliation.

The killing of Maesamasia

Maesamasia was another victim of the strict law of former times, whose story Michael Kwa'ioloa noted down from his father Alasa'a. She was the daughter of Kaoia of the Kwaru clan, descended in the male line from Fikiramo. Kaoia's younger brother had a son, Isulimae, who made his 'sister' Maesamasia pregnant. The normal penalty for fornication, let alone incest, was death, and Maesamasia was killed by Berote'e.

Berote'e presumably had his own reasons for killing someone, perhaps to avenge the killing over the gong. He then paid death-compensation (*toto'a*) for Maesamasia to settle and conclude the matter. Isulimae escaped and went to live in Western Solomon Islands, or he would probably have been killed too.

This must have happened in the 1900s or later, when opportunities for plantation work would have enabled Isulimae to go to the Western Solomons, at a time when, as Alasa'a says, he himself was 'big'.

Eating man

As Alasa'a's stories show, men sometimes ate the bodies of those they killed in retaliation for an offence, so adding insult to injury. Men who killed for the sake of eating, like the Kwaru ancestor Fikiramo, or 'Aramae of Gwauna'ongi (in Chapter 2), are regarded as monstrous cannibals or 'eaters' (*fafanga*). But for most men, eating man seems to have been a special and rather awesome experience. Alasa'a belonged to the last generation of Kwara'ae men to taste human flesh, before the British suppressed feuding and killing by 1920.

In 1987 Alasa'a described his experience of eating man as a boy:

> A piece of man is actually yellow. A bamboo-full lies in the fire, he splits it open and eats a part. If the juice flows it's luminous like sago-millipedes. It's actually like fireflies. That's what man is like. If I'd eaten it, I'd have eaten the leg. My father and my grandfather ate it but I'd gone. As I retched from eating it.
>
> Translated from Kwara'ae

Silas Sangafanoa of Ualakwai spoke in 1987 of his boyhood acquaintance with a notorious West Kwara'ae warrior, Rogokwau of 'Abara'i:

> Oh, his work was to kill and he'd eat the man, Rogokwau. If we killed anyone, wherever they killed a man, they'd carry him away and he'd eat him. He said it was good meat. Well, once there was a woman they killed, and this time I knew because I was big. They ate her and wanted to give a piece to me, but ... They baked her in a stone oven, cut her up, took out her belly, cut her into pieces and baked her. This was at 'Abara'i. It was in a tabu-place, they didn't do it outside, they came into the tabu-sanctum. . . . She was the wife of one of their men and had come in marriage to their home. But she didn't keep to her husband, she wanted to go around with other men.
>
> Translated from Pijin

Timi Ko'oliu of 'Ere'ere dictated these reminiscences in 1984:

> My father and others ate a man. I was born, it was when I was small they ate him. They ate him and said it was good meat, like pig. Those who killed the man had been sworn at: "You all eat women's arses." When they heard: "Hey, find the man, we'll kill him." They just went and killed the man who swore at them. They killed him to make themselves tabu. They took him to the place, you know the stream at Taba'akwaru? That's the place they cooked him, where they bathe at the stream. They singed him, then removed the hair, cut him up, filled up bamboos and cooked him on the fire. When you take this bamboo and you eat it, it's cold, not hot. It's not like pig when you lift it from the fire and it's hot. No, not man. When you lift it from the fire it's cold, like ice. So then, they ate him. "It's a good man," then they ate him all up. That's how it was.
>
> Translated from Pijin and abridged

Jonathan Didimae of 'Ere'ere repeated a rule for eating man in 1987:

> Our father has killed a man, so now we eat the man. We eat him and eventually you want to throw up, because they put medicine on it too and it turns your stomach, and if you throw up on the ground they'll kill you, the people of the man we've killed. If you throw up into my mouth and I swallow it down, they won't kill you, because the two of us are brothers, born of one man and woman. That's what my father told me.
>
> Translated from Pijin

Aia'a, 'unari, sa Ko'ola'a ka alua sa Mudi'a, sa Mudi'a ka alua sa Maeisua, ka alua 'i Ko'ongidu, nia'a nini nau ku firi ana kula ne'e kī sulia. 'Unari, 'i Ko'ongidu 'afe fuana sa Fane'a, ka alua sa Kamusudoe ne'e ki saea 'ania sa Fiu'adi, ka korea logo 'i Bingamae, ngela kini sa Maeisua, ka 'adoa logo Tolinga fa'inia Fairū. Sa Fane'a ka korea 'i Ko'ongidu, ka adoa logo Fairū fai'inia Tolinga. Nia'a nini'a nau ku firi sulia ana Fairū. 'Unari, sa Kamudoe ka futa logo ana 'i Ko'ongidu, ka korea ngwaingwaena, ngela sa Maeisua. Sa Maeisua ka sai ana, ka ogata'a ne'e nia korea, ka ore ana.

Sa Kamudoe ka nia 'i Gwaunafau, go'o kira ka saungia sa Maeisua, to'oba 'i Namo'isiu. 'O'a ka angi, nia ka ra'e ka ū go'o 'i Kwa'ifau, ka fata faifolo 'i fanoa sulia kira ore ana. Kira ka rīta'inia, "O kira ka saungia funga 'oe", ko'o nau ka foto ka leleka ka ū 'i Bulifau. Sa Ko'oū'a ka 'ui laelae sulia sa ngwane'e Rikifo'oa, nia saka ka saka na'a 'i māna sua ko'o nau. Sa Kamudoe ka dangulua sua ana, sa Bungi'a ka saka, sa ngwane'e Bakoi'a ka saka, ka to'osia fuadaro'o, ka oli ka saka 'i Gwaunafau. . . . Aia'a, kira ka tua 'i nai'ari, sa Maeisua kira ka kwaiatoa, kira ka teo ka dangi na'a, ko'o nau ka koso ka siu 'i Kwaitakea. Ka ngalia fa'i rufa ka fasia fāfia 'abuna, ka ābu ka leleka sa Fafau ka sungia. Nau ku sasi 'uana fasi nai ngalia saena kwauta. Nau ku saesae fasi nia ke kwatea ten paoni, nia ke sasi 'uana kwauta. . . .

Nau ku futa ana kini 'i Fairū kī ne'e, etana ne'e Ko'ongidu, ruana ne'e 'i Bingamae, ūla ne'e 'i 'Ofakao, faina ne'e 'i Lekafa'iramo. Ko'o nau ka lafua 'i Fairū, du'ua ngwai nia, funga nia, ka fo'o 'ania fai tafuli'ae kī 'ania maelana. 'Unari 'i Bingamae ka angi, saena babala 'i kō loni'a 'i 'Ado'alai, sa 'O'ota ka ū 'i māna fera lo 'i Ado'alai, ka rī fuana, rī fuana ko'o nia. Sa 'O'ota ne'e, ma'a sa Maeisua go'o, aibuira sa Mudi'a, ka 'uri, "Noa'a ta mani, ka noa'a ta gwata, ka noa'a ta lifa ī'a. 'Oke ngalia go'o ano nini'a kira saungia ma'a 'oe fa'asi'i kī." Ka kwatea 'Asida'ada'ai, ka kwatea Anokaulatae, ka kwatea 'Ado'alai, ka kwatea Anokō, ka kwatea Faulaua, Ngalisakikisi na'iri'a, ka toto 'ania fuana ko'o nau.

Well, so then, Ko'ola'a begot Mudi'a, Mudi'a begot Maeisua and begot Ko'ongidu, and it's through her I claim those places. So then, Ko'ongidu was married to Fane'a and begot Kamusudoe who they called Fiu'adi, and he married Bingamae, the daughter of Maeisua, and joined Tolinga with Fairū. When Fane'a married Ko'ongidu he also joined Fairū with Tolinga. That's why I have a claim to Fairū. So then, Kamudoe was born of Ko'ongidu and he married his sister, the daughter of Maeisua. When Maeisua knew, he was angry that he'd married her and shunned him.

Kamudoe was at Gwaunafau, then they killed Maeisua up at Namo'isiu. The gong cried out, he climbed up and stood at Kwa'ifau and spoke across to the home, because they'd shunned him. They shouted to him, "Oh, they've killed your father-in-law", and my grandfather rushed along until he stood at Bulifau. Ko'oū'a ran shooting after that man Rikifo'oa, and he emerged right onto the point of my grandfather's spear. Kamudoe let fly the spear at him, Bungi'a came out, that man Bakoi'a came out, he threw him to the two of them, returned and came out at Gwaunafau. . . . Well, they stayed there, they deposited Maeisua, they rested until day, and my grandfather went down to bathe at Kwaitakea. He took a *rufa* tree and planted it on his blood, it was tabu until Fafau burnt it. I tried to take him to court. I said he should give ten pounds, and he should try it on the court. . . .

I'm born of women of Fairū, the first was Ko'ongidu, the second was Bingamae, the third was 'Ofakao, the fourth was Lekafa'iramo. My grandfather elevated Fairū, avenged his uncle, his father-in-law, and offered four ten-strings for his death.[1] So then, Bingamae cried in the feasting shelter at 'Ado'alai, 'O'ota stood in front of the sanctum at 'Ado'alai, and she called for him, called for her grandfather. 'O'ota, a father of Maeisua, Mudi'a's younger brother, said "There's no money, no pigs, no dolphin teeth. Just take the lands your father left when they killed him." He gave her 'Asida'ada'ai, gave Anokaulatae, gave 'Ado'alai, gave Anokō, gave Faulaua, that is Ngalisakikisi, he compensated my grandmother with them.

1 The ten-string shell-moneys were for the funeral expenses.

How the Tolinga people came to Fairū

The Tolinga presence in Fairū began when Faneate'e married Ko'ongidu (as mentioned in Chapter 3). Ko'ongidu was the daughter of Mudi'a, and Fane'a came to live with his father-in-law, who by then had moved to Gwaunafau. Mudi'a gave some land to his daughter, the first of several pieces of land in Fairū to be inherited by Fane'a's descendants. Henceforth the Tolinga group formed part of the Fairū community, although they already had connections in the neighbourhood through Fanea's mother, who was from Marade in Latea, not far away.

The killing of Maeisua

Maeisua was Ko'ongidu's brother, and when her son Fiu'adi Kamusudoe took a wife within the family, Maeisua's daughter Bingamae, his close 'sister', Maeisua said he would never see them again until he died. The bad feeling in the family was only resolved when Maeisua was killed in a feud and Kamusu avenged his death. It is said that the ghost gave Maeisua to be killed because of this improperly close marriage.

In Alasa'a's account the significance of these events is in the land which Maeisua's 'father' O'ota (brother of Mudi'a), gave to his 'grand-daughter' Bingamae to compensate her for her father's death. In effect this legitimised her marriage in a way which Maeisua himself had refused to do, the land being inherited by her descendants and hence claimed by Alasa'a.

At the time of these events, which may have been in the 1830s, Mudi'a was living at 'Ado'alai and his son Maeisua had moved to Kwaiilia. These places were in the neighbourhood of their former home at Gwaunafau, where Kamusudoe was still living.

In 1987 Michael Kwa'ioloa dictated the story of how and why Maeisua was killed to illustrate the life and times of his great-grandparents.

Well, three generations ago my ancestor made a big feast at a place called 'Ado'alai, just near to Gwaunafau. Ko'ou'a was the man who made the feast, and O'ota, both from Fairū. You know preparations for a feast; at this feast the number of taros they used for making pudding was two thousand, with one hundred of the big fish called *gwa īla*. In our Kwara'ae language we call this *kō* [bake], meaning something very big to make everyone gather together for it.

At that time, a man heard the feast was happening and said "Oh, I must go and take part in this feast so they'll give me a bit of pudding." This man's name was Niutale'a, a man from Ubasi [in East Kwara'ae, further to the North]. When he arrived, you know formerly men were cruel and bad, only some of them were kind. So one of my ancestors saw him and was angry with him; "Hey, why's this man come to our feast? He's from somewhere else."

So while they were preparing the fire and bringing leaf to cover the oven, they'd play around while they were covering the oven for all those taros, taking leaves, throwing some on, then throwing some over him as they covered the oven, and funny things like that. But one of my ancestors, Bako, as he played he meant to beat up this man Niutale'a, who had arrived. So his play became more serious and eventually the man said "What kind of game are you playing with me? You're using the leaf to hurt me." So the man said "You don't understand do you? Why have you come here?" The man grabbed a stick and beat Niutale'a, the man from Ubasi. Beat him badly, and he went back to Ubasi.

When he got back to Ubasi they cried for that man. With his body wounded, he asked his cousins Rikifo'oa and Daununu to repay his wounds. They went back to Kwaiilia and that day the Kwaiilia and Ado'alai people had gone to an exchange market at Talaala'a. So the ghost gave Maeisua to be killed by enemies. When he went out to plant taro, Rikifo'oa jumped out and chopped him in the backbone with a tomahawk. On their way to escape Ko'ou'adoe came after them with spears, shouting "There he goes." So Kamudoe, Bungi'a and Bakoi'a killed him at Bulifau.

Translated from Pijin, with last paragraph edited from an English manuscript

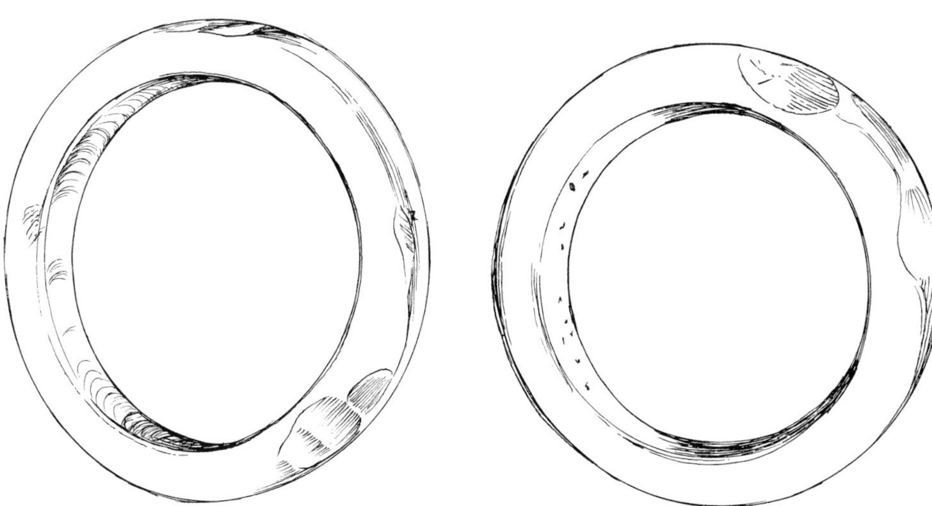

This pair of clamshell armrings, worn above the elbow, belonged to Fiu'adi Kamusudoe. They are of different sizes because he had a withered arm, and the chipped edges result from his fights. Such armrings were used to break a man's ribs while grasping him around the body, and perhaps to ward off blows.

Ka saea ngali ragi'a, "Ma'a 'oe sa Maeisua ragia, si mae fuli fa'inia, ka butā 'ae ngali na'a rū 'oe."

Ta ne'e nau ku firi ana Fairū sulia. Nia'a nau ku saea Kwaru ne'e rū nau, ta ngwae kesi ngenge nau la'u fa'inia. Nini nau ku fata saena redio ne'e fuana ngela nau, 'i leleka ngwae ka ngengeda kira ka rongoa fatalaku nairi'a nau ku 'iri firi 'o'o ana Fairū.

Aia'a ka 'unari, ka mango 'unari, sa ngwane'e To'ikwa'u ka koso ka folia 'i Marade. Ka fi'i alua sa Lobonunuba, ka fi'i alua sa Ko'ofiludoe, ka fi'i alua sa Sisilimae. Sa 'Aba'au ka dao, sa 'Aramae ifulanga'inia ma'i 'i Faureba. Ngwae 'i Maelifau nai'ari. Nini'a ka alu ngwae, sa Takangwane ka nia ana, sa So'ai ka nia ana, sa [Ramo'i]Tolo ka rora ka nau 'ania fanoa nau 'i Latea. 'Unari, sa Sisilimae alua sa Bakōmea, sa Bakōmea alua sa Ko'ofilute'e, sa Ko'ofilute'e alua sa Bakōmeate'e, ka alua 'i 'Urukwai. 'I 'Urukwai ne'e 'afe fuana sa Maelaua, ka alua sa Kamudoe, ka alua logo [ma'a nia] sa Fane'a. Na'i, nini'a nau ku firi ana fanoa ne'e 'i sulia, sulia 'abuku. 'Abuku nai'ari nau ngwae 'i Tolinga, nia fuli aku saena 'i Siale, ka 'iri fuli saena feraābu ta ngwae. Nia nini'a kira ngenge nau fa'inia, kira ka ngē 'uaku fa'inia. Bore ma kaili kwauta ma kira ke lulu fa'ua. . . . Sa Fane'a mae 'i fa'i? Nia mae 'i Gwaunafau. Sa Kaora ka alua nia ka ngalia, ka mae 'i fa'i? Nia mae 'i Gwaunafau. 'I Laguru nia inamae, 'uru na'a, ka oli fuana 'a'ai nia sa Kamudoe, ma nia mae 'i fa'i? Nia mae 'i Gwaunafau. . . .

Ne'e nau ku sai ana ko'o nau ka saea. Gwaunafau rū nau, etana tua'a nai saena fanoa nai. Ruana tua'a ne'e ko'o nau du'ua sa Tō, sa ngwane'e 'Anake 'i Alikwao, ka tua 'i nai'ari. Ūla, ko'o nau sa Francis Ko'odoe ka tata'e ka tua 'i nai'ari. Ūla mae ko'o nau ka du'ua sa Maeisua, ka ma'u go'o ka tafi ka oli ka tua 'i Buri'anaasi.

He said of the pollarded nut tree, "Your father Maeisua pollarded it, as it caused a feud, he wrapped up the nut trunk, now it's yours."[1]

It's through this I have a claim to Fairū. That's why I say Kwaru is mine, and people can no longer dispute it with me. That's why I'm speaking into this radio [cassette] for my son, so later on anyone who disputes with them can hear from my own words that I'm not making an empty claim to Fairū.

Well, so then, that can rest so, the man To'ikwa'u went down and purchased Marade. He then begot Lobonunuba, and he begot Ko'ofiludoe, and he begot Sisilimae. 'Aba'au arrived; 'Aramae banished him from Faureba. He was a man from Maelifau. So it was he who begot people, there's Takangwane, there's So'ai, and [Ramo'i]Tolo is wrong to say he owns my home at Latea.[2] So then, Sisilimae begot Bakōmea, Bakōmea begot Ko'ofilute'e, Ko'ofilute'e begot Bakōmea-te'e, he begot 'Urukwai. 'Urukwai was the wife of Maelaua and begot Kamudoe, she begot [his father] Fane'a. That's why I have a claim to this home, because of my blood. It's my blood, I'm a man of Tolinga and it originates with me at Siale, it doesn't originate in anyone else's tabu-sanctum. That's why they dispute it with me and challenge me over it. But if we go to court they won't know what's what. . . . Where did Fane'a die? He died at Gwaunafau. Kaora put him [his body] away, where did he die? He died at Gwaunafau. Laguru was without family, widowed, she went back to her nephew Kamudoe,[3] and where did she die? She died at Gwaunafau. . . .

So I know what my grandfather said. Gwaunafau is mine, my first presence in my home.[4] The second presence was where my grandfather repaid Tō, and a man called 'Anake of Alikwao lives there. The third, my grandson Francis Ko'odoe has begun to live there. The third is the feud when my grandfather avenged Maeisua, he was afraid and he fled back to live at Buri'anaasi.

1 This refers to the feud when Maeisua's brother Ko'ou'a ring-barked the nut tree and cursed the nut thieves. The two brothers seem to be identified together. The wrapping of the nut tree trunk was to heal it.

2 Ramo'itolo, descendant of Aba'au, was the father of Takangwane and So'ai, and Alasa'a's dispute with him is detailed on page 81.

3 Laguru was a sister of Kamusudoe's father Fane'ate'e.

4 That is, Gwaunafau was the home of Fane'a, the first Tolinga man to arrive in Fairū.

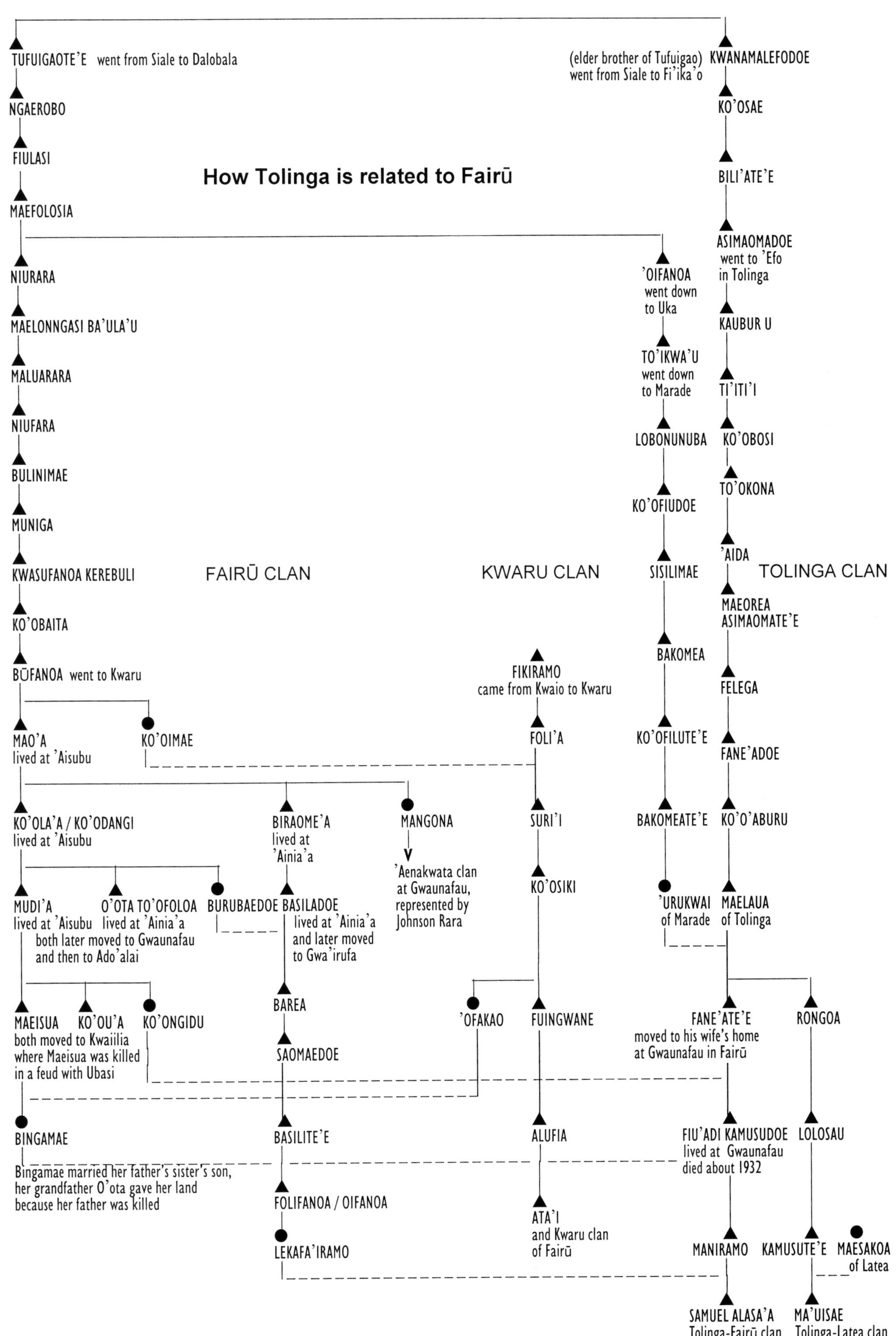

TUFUIGAOTE'E went from Siale to Dalobala
(elder brother of Tufuigao) KWANAMALEFODOE
went from Siale to Fi'ika'o
NGAEROBO
KO'OSAE
FIULASI
How Tolinga is related to Fairū
BILI'ATE'E
MAEFOLOSIA
ASIMAOMADOE
went to 'Efo
in Tolinga
NIURARA
'OIFANOA
went down
to Uka
MAELONNGASI BA'ULA'U
KAUBUR U
TO'IKWA'U
went down
to Marade
MALUARARA
TI'ITI'I
NIUFARA
LOBONUNUBA
KO'OBOSI
BULINIMAE
TO'OKONA
KO'OFIUDOE
MUNIGA
'AIDA
KWASUFANOA KEREBULI
FAIRŪ CLAN
KWARU CLAN
SISILIMAE
TOLINGA CLAN
MAEOREA
ASIMAOMATE'E
KO'OBAITA
BAKOMEA
FIKIRAMO
came from Kwaio to Kwaru
BŪFANOA went to Kwaru
FELEGA
MAO'A
lived at 'Aisubu
KO'OIMAE
FOLI'A
KO'OFILUTE'E
FANE'ADOE
KO'OLA'A / KO'ODANGI
lived at 'Aisubu
BIRAOME'A
lived at
'Ainia'a
MANGONA
'Aenakwata clan
at Gwaunafau,
represented by
Johnson Rara
SURI'I
BAKOMEATE'E
KO'O'ABURU
MUDI'A
lived at 'Aisubu
O'OTA TO'OFOLOA
lived at 'Ainia'a
both later moved to Gwaunafau
and then to Ado'alai
BURUBAEDOE
BASILADOE
lived at 'Ainia'a
and later moved
to Gwa'irufa
KO'OSIKI
'URUKWAI
of Marade
MAELAUA
of Tolinga
MAEISUA
KO'OU'A
KO'ONGIDU
both moved to Kwaiilia
where Maeisua was killed
in a feud with Ubasi
BAREA
SAOMAEDOE
'OFAKAO
FUINGWANE
FANE'ATE'E
moved to his wife's home
at Gwaunafau in Fairū
RONGOA
BINGAMAE
Bingamae married her father's sister's son,
her grandfather O'ota gave her land
because her father was killed
BASILITE'E
ALUFIA
FIU'ADI KAMUSUDOE
lived at Gwaunafau
died about 1932
LOLOSAU
FOLIFANOA / OIFANOA
LEKAFA'IRAMO
ATA'I
and Kwaru clan
of Fairū
MANIRAMO
KAMUSUTE'E
MAESAKOA
of Latea
SAMUEL ALASA'A
Tolinga-Fairū clan
MA'UISAE
Tolinga-Latea clan

Tuatua 'i Buri'anaasi, sa Tōdoe ifua ko'o nau 'i Bingamae, nia saeta'a go'o, ka oli ma'i, ka nia na'a 'i Gwaunafau. Ka nia 'i nini'a ka o'o 'i 'Asida'ada'a, . . . 'i Bingamae, ma'a nau ka leka na'a, 'i Mo'oso ai 'a'ana ka leka na'a. Kira o'o kira ka oli toli go'o 'i 'Asimoamoa ka rodo asoa. Ko'o nau ka o'omae, ka dao 'i Busui, ka dao 'i 'aena 'i Talakwata ka dangi logo. Ma'e tōtō nai nai'ari fuana tua'a nai 'i Gwaunafau. Noa'a nia 'iri mū fa'asia 'i Gwaunafau. Ka tuatua 'i nai'ari ['i Buri'anaasi], go'o sa Tōdoe ka fata fuana 'i Bingamae, ko'o nau ka mangosia saungilana, sulia kaela 'i Ko'ogao go'o. Sa Maelaua kera'a futa go'o sui ana sa Ko'o'aburu, kira futa ana kini 'i Ferasagwali. Go'o ka koso ka saeta'a, kira ka tuafia 'i Gwaunafau. * * *

While living at Buri'anaasi, Tōdoe ousted my grandmother Bingamae, she was angry and came back to be at Gwaunafau. While she was there she gardened at 'Asida'ada'a . . . Bingamae and my father went and Mo'oso his grown-up sister went. They gardened and returned down to 'Asimoamoa and night came. My grandmother lamented, she reached Busui, reached the foot of Talakwata and day came. That's my landmark for my family at Gwauna-fau. She wasn't cut off from Gwaunafau. She was living there [at Buri'anaasi] then Tōdoe propositioned Bingamae and my grandfather refrained from killing him only because he was a child of Ko'ogao.[1] Maelaua and he were both born of Ko'o'aburu, they were born of a woman of Ferasagwali. Then they went down, angry, and lived at Gwaunafau. * * *

Nau'a go'o ne'e nau ku etangia fanoa 'i Fairū kwa! Nau'a go'o ne'e nau ku 'abera 'ania to'a 'i Fairū kwa! Leleka nini kira ka mae, kira ka alua saena limaku. Kira 'uri "O noa'a na'a ta ngwangwane 'uri, 'oko futa ana kini bore, 'oko daua fanoa ne'e, 'oko 'abera 'ania kaimili, 'uri 'oke lia sulia fanoa ne'e. 'Aina, kafona, afu ano ana, rū 'oe leleka 'oko ngalia akalo ne'e ka nia na'a 'amu, leleka 'oko 'aila si kō 'oko fa'alia na'a 'amu." Fatalana sa Kalakini na'iri'a. Sa Kalakini ne'e moa 'isi fuaku, kamu firi ana ma kaumulu firi ana sulia tae? Kaulu firi ana ma sa tai ne'e ū fuana akalo saena kafo? Mulu saea. Akalo saena Kwaru satana sa tai? Na kui fu ke daungwae, satana, satana sa tai? Mulu saea re! Kaulu to'o ana ta ma'e toto 'i Fairū? * * *

It's I who leads the homeland of Fairū! It's I who cares for the people of Fairū! When they died they put it into my hands. They said "Oh, you're not on the male side, you're born of woman, but you've held on to this homeland, you've cared for us, so you look after this home-land. Its trees, its streams, its pieces of land, they're yours until you take the ghosts who are here, until you don't want to bake and you destroy them." That's what Kalakini said. Kalakini spilt it all out for me, and you all claim it, but what claim do you have? You claim it but who stands for the ghost in the stream? Say it. The ghost in Kwaru, what's his name? The dog which grabs people, its name, what's its name? Say it! Do you have a landmark in Fairū? * * *

Fa'uta ne'e sa 'Ata'i, sa Busuka ka mae ma nia ka leka sasi 'uana to'a Koio, ka kwaiatoa? . . . Leleka ki sasia ngada'a, ki ngalia bani'au nai, ka ngalia lima'ae nai, fa'afa'a nai, kira ka ngalia bani'au sa 'Una kira kesi du'ua go'o. Kira ka sasia ngada'a nai'ari kira ka kwatea fuana to'a Koio. Fa'uta ne'e sa Isusulia ka mae, ma ngwae nai'ari kesi kwatekwate ta mani? Nau ku 'oia bani'au ana. Fa'uta ne'e sa 'Ata'i ta'e ke lulu kwailiu, ke to'oto'o 'i Fulidaura'ia, ma ke to'oto'o 'i Malanga, ma ke to'oto'o 'i lo'oko 'i Fulisusuku, ma ke to'oto'o 'i Fauboso?

How is it that 'Ata'i, when Busuka died, went for the Kwaio people to deposit him? . . . Eventually we held the wake and took *bani'au*, took five-strings, *fa'afa'a*,[2] they took 'Una's *bani'au* and they couldn't repay it. They held the wake and gave it to the Kwaio people. How is it, when Isusulia died, those people couldn't give any money? I settled a *bani'au* on him. How is it that 'Ata'i set out searching all around, getting to Fulidaura'ia, getting to Malanga, getting over to Fulisusuku and getting to Fauboso?

1 To summarise this incident, Alsasa'a's grandparents Bingamae and Kamusu moved back to Gwaunafau after Kamusu's distant cousin Tōdoe propositioned Bingamae. Ko'ogao, one of the two orphans saved from scavenging on the rubbish tip, was the father's mother of Tōdoe and father's father's sister of Kamusu.

2 These are shell-money denominations. (The largest of them, *bani'au*, is illustrated on page 17.)

Alasa'a and Ramo'itolo

Alasa'a's reference to Latea (on page 78) reflects a longstanding rivalry with his brother-in-law Ramo'itolo ('Tolo') of Latea. Alasa'a traces descent from To'ikwa'u, who purchased Marade in Latea, through 'Urukwai, a woman of Marade four generations before. Ramo'itolo was descended in the male line from 'Aba'au, who came to Marade from Faureba in the central inland eleven generations before. (He was banished by 'Aramae, the famous warrior of Gwauna'ongi mentioned in the feud over the stolen bark on page 37.)

Ramo'itolo married Alasa'a's sister Siumalefo and the two men were close neighbours for much of their lives, until Ramo'itolo died in 1969. Their children grew up together (see Kwa'ioloa & Burt 1987:33-35) and Ramo'itolo's daughter Maefatafata cared for Alasa'a in his last years at Anofiu in Latea. But despite this, the two men were involved in bitter disputes over land.

In 1965 Alasa'a took Ramo'itolo to the Local Court over the boundary ('spearline') between Fairū and Latea. The court records provide a useful illustration of the issues at stake in Kwara'ae clan histories and an insight into local politics. Among other things, Alasa'a supports the claim of Ben Nongwae of the Bilubilu clan to leadership for Latea, the issue disputed between Ramo'itolo and Nongwae in the 1965 court case cited on page 55. (Note that these men's names are also used to refer to their ancestors many generations ago.)

The court decision identifies the motives underlying the dispute as fees for developments on the land. Of these, the establishment of the Council Headquarters is mentioned in Chapter 5, while the airstrip has still not materialised thirty-five years on. In the best tradition of Kwara'ae dispute settlement, the court decision is a compromise.

ALASA'A OF Fairu (Pltiff) Vs Ramotolo (Deft)
Pltff's <u>Claim</u>. ALASA'A not satisfied of Ramotolo's spearline between Fairu and Latea.
Statement.

ALASA'A said I want my land Fairu which Ramoitolo claim must be clear on the boundary so that Ramoitolo and his side not head over, even our land lies together he must have the right to claim his side not mine.
Plaintiff Swear to tell the truth.

I said the place Marade was Nowae's. He is the man that invite Ramoitolo to his place. He did invite me also. My heart object Ramoitolo for trying to reject me. Only Nowae who invite us both. Everything happen in Latea it is Nowae who should be our first man. Nowae should talk [give directions] to Ramoitolo and me because he gave lands to us.

Only this spearline between us is not straight. Ramoitolo moved the foot of my boundaries where the Council Headquarters settled he made the foot of Fairu boundry sharp as a spear head that is why I like to review the case. My ancient places which is Kwaililia and Kwaru Ramoitolo took away that is why I not satisfied about.

Another is Fauanameaoa Feraauagona Ada'adaasi Fiu inao Fiu buri Gwaiu'ula. All this my tambu places which I fought after. I did not remove towards Ramoitolo's land. All this place Ramoitolo have nothing of his inside. I have my dead bones stone walls, still remain today. Also all this is at the back of Faumamanu Council Headquarters in the spearline which I now mention in the Court today round it all. That is the end.

Ramo'itolo then questions Alasa'a, witnesses speak for Alasa'a and his version of the boundary, and he recites his genealogy and 'ancient places'

Defendant Ramoitolo said:- Sworn states

About Alasa'a's spearline I did not proved because they have move this all about, I did not know that ALASA'A claim MARADE all these places he claim was not his because he did no sacrifice there I did not know ALASA'A today no pig of his died at those place he claim.

I did not know where ALASA'A come from no sacrifice on those places. His spearline I object. That is the end.

Alasa'a questions Ramo'itolo, who then recites his genealogy, tabu places and version of the boundary

Decision

Court having heard the evidence and was satisfied that both side should share in the Council Headquarter area and air strip land because both side cannot agreed for the spearline they put themself so the Court must set the boundry for them. Also the Court found out that on the bush side there has been a set boundry no doubt of that only on the sea side which is no proper boundry before, and the quarrel only start because if the Council will pay for land fee and one side will take the money however they can share it. Also Court cannot deny Alasa'a because he was the one who first let the land for Council when there was no one allows any land. However the Court must recognised him for being generous to help the development of Kwai side and he should share with the fee also. Lot of people want to argue but the two heads is Ramoitolo & Alasa'a.

Judgement

The boundry is set at the midst of Council H.Q. & air strip Ramoitolo on the north and Alasa'a on the south side. Court found out that these two people even olden days they used to live together and intermarried now the Court cannot divide but each should see for his side boundry set on 7/4/65.

Solomon Islands National Archives BSIP 25 IV/30, original English

Ka leleka kaida'i ana mola'a, nau ku fikua fa'i niu, sa Bitareo ka sai go'o ana, sa Nongwae ka sai go'o ana, lia 'i Ta'efa'i ka sai go'o ana. Kira ka sasia sau'a nai'ari. Lima'ae ne'e sa Nongwae ngalia, lima talanga'i alo kī. Fa'afa'a ne'e sa Ladusu ka ngalia, fai talanga'i alo kī ki lae 'usi'i 'i Taulaungi, 'i Ko'omali ne'e lae ka foe'e go'o. Talanga'i alo ne'e sa Diosi foea kwau ka dao fa'inia, nai lisia, nau'a ne'e nau ku sasia maelana. Ka 'unari, kana nai'ari, nau ku ra'e ku ngalia akala'i afu ana sa Maelu'ia, nau ku du'ua 'ani gwata. Nau ku ngalia ta akala'i afu 'i Faumamanutolo ana 'i Ko'obulu, sa Samani, nau ku du'ua 'ania akala'i bī.

Sa 'Ata'i ka mae, kaili ka ngalia 'uana 'i Fa'imalasata nia tau. Sa [Ramo'i]Tolo ne'e mae na'a, sa Dasa ka mae na'a, sa 'Ui ka mae na'a, nau'a go'o nē ngwae ne'e nau ku ngalia. Ngalia ka leleka mili ka kwaiatoa 'i Fa'imalasata oli ka dao, nau ku 'oia fa'afa'a na'a, gairabi, kwalu la'usu'u kī. Sa Dasa, sa Tolo kera'a ngalia go'o fa'afa'a. Kwalu la'usu'u kī fuana sa 'Ui du'ungana maelana ka sui. Nia ne'e nau ku firi sulia, nau ku firi ana Fairū. Sa Kalakini ka mae, kira ka ngalia go'o saena tafe, nau ku kwaiatoa nau ku musia bani'au, bani'au ono. Sa [Bita]Reo fa'ida sai ana, sa [Gwa]Lebe ka sai ana, to'a ne'e kira ngalia sa tafe. Ka dokodoko, ta kwalu la'usu'u nau ku ladoa 'ania. Ma kira tuatua 'i fa'i nau ku siroro fa'inida, nau ku usuta'i fa'inida ma ta ngwae kesi dao, ta ngwae kesi nagu. . . . Nau'a go'o, nau'a go'o ne kwā! Nau'a sa Alasa'a ngwae nini'a kira tofe nau. Nau'a go'o nau ku to'o ana gwata nau ku kwatea fuana te'a nau, ka sarea ka sasia 'ania maoma. Gwata nai ke do'ofia ana sa Ko'odangi, gwata nai ke do'ofia ana sa Mudi'a, gwata nai ke do'ofia 'i Faunamoa ana sa Mao'a. Ka leleka ta'ena ngwae kī malata'a aku fa'inia ngela nau kī, kira ka firi ana kula nau. * * *

'A'erū Fairū nai kwa, 'a'erū nau ku kwa'ia ka sui na'a, gwa'irū nini'a nia 'ua. Di'ia ngwae oga ke fa'ita'i nai'ari ma nia ke liu fauta Michael, 'oko foneda na'a 'i nai'ari, . . . Sai, 'oko tua to'o 'oke tasa'ia ogaku. 'Oke tua sulia ta fita bongi, o ta fita beba ne'e 'oke keresia. Kwate'a ne'e god kwatea fuaku, nia liufia rū 'oro kī fuana bubunga ne'e. Fuana nai ta'ea 'ania kastomu ke ū 'ana ti'ana, na lō ka noa'a na'a.

When it came to the time of the normalisation, I gathered coconuts, Bitareo knows it, Nongwae knows it, and the onlooker Ta'efa'i knows it. They made the pudding feast. The five-string Nongwae took, for 500 taros. The *fa'afa'a* Ladusu took, for 400 taros, we went for them at Taulaungi and Ko'omali went to carry them. The hundred taros which Diosi loaded up and came with, I saw and it was I who made the death feast. So then, at the chanting I went up and took ten rolls of tobacco from Maelu'ia and I repaid it with a pig. I took ten rolls of tobacco at Faumamanutolo from Ko'obulu and Samani, and repaid it with ten bamboos of nuts.

Ata'i died, and we took him to Fa'imalasata far away. [Ramo'i]Tolo has died, Dasa has died, 'Ui has died, and only I can speak as one who took him. We took him and eventually deposited him at Fa'imalasata and came back, and I threw in a *fa'afa'a*, a *gairabi* and eight elbow-lengths. Dasa and Tolo just took a *fa'afa'a*. The eight elbow-lengths were for 'Ui, to repay the death. That's why I have a claim, I have a claim to Fairū. When Kalakini died they took him to the platform, I deposited him and I parted with a *bani'au*, a six-string *bani'au*. [Bita]Reo and the others know, [Gwa]Lebe knows, the group who took him to the platform. It was short and I joined on eight elbow-lengths. Where were they living while I struggled for them, I strove to support them, and no-one came, no-one mourned. . . . Just me, it was just me! Me, Alasa'a, the man they deny. It was just me, I got pigs and gave them to my mother to feed and use for festivals. My pig was cooked for Ko'odangi, my pig was cooked for Mudi'a, my pig was cooked at Faunamoa for Mao'a. And eventually today people abuse me and my sons, they claim my place. * * *

That's the basis of Fairū, I've finished relating the basis, there's still the effects. If anyone wants to turn about, however they go about it, Michael, you shut them off here, . . . Eh, you stay put and carry out my wishes. However many days you have to stay or however much paper you have to write on. The gift god gave you surpasses many things for this island. So I can revive custom to stand by itself, not by the law.

Alasa'a and the old men of Kwaru

Having set out his inherited claims to Fairū, Alasa'a goes on to talk about his personal relationships with the senior generation of the clan, in particular with his uncles of Kwaru, the priest Ata'i and his brothers. In so doing he demonstrates another essential principle of Kwara'ae land tenure, that claims to the benefits of clan membership depend on fulfilling social and religious obligations to other members. Hence Alasa'a's reference to the pigs he baked for his Fairū ancestors Ko'odangi, Mudi'a and Mao'a demonstrates his claim to inherit from them.

Alasa'a's uncles and grandparents on his mother's side were the last generation to live and die under the religion of the ghosts, and his last services to them were to help with their considerable funeral expenses. Among the other contributors he mentions are members of the diminishing community of ghost-worshippers in neighbouring Latea; his brother-in-law Ramo'itolo of Faureba-Latea, Nongwae of Bilubilu-Latea and Gwalebe of Atōbi-Latea.

Alasa'a details the shell-moneys paid to those engaged to dispose of the dead (as described on page 39) and to commission food for the funeral feasts. Most of these are denominations of the southern kind of money used in neighbouring Kwaio (with untranslatable names). References to people going to Kwaio and other distant places for help reflect the reluctance of the local Christian majority to contribute to these 'heathen' funerals.

In East Kwaio many people still maintain the kind of funeral ceremonies mentioned by Alasa'a but long since abandoned in Christian Kwara'ae. These men are making public presentations of shell-money from the platform at a funeral feast as a contribution to the funeral expenses, in 1996.
Photo by David Akin

The tabu-sanctum at Fiu

The tabu-sanctum at Fiu illustrates the history and ritual organisation of Fairū. It was founded by Būfanoa, the tenth tabu-speaker of Fairū, who came to live in Kwaru. He placed his father's bones there, and he and his son Mao'a had their bones deposited there in their turn, in the area known as Former Fiu (Fiu 'i Na'o). The bones of Fikiramo, the Kwaio fugitive adopted by Būfanoa, were laid nearby, and the bones of Fikiramo's sons, whose families were afflicted by Mudi'a's curse, were laid in the area known as 'Ada'adasi.

Several generations later, when Alasa'a was young, the tabu-speaker for the Kwaru clan, Ata'i, was also caring for the Fairū ghosts (the ancestors of his in-laws, from whom he was also born of woman: see genealogy page 79). Ata'i took all the bones from the tabu-sanctum at Gwau'ulu, where Būfanoa's descendants at 'Ainia'a had held their festivals (see page 60), and brought them to Fiu for safekeeping. The place they were deposited was known as Latter Fiu (Fiu 'i Buri).

When Ata'i died in the 1930s, Alasa'a contributed to his funeral expenses (as he says on page 82), and became caretaker for the shrine, but by then most of the Fairū and Kwaru people were turning to the church. When Alasa'a himself took up Christianity in the 1940s, the shrine at Fiu was finally abandoned to the encroaching forest.

Surveying the Fiu shrine

In 1979 Alasa'a took his sons to see the abandoned shrine, in order to pass on his knowledge of the site and validate their descent from the ancestors who had lived and worked on Fairū land before them. Afterwards Kwa'ioloa drew a plan (opposite) showing the different clan areas, as well as other details such as the site of the wild dog ghost. Piles of oven stones show the 'restricted hearths' (*fu'a ete'a*) where, before festivals, preliminary sacrifices were offered to particularly tabu ancestors and eaten only by their direct male descendants, and 'festival hearths' (*fu'a maoma*) where food was cooked for the festival congregation as a whole.

Skulls (drawn in profile) and bones show where the ancestors' remains lie, but we have had to delete their names. As the 'confidential' heading indicates, such details should be shared only by clan members who may some day need to prove their claim to the land by demonstrating their historical and genealogical knowledge. The plan is published here to show how the Kwara'ae deal with such historical evidence.

Kwa'ioloa has described their visit to the shrine in his autobiography, *Living Tradition*:

Me, my brother Maniramo and another brother Rex Di'au, my cousin Filiga Takangwane and Festus Fa'abasua, we all went to a sacrificial shrine of ours at Fiu. We went for the whole day, to survey it, look at boundaries and things like that. It was so we could see all the ancient things to do with the ghosts, because we'd only heard about them and not seen them. The place had been killed off in the name of Jesus by the missionaries and we thought it had been finished. But my father wanted us to go to a place where there was the tooth of the white dog of A'arai, which in the past was a ghost which used to kill people. It died long ago but its spirit remained and it used to grab people and they'd die, beside the A'arai river.

When we reached the place where they used to sacrifice to the ghosts, my father directed us to the red tooth of this wild white dog. He told us to dig a hole the full length of an arm and when we reached it we took out two skulls. They'd put the skulls of two women on top of it, to feminise it as we say. I won't mention their names, but they were two of my ancestors and they'd put them on top of it to sort of dilute it, so it would be feminised and not powerful. First they'd cut a stone in half and hollowed out both sides, put the tooth in the hole and joined them both together. Then, before they put the skulls on top, they put it in a deep hole in the ground at the base of a very strong tree.

When we dug it up and took it out, what should happen but a heavy fall of rain; we weren't expecting rain. We were in a bad way. Then as we watched we saw a tall man who took one long stride, squatted down, and disappeared. We all saw him; he bent down and he was gone, we didn't know where. Then before long my father began to pray, to get rid of him. I was a pastor at the time and when we prayed we felt him go away and our situation and the place where we were felt better, with nothing to harm us. My father took out the tooth, held it and he could somehow feel the power it had. As he held it he prayed, calling the name of Jesus. Then everything was put back in the same place.

From *Living Tradition,* by Michael Kwa'ioloa and Ben Burt, 1987, pages 162-3

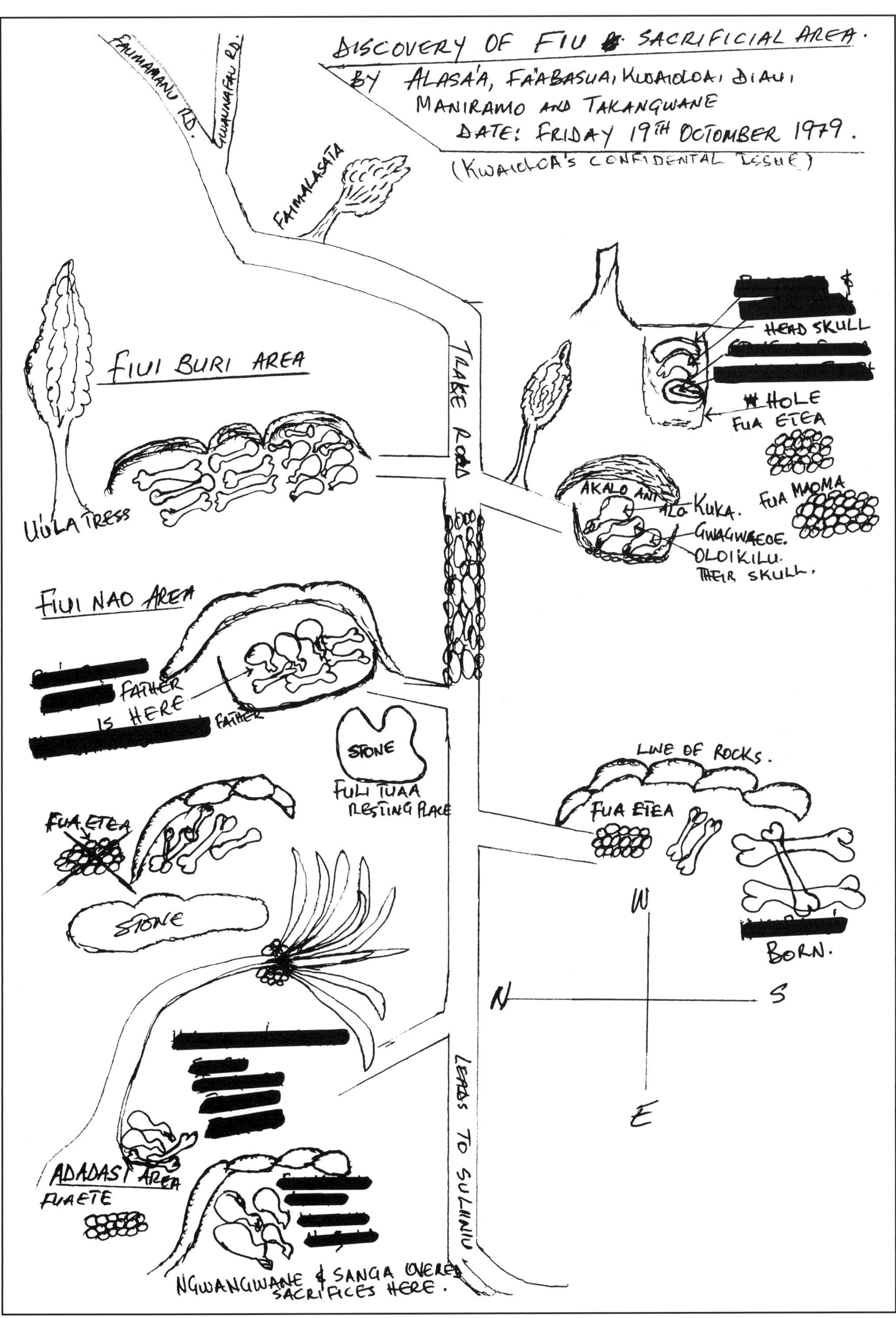
DISCOVERY OF FIU SACRIFICIAL AREA.
BY ALASA'A, FA'ABASUA, KWAIOLOA, DIAU, MANIRAMO AND TAKANGWANE
DATE: FRIDAY 19TH OCTOMBER 1979.
(KWAIOLOA'S CONFIDENTAL ISSUE)
FAUMAMANU RD.
GWANAFAU RD.
FAIMALASATA
FIUI BURI AREA
U'ULA TRESS
TILAKE ROAD
HEAD SKULL
HOLE
FUA ETEA
AKALO ANI ALO KUKA.
FUA MAOMA
GWAGWAEOE.
OLOIKILU.
THEIR SKULL.
FIUI NAO AREA
FATHER IS HERE
FATHER
STONE
FULI TUAA RESTING PLACE
LINE OF ROCKS.
FUA ETEA
FUA ETEA
STONE
BORN.
W
N
S
E
LEADS TO SULIMU
ADADASI AREA
FUAETE
NGWANGWANE & SANGA OVERED SACRIFICES HERE.

4
Kaida 'i Buriana Faka kī ni 'i Dao ma 'i.

Aia'a, nau ku ala'a sulia kaida'i nau ku te'ete'e. Nau ku futa na'a, ku doe na'a ku rongo sulia ne'e ko'o nau fa'ida kira ala'a ana faka, etangilana laungwae'a saena fanoa 'i Malaita. Aia'a, faka nai'ari, no 'iri lekaleka ma'i. Aia'a kingi 'i Inglana mala nai'ari, kira saea 'ania Fauikuila. Nia lialia saena 'abuka nia, kira saea 'ania buka ābu, ka falia na'a 'i saena faka nia kira saea 'ania Gorai'alosina. Go'o ka 'ato na'a 'uana 'i Malaita, leleka ka ōlo 'i Kwai. Nia ōlo 'i Kwai, 'i Tala'ionegere, ka mamākela'ia kwalu'ani malitako. Ta ngwae 'iri ra'e. Ka rao na'a 'uana kwanga ābu nia, ka 'ui 'ania, ka talofia na'a, ngwae ana tolo kira ra'e ka sui. Nia ka olia na'a fa'inida, kira ka kurū na'a 'i matako. Etangilana laungwae'a nai'ari. Noa'a kira 'iri leka rao na'a ana ta kula, kira mae go'o 'i ne'e saena asi.

Aia'a, kaida'i nai'ari, buriana faka ka dao ma'i, ko'o nau fa'inia ma'a nai kira lisia kira saea 'ania gwa'i mae'a, kira tafi la'ala'u. Fanoa 'i Malaita ne'e 'unari, kira kina, ne'e nau ku doe ku rongoa kira ka ala'a ana go'o. Ne'e 'i ta'ena nau ku lisia rū 'oro kī, ma rū nau ku rongo'i kī nini'a. Ala'anga nai sulia laungwae'a ka dao go'o 'unari. Kira etangia laungwae'anga 'i Kwai, nau ku rongoa na'a. Na ala'anga nai'ari sui na'a. * * *

Nai ala'a la'u sulia nai, rū ne'e eta fuli saena fanoa 'i Malaita kī. Ma'a nau 'alako, sa La'ugeredoe, sa Sinamudoe, kira 'ui ta'a ana bauta kī ana ara'ikwao ne'e leka fa'ara'e saena su'u 'i Nāfinua. Ara'ikwao nai'ari ka oli ka dao 'i lo'obo, ka ngalia ma'i ngwao. Noa'a ki 'iri saisai ana ngwao. Fanoa kami na'o ma'i kira saea ngwao 'ania manungwao. Kira ka tua 'i Lili ka 'ui. To'a asi ne'e kira ū fa'inida, kira lisia go'o ta gwa'i mafula ne'e du'a ana ta o'olā, kira ka 'uri "Ta ma'e fanoa lō", ta fa'i bomo ka liu. Ta fa'i ai ne'e to'o saena ano nau to'oba saena Kaole, kira 'uia gwa'i mafula ma'a nau, ka tafi na'a fa'asia. Aia'a, ta fa'i ai ne'e ōlo 'i Darioga, ta fa'i ai ka ōlo 'i to'oba 'i 'Aitanga.

4
The Time After the Ships Arrived

Well, I'm talking about when I was small. When I was born and was big I listened to my grandfather and others talking of ships, the beginning of man-seizing in the country of Malaita. Well, the ships hadn't travelled here. Well, it was the king of England, called Fauikuila. He looked in his book, called the tabu book, and stepped into his ship called Gorai'alosina. Then he headed for Malaita until he landed at Kwai. He landed at Kwai at Tala'ionegere and sought out a number of passages. No-one came aboard. He reached for his tabu gun, shot it and sounded the news, and the men of the inland all climbed in.[1] He returned with them and they drowned in the ocean. That was the beginning of man-seizing. They didn't go to work anywhere, they just died there in the sea.

Well, at that time, after the ship arrived, my grandfathers and fathers saw what they called a dying-off, and they escaped that too.[2] The country of Malaita was such that they didn't understand, and when I was big I heard them talk of it. Up to today I've seen many things, but these are things I heard about. That's where my talk about man-seizing comes to. They began the man-seizing at Kwai, as I've heard. That's the end of that subject. * * *

I'll talk more about the things which happened before in the country of Malaita. When my father was a youth, La'ugeredoe and Sinamudoe took a mis-shot at the boats of a whiteman going to recruit in the inlet at Nāfinua. That whiteman went back over there and brought a warship. We didn't understand about warships. At home formerly they called warships man o' war. They stayed at Leili and shot. The sea people stood with them, they just saw some smoke from the burning of a garden and said "There's a home", and a shell went off. One of them struck in my land up in Kaole, they shot at my father's smoke, and he fled from it. Well, another one landed at Darioga, another one landed up there at 'Aitanga.

1 Once the labour trade had been established, ships recruiting plantation workers announced their arrival and the duration of their visit at navigable passages by firing a cannon which could be heard far inland.

2 Epidemics of new diseases were an effect of early European visits to Malaita which is still associated with the first ships.

The colonial period

Chapter 4 begins with the arrival of Europeans, who began to recruit plantation labourers from Malaita in the 1870s. It continues with Alasa'a's own recollections of the early colonial period and the arrival of missions and government, to show how times have changed. But in editing his text we have also included the story of a feud which he recorded to support his claim to Fairū land. As an incident of his own youth, this illustrates his memorable experience of inter-clan feuding.

Alasa'a's age

It is difficult to be sure when Alasa'a was born. In 1984 he claimed to be 107 years old (see page 96), but how he made this calculation is unclear. He once said he was 'big' and walking around when the missionaries arrived (in 1905) and 'adult' by the time he went to work abroad (in 1918). All we can say is that he was born some time around 1890.

The labour trade

In 1984 Andrew Gwa'italafa of Ubasi dictated a story which summarises the early history of the labour trade in Malaita. At first men were kidnapped and taken to unknown destinations as plantation workers, but some later returned and encouraged others to recruit willingly. The first documented ship to take men from Kwai was the notorious *Nukulau*, kidnapping for Fiji in 1871 (see Burt 1994: 88-89). Gwa'italafa's story must date from about the same time.

Andrew Gwa'italafa of Ubasi, 1984.

There was one of our men whose name was Misuta, a man of Kwakwaru, the district known as Kwai at present. So one day this man Misuta was out with some people fishing between Leili and the two islands called Kwai and Ngongosila, and eventually they saw something big coming. They thought it was a big flying fox. They saw a lot of cloth out on the masts and it looked beautiful. They were frightened and wanted to run away, but they saw people standing in the ship. They looked very white, and they beckoned to them, so they went closer and the whitemen started to make friends with them and tried to invite them. Eventually they came close to, then they tried to catch them and the crew took their guns into the boat and chased the people in the canoe. They chased them, caught them and tied them up. And one man we know they tied up and took was Misuta, from Kwakwaru.

When they took them away many of our people thought they were lost. They baked pigs for divination, to find out whether the people they took away were alive or dead, killed by them. And often the people sang about them, thought about them and thought they were lost.

Eventually they saw them bring back this first group. When Misuta landed at Kwakwaru, my word, the people were very very surprised. Then Misuta began to talk about whitemen, to talk about wealth, and our people saw him with his wealth and all the things this man had come back with. So the story sped up inland, via the market, of how Misuta had come back wearing a jacket and trousers, talking in a different language and things like that, wearing big boots and everything. Then, when it had spread around and our people came to exchange taro for fish, marketing and being sociable, Misuta began to preach about the white people. He said "The ship will come back, and take some people away again."

So then another ship came and this man Misuta went first and met them. They came into harbour at a place near Faumamanu. When they had anchored many people came; the inland people heard that the ship had come because it was market time. It probably anchored for quite a long time, and it was then another group of our people went inside. One man who left us was named Ramonia. Another was Ri'asi. Another was my namesake Gwa'italafa, my real grandfather, who my father was born of. They were all born of one man.

Well, Ri'asi went on a ship to Australia, Ramonia went on a ship to Australia, and Gwa'italafa went on another ship which just went to Fiji, on a second trip. When Ramonia came back he talked about the places he'd worked: Bundaberg, Rockhampton, Mackay, Cairns. When I was a boy he told me stories of the places he'd worked. But Ri'asi was separated into another ship and the ship sank with him, when Ramonia was already in Australia. Well, then our people baked a sacrifice to find out whether the two were in Australia and if they were alright or not, and our priest said "Oh, I think this man Ri'asi is dead; I heard his cry when the ship sank down with him."

Translated from Pijin and abridged

An attack by a man o'war

Alasa'a's account of his fathers' attack on the labour recruiters and the retaliation by a warship is corroborated by British naval reports published for parliamentary enquiries into the labour trade. Some of the differences between them may reflect the British reliance on information from the sea people of Kwai ('Quoi' or 'Kwi') island, or mutual misunderstandings. Bungia ('Boon-Year'), the old leader leader of 'Aita'e ('Ai-Tai') in the British account, was presumably a 'father' of the attacker Sinamu (himself still active almost twenty years later, see pages 94 and 95).

Something Goodrich should have known was that HMS *Royalist* had already visited Kwai in 1891 to bombard a village in neighbouring Kwaio. This was in retaliation for a similar attack on the same recruiting ship, the *Sybil*, at the Kwaibaita river on the border between Kwaio and Kwara'ae. As Goodrich noted elsewhere in his report: "The bush tribes living at the back of this part of Malaita are undoubtably the most troublesome in the whole group" (of Solomon Islands).

Some of the places mentioned in this story are shown on the map on page 57.

[*Appendix B.*]

EXTRACT from the Government Agent's log while anchored at Quoi, Malayta, 7th January, 1894.

At 4 p.m. canoes came on board and cautioned us against the bush natives, saying they have threatened to fire on the boats the first chance, and they are banding together in large numbers, being well supplied with rifles and ammunition, got, the natives told me, from Samoan ships. Their object in killing a white man is: Two bush chiefs whose sons came to Queensland are said to have died there, and this is to be their revenge. It seems they nearly accomplished their object the last recruiting trip of the "Sybil," when they tried to kill the recruiter. Had they done so they would have been satisfied. If one of H. M. ships were to call and caution them it would have the effect of making them quiet.

* * *

Sir, H.M.S. "Royalist" at Ugi, Solomon Islands, 29 August, 1894.

* * *

2. With respect to Appendix B, of case J, I beg to report that I anchored at Kwi Harbour on Sunday 19 August, and was immediately boarded by seven or eight leading natives, most of whom talked a little English. Gooreah, the Chief of Kwi Island, gave me a letter, signed by Mr. Stillingfleet Bowles, Government Agent of the labour vessal "Sybil," stating that her boats were fired upon by the Boon-Year tribe, of Ai-Tai village, on the 11th of last month. This deliberate act, taken in connection with the threats and attempts mentioned in the above-mentioned Appendix B, Case J, made me decide that some show of force at all events was necessary. The chiefs of Kwi were most pressing in imploring me to fire on Ai-Tai, but their wishes had little weight with me, as undoubtedly they now see their interests lie with making recruiting easy. The village or district of Ai-Tai is on the side of a hill, between 5,000 and 6,000 yards in a direct line from where the ship was anchored, and the most satisfactory method would have been to have marched there and burnt the village, but Gooreah declared he could not possibly get anyone to guide me, and as the first two miles would evidently be through mangrove swamp, which might take a party half a day accomplishing, I reluctantly gave up the idea of landing, and the following day shelled the district with the ship's guns and a seven-pounder mounted in one of the cutters. Gooreah and all his colleagues were enthusiastic over the good I had done, and said now the bushmen would give no trouble. I told them I should call again in October, and that the first opportunity they were to inform the bushmen I was going to do so, and also to tell them that unless they promised to give up firing on white men, I should land and march to their village. Gooreah promised me that on my return if the Ai-Tai people were still threatening to fire on labour boats, he would do his best to procure guides for me. Although the punishment inflicted was probably very small, there is a fair chance that the Ai-Tai tribe may have had a good fright, as no man-of-war seems to have visited Kwi for many years, and in all probability this is the first ship that has ever been there with guns that could reach their village.

3. Trusting that my proceeding in this case will meet with your approval.

I have, &c.,

JAMES. E. GOODRICH,

Commander.

From: *Correspondence respecting Outrages by Natives on British Subjects, and other matters which have been under inquiry during the year 1894 by Her Majesty's Ships.* Public Record Office, London (ADM/7252)

The British 'apologise'

A year after Goodrich tried to shell 'Aitat'e (and hit several other places instead) another commander of the *Royalist* pursuaded Bungia and his men to meet him on the coast at 'Adako'a. Alasa'a (on the next page) describes the meeting as a court, resulting in an apology from 'government' in the person of E.G. Rason, the ship's commander. Rason evidently saw the outcome as an acknowledgment of British authority, as this extract from his report shows.

Note:*'natives killed' probably means 'struck' rather than 'dead'; a misinterpretation of local English.*

. . . I found Boon Year, surrounded by several armed bushmen, seated under a tree - an old man, with some pretension to dignity, but very nervous. On my side I had all the "salt-water" men as a voluntary retinue. . . .

2. Boon Year at once opened and said what a lot of damage man-of-war had done him last year, and that he never intended to hurt "Sybil" but that, as his son had died in Queensland, he did not just then want any more recruiting from his tribe. I condoled with him on the death of his son, and observed that all men must die, and because his son died in Queensland it was no reason he should fire on a labour schooner. He said he was overcome at his son dying away from him, but that he would not fire on labour schooner any more.

3. Taking into consideration the punishment he received last year, when, as far as I could learn from him and other native sources, three natives were killed and several wounded, three or four huts burnt, and all very much frightened by the shell bursting, throwing bits of stone about everywhere, and cutting large trees as if they were reeds, I said that I would take his promise and consider the matter over. . . .

From: Letter to Commander-in-Chief from Commander Rason, H.M.S. Royalist, Rendova 19 September 1895

HMS Royalist*, the warship which dealt with the attack on the* Sybil*, under steam power with sails furled, in 1898.*
From the National Maritime Museum, London (N1241)

This photograph shows the ship's company of HMS Royalist *raising the British flag in the Western Solomons, on the same voyage that it came to bombard 'Aita'e in 1894. Unfortunately there do not seem to be any photographs of the action at Kwai.*
From an album in the Fiji Museum, Suva, with thanks to Andrea Tuisavuna

Go'o kira, "'Ae 'oko 'uia na'a rō ngwae baera kī loko, 'oko 'uia fanoa kira." Go'o ara'ikwao nai'ari ne'e kira saea 'ania gafamanu ne'e ngalia ma'i ngwao nai'ari, ka 'uri "'Ira kira ke leka ma'i nau ku kwaimanata'i na'a." Kira ka ba'ea ma'i sa ngwane'e Sinamudoe fa'inia sa La'ugere, kira ka kwauta na'a ana fa'i kwauta ne'e 'i māna 'i 'Adakoa kira saea 'ani Fa'ikwauta. Kwaukwauta go'o, rō ngwae nai'ari kī ka fata 'uri go'o, ko'o nau fa'inia ma'a nau,"Sai! 'oko 'uia musia na'a fanoa kero'o kwa!" Go'o nia ka 'uri "O kwaimanatai, sui na'a." Rū nai'ari ne'e ni'i fuli ma nau ku sai ani kī nai. * * *

Ana asoa ne'e nau ku oga nai kwa'i sulia ti'iti'ilaku 'i ne'e ngela nau ke rongoa fani sa Ben. Nau ku futa ana asoa nai'ari kira saungia ngwae ana, sa Bakete saungia sa Sau'i. Te'a nau 'i Lekafa'iramo leka ka lia saena labata ma ngwae kwa'i belabela na'a. Ka ngalia ngwa'i, mani nia 'i saena, ka ngalia ka sofongani. Kira ka koloa na'a, kira ka 'uri "Ta ngwae loni'a saungia sa Sa'ui." Te'a nau ka 'uri "Nau'a ne'ana nau ku lisia ne'e kira saungia." Kira ka 'uri, "Ma bani'au teoteo saena ngwa'i mo?" Te'a nau ka 'uri "Noa'a ta mani saena ngwa'i nia, ngwae siroro'a ne'e noa'a kesi to'o go'o ana ta mani." Leleka ka 'unari, nia 'usu ma ngwane'e sa Sau'i ne'e nia du'ua 'ani. . . .

Kaili ka tua 'i nai'ari ka leleka kira ka saungia go'o 'afe sa Filiga 'i Angitā ne'e alua sa Ramo'itolo fani 'i Aderamo. Sa Laua'a kira tata'e kira ka saungia 'i Angitā 'i Rakufaolu. Kami ka tafi ma'i kami ka tua 'i Kwa'itakea. Kami ka tua 'i nai'ari leleka rū nau ku tua ku lisi'i kī, ne'e ma'a nau fa'ida kira sasia talo'a 'oro. Kira ka 'uia fa'i ngali loeri kira ka sasia siufa ma nau ku 'a'ana na'a, nau ku leka na'a, nau ku 'ani'i na'a. Mae ka saungi kami, kami ka takalo na'a.

Then they said "Well, now you've shot those two men over there, you've shot their home." Then the whiteman who they called the government, who brought the warship, said "If so they can come here and I'll apologise." They summoned that man Sinamudoe with La'ugere and they held court at a court place in front of 'Adakoa called Fa'ikwauta [the Court]. In court those two men just said, my grand-father and my father, "Hey, you shot and broke up our home!" Then he said "Oh, sorry; it's all over with." Those are things which happened and I know about. * * *

Today I want to tell about when I was small, so that my son can hear, with Ben.[1] I was born on the day they killed a man; Bakete killed Sau'i.[2] My mother Lekafa'iramo went to look in the yard and a man had been struck down flat. She took his bag, his money was inside, she took it and hid it. They didn't see, they said "Someone has killed Sa'ui." My mother said "I was there, I saw them kill him." They said "And was there a *bani'au* [shell-money] lying in the bag?" My mother said "There's no money in his bag, he's a poor man who doesn't have any money." And that's how it went, he fornicated, this man Sau'i, and he paid for it. . . .

We lived there until they killed Filiga's wife Angitā, who bore Ramo'itolo and Aderamo. Laua'a and others set out and killed Angitā at Rakufaolu. We fled and came to live at Kwa'itakea. We lived there and later on the things I saw were my father and others making many feasts of fame.[3] They pounded the nuts and made pudding-feasts and when I was grown up I went and ate at them. A feud struck us and we scattered.

1 This is the beginning of Alasa'a's recording for Ben Burt in 1987.

2 Arumae Bakete ('Bucket') of 'Ere'ere, the killer of Sa'ui, was the father of Alasa'a's wife Arana. He was a noted warrior (one of whose exploits is mentioned on page 71) and a comrade of Gwagwaofilu and Iro'ima, who appear later in this chapter.

3 These were the kind of feast described on page 77, made to gain renown for a display of generosity.

The killing of Angitā

Angitā, mother of Alasa'a's brother-in-law Ramo'itolo of Latea, was yet another innocent victim of inter-clan feuding. In 1897 Maefatafata, Ramo'itolo's daughter, recalled the details, with comments on the kind of offences for which women might be killed in those times.

My grandmother didn't misbehave at home, didn't have a period in the house, didn't go to the toilet by the yard, she always lived correctly, she did, but men who were seeking restitution killed my grandmother while my father was small and they returned and proclaimed it at their homes.

Fane'auroro and others had killed a grandmother of mine, and others had gone and killed Maelengu over there, Tafanga's father and others, and Nakisi and others, they went and repaid the death of their sister, they killed the people over at 'Atori. They [the 'Atoris] went to get restitution and killed my grandmother at Rakufaolu, while my father was small, and my aunt, they killed her and then they [the Lateas] took them [the children] off down to the sea. They stayed with my grandfathers Maebu and Amasia. If they'd remained and they'd come again they would also have killed my grandfather.

It's not as if they killed her over having periods or misbehaviour, but for that. They took them down and lived there and when my father and the others were full grown they returned them inland. They came back and lived with Kamusudoe right over at Kilugwari.

Translated from Kwara'ae

Maefatafata, 1987

Tolinga and Latea

Although Alasa'a refers to the killing of Angitā only in passing, a closer look at the relationship between the Latea and Tolinga clans shows that it was also a crisis for Alasa'a's family.

Rakufaolu, where Angitā was killed, is close to Gwaunafau. She and her husband Filiga of Latea lived there with the Tolinga people, probably because Filiga's sister Maesakoa was married to Alasa'a's 'father' Kamusute'e. So when Filiga's wife was killed, Alasa'a's family also felt threatened and fled their home.

There had long been enmity between 'Atori and Latea. When Filiga fled with his children to Kwai island, he was returning to his place of refuge as a small child, when his own parents were killed by the 'Atori warrior Ko'odiko'a. Kwa'itakea, where Alasa'a's family fled to, is in Latea and, as he mentions below, he was living there by the time of events which occurred in 1912.

The close relationship between Tolinga and Latea continued, with Tolinga families taking up long-term residence in Latea because of their descent from Filiga's sister Maesakoa. When Filiga's son Ramo'itolo grew up and returned to the mainland he married Alasa'a's sister Siumalefo, and their son, Alasa'a's namesake, married Alasa'a's daughter Sango'iburi.

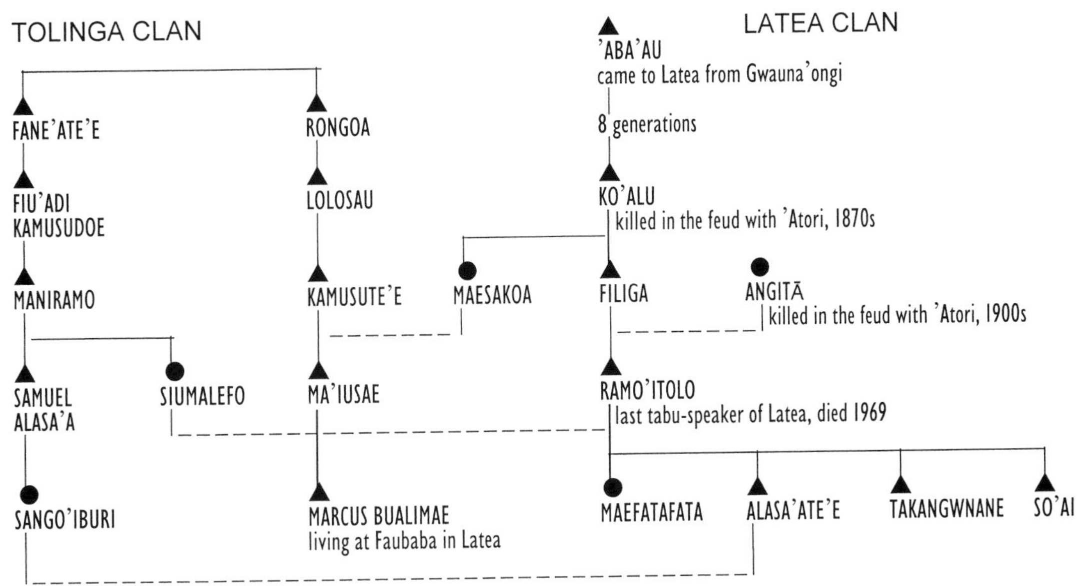

Kami ka tua 'i Ra'iako, sukulu ka dao. Ka ru'u 'i Kwaruakalo, ka ru'u 'i Aufana, sukulu eta dao 'i Faumamanu, noa'a ta ngwae kesi daodao 'ua fani sukulu 'i na'o. * * *

Aia'a, nau ku doe na'a, 'i buriku nau ku 'iri sai ana, nau ku leka na'a, nau ngwae 'a'ana na'a, sukulu ka dao 'i Onepusu. Sa Misita Dek, 'i Misis Dek, ngwaingwaena nia ne'e kera'a ngalia ma'i, kera'a ka etangia 'i Onepusu. Aia'a, ma'a nau fa'ida ne'e kira leka 'i Kwinsilan, kira ka sukulu ana; sa Sele'au, sa Bita Kabulanga, sa Anikaru, sa Noa Fa'asalo, Kailaua Samuele, sa Diau Ngwaki, sa Mosisi Gwagwaofilu, sa Dionatana Ngwalasi, sa Samuel Kelema. Kira ka dao fa'inia 'i Ngongosila. * * *

Ta ngwae 'iri tuatua 'i Faumamanu, 'unari ma'a nau fa'ida ka 'uri, "Kulu leka dao fuana to'a 'i Fairū, kulu ka gania sulia asi lo'oko, kulu ke saungani ta babala, kulu ka sasia sukulu." Kira saea 'ania gospel, maelana sa Jisas ka fa'a-mauria ngwae kī sui saena fanoa ne'e 'i ano. Kami ka ra'e ka dao 'i Afufana na belo loeri ka angi. Ma'a nau, sa La'ugere, ko'o nau sa Fiu'adi fani sa Dadao kira lau ra'unga ma'i, "Mulu lakusia!" Kira ka taga'a tala'i lima, ka 'uri go'o ne'e fani ra'unga kira kī. Kira ka dao, ma'a nau ka 'uri fuada "Noa'a la'u fu'anga'a nini'a bore ma na gospel lala nini'a." Kira ka 'uri "Gospel nai'ari nia 'i fa'i?" Ma'a nau ka 'uri "Maelana sa Jisas." Kira ka 'uri "Jisas nai'ari nia 'i fa'i?" Kira ka ala'a ka leleka sa Sausaungia, sa Kalakini, sa So'ofia, sa Sili'ota, sa Busuka, sa Arasimae, sa Ata'i kira ka 'uri "Ō, nia le'a. Mulu koso mulu ka tuafia fafona asi fuiri, fuana kī saka bore ana asi ki dao ana kula madako." Kira ka fulia sukulu ana kula fu sa Taemana Ngwasangwane tua ana, * * * kira ka koso ka fulia 'i Faumamanu. Kira ka fi'i tua 'i nai'ari, kira ka sasia babala kī ma kira ke teo 'i aelana. Kira ka ngalia ma'i fa'i niu fuiri kira ka fasia.

'Unari sa Ngwaki ka oli na'a 'i tolo kira saea 'ania sa Diau Ngwaki, Mosisi Gwagwaofilu ka oli na'a 'i tolo, sa Ngwalasi ka oli na'a 'i tolo, ka uikiti lala nai. Kira ka olita'inida 'ania ma'e fata'a 'i na'o kī. Sa Sele'au, sa Kabulanga, rō ma'a nau ki, kira na'a 'i fuiri 'i Faumamanu, ma kira ka oli kike teoteo 'i aelana, ka dangi kira ke kosokoso ma'i.

We were living at Ra'iako when the mission arrived. It came in at Kwaruakalo, it came in at Aufana, the mission first arrived at Faumamanu; no-one had come with the mission before. * * *

Well, I was big, it was after when I didn't know anything, I was going about, I was a grown man, when the mission arrived at Onepusu. Mr Deck and Miss Deck, his sister, it was they who brought it and started it at Onepusu. Well, my father and others went to Queensland, they went to mission there; Sele'au, Peter Kabulanga, Anikaru, Noah Fa'asalo, Kailaua Samuel, Joe Ngwaki, Moses Gwagwaofilu, Jonathan Ngwalasi, Samuel Kelema. They came with it to Ngongosila. * * *

No-one was living at Faumamanu, so then my father and the others said "Let's go to the people of Fairū and ask for the sea-side over there, we'll build a shelter, we'll make the mission." They called it the gospel, the death of Jesus gave life to all men in this home on earth. We went up to Afufana and the bell cried out. My father, La'ugere, my grandfathers Fiu'adi and Dadao, they seized weapons: "Hurry up!" They all raised hands, doing so with their weapons. When they arrived my father said to them "This isn't a fight, this is the gospel." They said "Where is this gospel?" My father said "It's the death of Jesus." They said "Where is this Jesus?" They talked on until Sausaungia, Kalakini, So'ofia, Sili'ota, Busuka, Arasimae and Ata'i all said "Oh it's alright. You all go down and live on the sea-side, so when-ever we come out at the sea we'll come to a clear place." They founded the mission at the place where Taemana Ngwasangwane lives,* * * they went down and founded Faumamanu. They lived there, they made shelters but they'd sleep on the island. They brought those coconuts and planted them.

So then Ngwaki returned inland, he was called Joe Ngwaki, Moses Gwagwaofilu returned inland, Ngwalasi returned inland, and became heathens. They brought them back with words of the past.[1] Sele'au and Kabulanga, my two fathers, they were down at Faumamanu but they'd return to sleep on the island and when day came they'd come down [to the mainland].

1 That is, their relatives brought them back to the ancestral religion by invoking the ghosts (see page 101).

The early Christians

The first Christians in the East Kwara'ae area were labour migrants who converted in Fiji and Queensland and returned home from 1900 onwards. Their religion became known as 'school' (*sukulu*, translated here as 'mission') after the mission schools of Queensland. They lived at first on the offshore islands of Kwai and Ngongosila, where the British colonial government and navy could give a little protection against persecution.

Australian missionaries of the Queensland Kanaka Mission, which later became the South Sea Evangelical Mission (SSEM), first visited this Christian community in 1905. They founded the mission's training school at Onepusu on the West coast of Malaita in 1906. The Deck family were prominent in the SSEM on Malaita for many years thereafter.

John Sele'au and his brother Peter Kabulanga, who founded the Christian settlement of Cherith or Keret at Faumamanu, were Tolinga men, sons of Kaobata, who was a brother of Alasa'a's grandfather Fiu'adi Kamusudoe. They became Christians in Queensland and on return lived on Ngongosila, where the SSEM opened a mission station in 1906. They founded Keret the same year with the permission of their Fairū in-laws, the Kwaru group descended from Fikiramo, who Alasa'a lists as sharing this decision (and who appear in the genealogy on page 67). But the Christians were persecuted by other inland people; hence their practice of spending the nights on Ngongosila island.

A valuable source of information on the spread of Christianity on Malaita is the SSEM newsletter *Not In Vain*. The following extract from Northcote Deck's report in the 1914 issue summarises the fortunes of these East Kwara'ae Christians.

A group of Onepusu students at a school at Baunani in south-west Malaita, which was founded in 1911. They include future leaders of the SSEM from Kwai and Ngongosila: Stephen Sibolo (back row left) Shadrach (Amasia?)(middle row right) and Timothy Anilafa (front row right). Their smart European clothes symbolise their Christian identity.
From the South Sea Evangelical Mission archive

Mr. Watkinson was the missionary then, who had his headquarters on Nongasila, while he visited up and down the coast, establishing mission villages, with the native Christians, who at that time had been newly returned from Queensland. With his help and encouragement a station was formed on the mainland opposite Nongasila by a band of five bush Christians, who hoped by settling there to win the people of their tribes living on the mountains round about.

With unconscious foresight the little village was named CHERITH. The name was prophetic of the place, for Cherith literally means "cutting or slaying," and well this little forlorn hope earned its name. From the very beginning the place seemed doomed to trouble. We found it was really a battle ground, where the warring mountain tribes met for markets, and where there were constant skirmishes and fighting. Yet no other site was safer, or available. Gradually bush folk drifted down and joined the village, attracted by the teaching, but were picked off one by one by the menslayers, or, taking fright, relapsed back to the heathen. Sometimes there would be a lull in the murders, and the numbers would increase, but the finale was the same, and one more little mound took its place in the little burying ground. Strangely enough, none of the original band who began the village have been killed, though for five years they have lived in almost constant danger of their lives, and faithful old Joshua Fosalo has a wheal across his forehead where a Snider bullet gouged its way. He with two others of the band, Luke Neomea and John Selou, were the guides when we first crossed the island. At that time John was the leader; he was very bright in spite of all the killing and discouragements, and constantly risked his life, preaching at the markets.

Then came a longer lull than usual without trouble, and a fine young Christian, Barnabas, joined the other Christians; this greatly encouraged them and we hoped better things were in store for Cherith.

From *Not In Vain* 1914

Kira etangia na'a sukulu nai, ne'e ka dao saena fanoa kia. Nau'a noa'a la'u ta ngwae te'ete'e, nau ngwae ngwaro na'a, nau ku lisi'i na'a, ku rongo'i na'a. * * * Buri'ana, to'a nini'a 'i Fakula'e, sa Angitafe kira 'uia sa Kelema Samuole saena 'i Faumamanu. Go'o kira ka osia sukulu, kira ka oli kira ka tua 'ada 'i aelana.* * *

'Una'ari go'o, kira ka oli kira ka tua nama 'ada 'i Ngongosila fani sukulu. Kira ka tua leleka sa Sinamudoe nia tua 'i Taradunga, 'una'ari ngela nia ka mae, sa Ganifiri ka koko gwata ka noa'a na'a ta gwata. Kira ka oli kira ka leka na'a 'ada sulia talada, kira ka tua na'a 'i fafona asi. Sa Sele'au ka koso, sa Kabulanga ka koso, kira ka 'uri "O nau ku sasisasi fani akalo ma inamauri nau ka mae na'a. Ala 'ani nai leka ki ola'a na'a 'aku."

'Unari kira ka fata 'uri fuadaro'o "'Uri ma angita ne'e koro ke koso ma'i 'i sukulu?" "Kero'o ke koso ma'i ma kero'o ke saungani ta babala ma kero'o ka sukulu na'a, fani ngela nau." Sa Sinamu ka alua 'i Safina fani sa 'Ilaisa Sareto'ona. Sa 'Ilaisa ka alua 'i Alari'i fani sa Kamusu. Go'o nia ka oli ka dao fuana ko'o nau 'i Kwa'itakea. Ko'o nau ka 'uri "'Aeo ngwae nini 'oko ābu," ka 'uri, "'Oko teoteo ko saea 'uli 'ai fuana ngwae, ma rorodo bore nia mae na'a, noima kira ka saungia na'a." Ma nia ka 'uri "Nau ku 'aila na'a, ma nau ku 'aila kesi sasi na'a fani akalo, sulia ngela nau kī mae ka sui na'a." Kira ka koso kira ka 'oia 'i Gwaubusu, mala ngwae kī ka fi'i koso ta'ifau 'i sukulu. * * * Sukulu nai'ari nai. 'Oko lisia sulia asi fūri ka fi'i doe, kira o'olia musia, nini'a nau ku lisia 'i ta'ena.

Aia'a, ruana ai la'u, gafamanu ka dao, sa Kabolo dao 'i 'Aoke ka folia go'o kula 'i Ābu loere. Ka folia 'ania fa'i bā, ka folia 'ani akisi, ka folia 'ania naefi, fa'i biala go'o fuana sa Subua, ngwae 'i Ābu, ka etangia go'o ana sa Subua na'a. Gafamanu na'a 'i nai'ari nia 'iri saungia ta ngwae, ka noa'a ta kwauta, lō dao go'o ana sa Misita Belo, ka lomotā fanoa 'i Malaita. Sukulu ne'e eta dao, ka lomotā fanoa 'i Malaita.

They began the mission, and so it came into our country. I'm no longer a young man, I'm an old man now, and I've seen it and I've heard it. * * * Afterwards the people of Fakula'e, Angitafe and others, shot Samuel Kelema at Faumamanu. Then they broke up the mission and they returned and lived on the island. * * *

So then, they returned and they had to live on Ngongosila with the mission. They stayed on until Sinamudoe, who lived at Taradunga, so then, his child died, Ganifiri had baked pigs until there were no more pigs. They returned, they went off by themselves, they lived at the seaside. Sele'au went down, Kabulanga went down, and they said "Oh, I was dealing with the ghosts and my family has died. So be it, I'll go and we'll be defiled."[1]

So then they said to the two of them, "So, when will you two come down to the mission?" "We'll both come down and build a shelter and we'll go to the mission, with my child." Sinamu begot Safina and Elijah Sareto'ona. Elijah begot Alari'i and Kamusu. Then he came back to my grandfather at Kwa'itakea. My grandfather said "You're a man who's tabu," he said "You can lie there and say tree-bark magic for a man and tomorrow he's dead, or they've killed him." But he said "I reject that now, and I reject dealings with ghosts, because my children have died." They went down and they settled Gwaubusu and only then did people all come down to the mission. * * * That was the mission. You saw along the sea-side getting bigger as they gardened everywhere, and that's what I see today.

Well, the second thing was that government arrived, Campbell arrived at 'Aoke and bought the place at Ābu. He bought it with crowbars, he bought it with axes, he bought it with knives and sticks of tobacco, from Subua, a man from Ābu, he started it with Subua. The government there didn't kill anyone, there was no court, the law only arrived with Mr Bell and spread over the country of Malaita. The mission was first to come and spread over the country of Malaita.

1 For senior men like Sinamu, Christianity was defiling because of its wilful breach of the rules of tabu required by the ancestral ghosts.

The foundation of Gwaubusu

Northcote Deck's 1914 report for *Not In Vain* continues with the destruction of Keret, which Alasa'a attributes to the people of Fakula'e. Then in 1912 the Christians' fortunes changed with the foundation of Gwaubusu in Latea by the warrior Sinamu of 'Aita'e. Sinamu was one of the men who attacked the recruiting ship *Sybil* in 1894 and it was his home at Taradunga that Commander Goodrich of HMS *Royalist* had attempted to bombard.

The next time we came round in the ship we landed at Nongasila, full of hope for the school on the mainland. But we had no sooner stepped ashore on the island than the whole band crowded down to us with their bad news. Soon after we had left, Barnabas had been shot dead while working in the field, the gardens themselves had been raided by large numbers of bush-men, and a determined attempt had been made to massacre the whole school. So they had all left to take refuge on Nongasila. It really seemed the only thing to do to save their lives.

* * *

A month or so after we left them, a ship anchored in the bay. By then the Christians were restless again, and Luke arranged with the captain to sign on next morning as boat's crew. But when the morning came, the ship sailed without him, for he was down with fever! Surely it was God's over-ruling hand, for a few days after that, a stranger thing happened. A powerful chief, Sin-moo, who was a big fighting man in the bush, lost his only son through sickness. The old man was so angry with the Akalos, whom he worship-ped, that in spite of all the protests of his people, he determined to go down to the coast; adopt Luke, who was a distant relation, as his son, and come to school!

He was determined to make a clean break with the old way, so he came over to Luke on the island, and in spite of the consternation and protests of Maifo, and the other heathen chiefs on Nongasila, he in-sisted in sleeping in the church. The old man was really still in fear of his old deities, and thought the church the safest place! Luke, of course, was overjoyed, and quickly made arrangements for him to bring down his family and yams. And here comes the most wonderful part of God's provision for the evict-ed Christians. Sinmoo was so dreaded as a fighter, that any vil-lage he founded would be safe from attack. A new site was chosen at GWOBUSU, half a mile north of Cherith, at the mouth of a river.

Here for about two years God's work has gone steadily on. The numbers have grown till now there are about thirty attending school.

From *Not In Vain* 1914

The arrival of government

The government station of 'Aoke (officially mis-spelled Auki), now the provincial capital of Malaita, was founded in 1909 by T.W. Edge-Partington as Resident Magistrate for Malaita. F.M. Campbell, whom Alasa'a recalls, was posted there as Police Officer from 1911. Ābu was added to the station after 1912.

These colonial officers and their successors are what Alasa'a means by 'government'. The difficulties they faced are detailed in bad-tempered reports from Edge-Partington to his superiors in the colonial capital at Tulagi. This extract comes from a letter of December 18th 1909.

Note: *In this letter, Langalanga is the home of the sea people of the west coast of Malaita, Quai is the district of Kwai (including East Kwara'ae), and Fiu is on the West Kwara'ae coast (not the Fiu in Fairū).*

Will you let the Belama get me some more police from somewhere as the number I have got here is not sufficient. Unless I have my complement of 40 police and 40 rifles I have not got a hope of doing anything here in the bush. If I go away anywhere I must leave IO good boys behind me to guard the station, and 30 is none too many to go into the heart of the bush here. There is a tribal War on at present in the bush opposite Langa langa and I can hear the drums beating every day. One whole village of about 60 or IOO fighting men came over from Quai and attacked a bush village at Langalanga. They expect me to have a lot of police here and have absolute-ly no fear of the government. They laughed at me the othr day when I went down to Fiu about a murder and took I7 wi with me all I could spare, leaving 6 to guard the station Jacky Fiu told me it was useless to go into the bush with only I7 as when I attacked the first village would beat a dru and a mob would collect as they know exactly how many police I have got. I could manage if I had 40 here as I

From the Solomon Islands National Archives

Ta'ena, nau ku lisia ko'o ma roki 'i ngwae 'i nini'ari kira kina, kira fīa fasi rū nai'ari kī rū 'ua kī na'a. Noa'a, ni'i dao ma nau ku doe na'a. Nau ku tua na'a sulia talanga'i fa'i ngali ma fiu fa'i ngali aku nini'a nau ku ala'a na'a ana. Nau'a ne'e nau ku dao 'unari.

Nau ku ngwaro na'a ne, ma nau ku eta tua na'a ne, ma nau ku 'iri 'ani'ania ti rū 'oro. Ta'ena na rū 'oro nini saka 'i ta'ena kī. 'I na'o ma'i, etangilana bubunga nai, ra'i sao bore noa'a. Kira ke usa go'o rauna felofelo, kira ka tolea 'ania luma kī. Kira ka usa go'o rauna mafusu tolo, kira ka tolea 'ania luma kī, ka leleka sao ka fuli ma'i 'i Bina ka dao, ki fi'i sasia babala 'i sao kī. Ta'ena luma nai'ari kī sui na'a. Kaba nini'a ōlo na'a, ta ngwae bore tua na'a saena fera 'i kaba, ka tua ana ta fera 'i tiba, nau ku lisia ku arefo ana. Bore ma kaida'i nau ku te'ete'e nau ku siroro'a na ma'a nau ma ko'o nau fa'ida. Fatalaku dao 'unari. * * *

Nau ku oli 'uana 'i Faumamanu, na rū nau ku lisi'i kī noa'a 'iri fulifuli. Ru nau ti'iti'i ku lisi'i kī noa'a 'iri fulifuli. Nau ku ti'iti'i nau ku 'ania da'u. Kami ke 'ara, kami ka kōngia ka sui kami ka fi'i 'ania. Kami ka 'ania sao, rū gwa'abīa. Na bō 'i rū fuana la'usu'u, na afurū, fuana gwata. Kami ka siroro'a, kami ka fa'asinafia 'abana alo, ka du'a mala kami ka fi'i 'ania. Na falisi go'o fani alo go'o. Ru ne'e dao ma'i 'i na'o kī, ne'e nau ku lisi'i ne'e, kaibea meo fani baenafa meo. Kira ka dao fani butete satana sarere. Ka 'unari te'a nau ka memea ka sarea 'ania aiburiku sa Tolosau. Ngwae nai'ari mae na'a 'i Guadalacanal. Nia ne'e te'a nau ka fa'asata 'ani sa Kwalafanga sulia nia 'ania kwala butete. Nia ne'e kira ka fa'asata logo 'ania sa Kumara, Kele. Nia fi'i maemae go'o 'i Faubaba. Ba'u faga dokodoko fani ai keta fani butete, ni'i ka teo ma ka fonea fiolo'a ma ngwae kī sui ka mauri 'ania. Leleka karai bore noa'a 'iri teoteo saena fanoa ne'e, sa Laugere ka ngalia ta'i, ngwae ne'e nini'a alua sa Sareto'ona. Kira fa'asata 'ania kuakua fani toatoa. Na karai nai'ari nia meo ta'ifau ma 'aena ka lafua.

Today I see grandchildren and the present generation are unaware, they believe these things are old. No, they arrived when I was already big. I've now lived for a hundred years and I've had another seven years as I speak now. Me, that's where I've reached.

I'm old now and I started living first, but I didn't eat many things. Today there are many things which appeared today. Formerly at the beginning of my island there was not even sago leaf. They just sewed rattan leaf and thatched houses with it. They just sewed ginger leaf and thatched houses with it, until sago-palm originated at Bina and arrived and they then made sago-leaf shelters. Today these houses are finished. Sheet-iron has arrived and some people even live in sheet-iron houses, live in timber houses, I've seen it and I'm astonished. But when I was small I was poor, my fathers and my grandfathers and others. That's what I'm saying. * * *

I'll return to Faumamanu, to things I saw which hadn't happened before. Things I saw when I was small which hadn't happened before. When I was small I ate *da'u* yam. We'd grate it, we baked it and then we ate it.[1] We ate sago [pith], cooked in the oven. A block of it for an elbow-length money, pieces for the pigs. When we were poor we put taro leaf out in the sun and when it was well cooked we ate it. Just yam and taro. Things which arrived before, which I saw, were red tapioca and red pineapple. They came with the [sweet] potato called *sarere*. And so my mother chewed it and fed my younger brother Tolosau with it. The man who died on Guadalcanal. That's why my mother named him Kwalafanga [Vine-eater], because he ate potato vines. That's why they also named Kele Kumara [Potato]. He has just died at Faubaba. Short foreign bananas and long ones and potatoes, they stopped hunger and everyone survived on them. Eventually, although there were no chickens in this country, La'ugere brought one, he was the man who begot Sareto'ona. They named it *kuakua* and *toatoa*.[2] This chicken was all red and its legs were long.

1 *Da'u*, the wild variant of aerial yam (*Dioscorea bulbifera*) is a famine food, which has to be grated and soaked in running water for three days to make it edible.

2 As *toatoa* is Fijian for chicken, this may indicate where La'ugere got it from.

Trade goods

Douglas Rannie, a government agent supervising the recruiting of Pacific Islands labour for the Queensland plantations, listed the goods given as an advance 'beach payment' on a visit to East Kwara'ae in 1886.

After a long confab half a dozen young fellows recruited; and in return for doing so each received a half-case of tobacco, an axe, a tomahawk, and a twelve-inch knife, together with a miscellaneous lot of pipes, beads, paint, jews' harps, matches, a sun-glass, as well as a small hand-mirror, all of which they handed over to their friends.

From *My Adventures Among South Sea Cannibals* by Douglas Rannie, 1912, page 181

The new imports

The crops Alasa'a describes as improvements to the food supply were acquired by Malaitans on their travels overseas from other Pacific Islanders.

Another import which he does not mention is guns, greatly valued for fighting. Because of the threat they posed to traders as well as local people, the British made it illegal to import guns into Solomon Islands after 1884. But returning labourers continued to smuggle them home, as Silas Sangafanoa of Ualakwai recalled in 1987.

When they'd finished three years and came back, one thing they did was steal rifles. Steal rifles into Solomon Islands, their home. Well, he'd take the rifle and put it inside a box. He'd do it by putting another plank in the bottom of the box and covering it up. And cartridges. When it was covered by the planks, cloth and other things went on top. When they went to the wharf to come back to Solomon Islands, well, the soldiers [police] stood there and took everything out, took out the cloth, but the rifle was underneath. Everyone did it, everyone from Solomon Islands, who went from Malaita, did that. So that when they came back they could use rifles for feuding. They left off bows and arrows, left things for killing such as clubs and used the rifles they'd brought from Australia, from Queensland. My father talked about this. Well, they went on bringing them, all these rifles, there were loads of them in Malaita. They called it an opening gun [breechloader], because he'd open it, put in one bullet, and close it again. I've seen them too, these rifles.

Translated from Pijin

Silas Sangafanoa in 1987.

This photograph from 1906, at the end of the Queensland labour trade, was taken by J. W. Beattie at Fote in West Kwara'ae (on the same occasion as the photo on page 63). One man has an old muzzle-loading gun, one of a wide variety of firearms imported into Malaita from the 1870s onwards and commonly known as 'sniders'. A boy has dressed in a prized vest and calico, and they smoke European pipes.

From the British Museum Ethnography Dept. pictorial collection

Iu, ta'ena nau ku oli la'u 'uana 'i buriku, 'uana rū 'i na'o kī. Na dao'a nai'ari kira dao fani naifi fani akisi fani toro kī. Na faka ne'e dao fa'ini'i. 'Unari 'afe kī kira 'uia 'uli 'ai kī, kira toro 'ani'i. Kami'a ngwae kī kami ka tua dadara go'o, noa'a kami 'iri toro 'ania ta rū. Di'ia nau ku toro ta ma ra'i 'ai go'o. Nau ku sofongani go'o na'ofaku.

'I na'o ma'i ko'o nau fa'ida kira tufu 'ania naki. Noa'a ta naifi. Kira ka diua go'o fa'i kwalo kī 'ania 'abala 'i 'ai, kaida'i ana o'onga'a kī. 'Unari ifi 'ai, kini kī kira ke kwa'ila'inia go'o ka foga fuana du'anga'a. Kaida'i rū kī ato 'ania ko'o nau fa'ida, nia ta'a liu. Noa'a ta ara'ikwao kesi 'afida, ka noa'a ta 'aria kanaselo saena fanoa ne'e, noa'a ta takis 'i saena fanoa ne'e, ka noa'a ta lo saena fanoa ne'e. Nau ku tua 'aku talaku. Nau ku nonifi ku ulafu. . . .

Nau ku olitani la'u ma'i. 'I na'o ma'i falisi go'o, alo go'o, fani fana go'o. Ka 'unari di'ia o'ola 'oe le'a ta ngwae mamata lala ne'e ke kwako ma'i saena rodo ke bilia. Noima 'oko saungia ta ngwae ne'e dao ka fiolo logo, 'oko fiolo logo. Ta nini'a nau ku tua ma'i ka dao 'i ta'ena, ti ngwae ne'e kira fi'i futafuta go'o kī kira oga kī ke ngenge nau fani rū saga ne'e nau ku sai ani kī. Nau ku sai ana ne'e noa'a na'a ta ngwae di'ia nau'a nini'ari. * * *

Kaida'i nau ku te'ete'e nau ku ma'u. 'Oko tata'e ko lae kabara bore, ngwae lia logo suli'o, ke lae ke ū kalio 'oko lae kabara ko oli na'a mo. Ngwae ū 'i māna o'olā, di'ia kira dao kira ka "Kulu leka," ta ma kulu tafi kulu ka leka na'a nai. Nau ku lisia ana ma'a nau, nia ke kilu ka alua ngwa'i 'o'o, alu ka teo 'i fafona biru ne'e fa'inia fa'i bila, kufikufi fena 'o'o. Nia ke kilukilu ka labunga'inia go'o suba'e ka afila ka leka. Ngwae kira leka ma'i fasi kira ke saungia ki lisia ngwa'i, kira ke 'uri "Nia ke oli logo ma'i, ngwa'i teo liu," na ngwa'i le'a nia nia 'i fanoa. Nau ku te'ete'e ana rū ne'ekiri. Nau ku ma'u 'i 'aena ma'a nau fa'ida. So'olafi ma'i kira ka "Rela, kulu 'isi sai ana so'olafi ne'e, nia rodo ka alifa'i ka dao na'a 'uri ma nia le'a na'a." La'a, karangi ke la'a go'o kira tata'e kira ka fa'aadā na'a, saea "Ada! ada! ada!" Nia ne'e nau ku fata sulia nau ku te'ete'e saena mae ne kwa, nia ne nau ku ala'a 'i sulia ta'ena. * * *

Yes, now I'll go back again to before my time, to former things. To when they arrived with knives and axes and clothing. The ships came with them. So then, women pounded the bark of trees and dressed in it. We men just stayed naked, we didn't dress in anything. If I dressed then it was just tree leaves. I just concealed my front.

Formerly my grandfather and others chopped with flint. There were no knives. They just slashed vines with a plank of wood, while making gardens. So then, a log of wood, women would just strike with it to smash it for burning. When things were hard for my grandparents and the others, it was very bad. There was no white-man to help them, no Area Council at home, no taxes at home, no law at home. I lived all on my own. I suffered and struggled. . . .

I'll go back again. Formerly it was just yam gardens, just taro, just pana-yam. So then if your garden was good another man would sneak up in the night and steal it. Either you killed a man who came hungry or you were hungry too. This is it, I've lived until today and some men who have just been born want to argue with me over the true things I know about. I know that there's no other man like myself at present. * * *

When I was small I was afraid. Even when you set out to the latrine, someone looked after you and stood waiting for you to go to the latrine and come back. Someone stood in front of the garden and if they [enemies] came, said "Let's go," so we'd flee, we'd be gone. I saw it with my father, as he planted he'd put an empty bag to lie on the border-pole with a pipe and an empty lime-bottle [for betelnut]. He'd plant and stick in a digging-stick, leave and go off. If men came to kill him and saw the bag, they'd say "He'll be back again, his bag's lying there," but his good bag was at home. I grew up with these things. I was afraid on behalf of my father and others. When evening came they said "Hey, we didn't expect to see the evening, night's come round so all's well." At dawn, when it was almost dawn, they arose and woke them, saying "Wake, wake, wake." That's what I'm saying about when I was small during a feud, that's what I'm talking about today. * * *

The former technology

By the time Alasa'a was born, imported steel tools were in general use for tasks such as clearing forest and cutting wood for fuel, building and carving, and metal utensils and manufactured cloth were also common. But older tools were still familiar and some ancient technologies continued in use throughout his long life.

The standard woodcutting tool was an adze, with a blade of chipped flint lashed with rattan strip to a haft cut from a forked branch. Shells provided many useful tools which imported goods did not entirely replace in Alasa'a's lifetime.

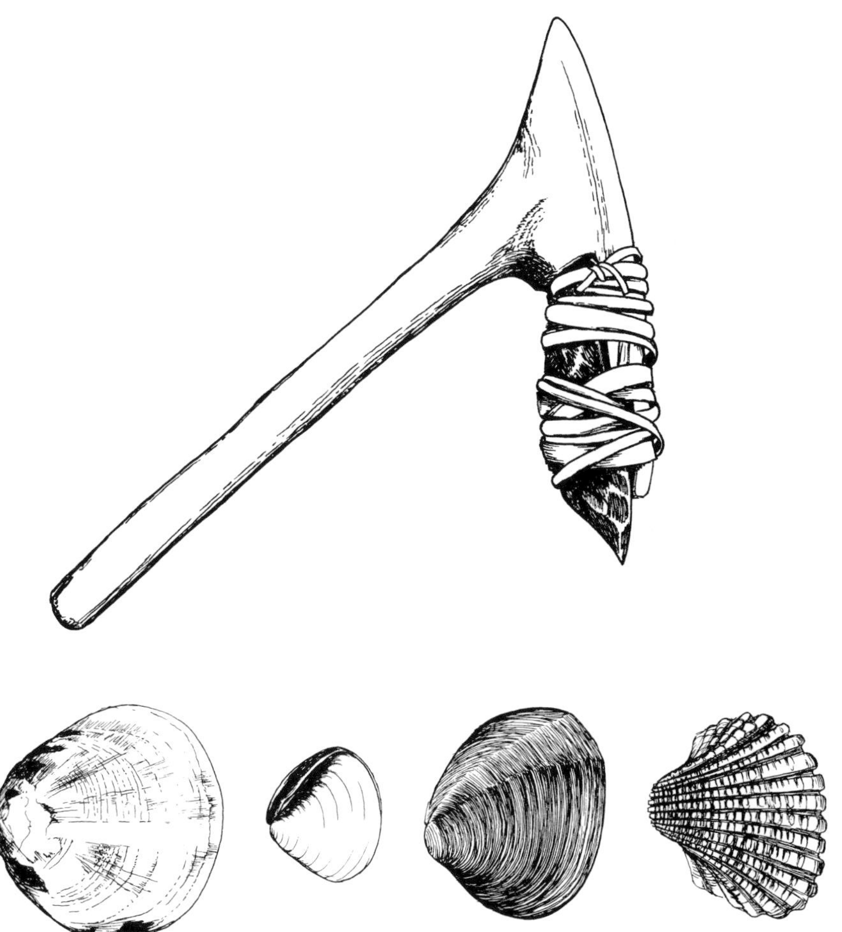

This adze was kept as a memento by Timi Ko'oliu of 'Ere'ere. The shell tools include a ground and polished pearl-shell knife for preparing root-vegetables, a pair of clam-shell tweezers for shaving, a black clam-shell serving as an improvised spoon and scraper, and a cockle-shell used for grating coconut flesh and beating barkcloth.
(All about a third actual size)

In Alasa'a's youth, when killing in restitution for grievances was still common, men carried weapons for their own security as a matter of routine.

In 1917 this band of armed men came to see District Officer William Bell on one of his early police patrols to establish British colonial authority in the Kwara'ae inland. Martin Johnson, an American traveller who accompanied the expedition with his wife, took their photograph.
From the Martin and Osa Johnson Safari Museum

Lisia, sa Tongala, sa Laua'a, sa Lafua, kira tuatua lala 'i 'Aitanga, kira ka tuatua lala 'i 'Aufaolu. Mae go'o ne'ana kira fikua. Sa Iro'ima ne'e fikua mae nai'ari, maelana sa Kwasufo'oa. Sa Kwasufo'oa ne'e korea go'o 'i Kalifaka, sa Gwagwaofilu ka saeta'a, ka kanusua akalo kelema saena ka'o to'oba 'i Makwasi, sa Kwasufo'oa ka kwa'ufia go'o ka mae. Sa Iro'ima, sa Geobauta, Kwa'ilalamuadoe kira ogata'a go'o, kira ka kwaiatoa ka sui, kira ka koso 'i Lalibubu.

Kira ka tua 'i nai'ari, kira ka leka adaada 'i Talakali fu kira ka adaada to'ona. Kira ka fikua mae, akalo 'i Talakali ka dao, kira ka labua unu 'i lo'oba 'i Maku, kira ka 'olea asoa ke dao ana. 'Unari, Tongala leka saena mae 'oe, sa Laua'a ka leka saena mae nai'ari, sa Lafua ka leka saena mae nai'ari, kira fikua 'i Lalibubu. Sa Alaisae nia saena mae nai'ari, sa Diosi nia saena mae nai'ari, sa Kwalemanu nia saena mae nai'ari, sa ngwane'e Salofafo nia saena mae nai'ari, Talaumae nia saena mae nai'ari, sa Fangamae nia saena mae nai'ari, sa ngwane'e Manukao nia saena mae nai'ari, ara'i sa Kekea nia saena mae nai'ari, sa Ngūta nia saena mae nai'ari.

Kira fikua mae nai'ari, sa Iro'ima ka rī kwau 'uana ma'a nau, ma sa La'ugere. Tafi kira ka teo na'a 'i Ngalimatanga. La'ugere ka 'uri, "Maniramo, koro leka lisia sa Iro'ima." Sa Kwa'ioloa ka leka rongoa, sa Fatangasi ka leka, sa Kele ka leka, sa ngwane'e Kwasite'e ne'e alua sa Defene nini ka alua sa ngwane'e Niufilia. Ka tata'e, sa Galisu'u ka leka, nau ne'e ku leka. Daua go'o saena babala nai'ari, nau ku lisia to'a nai'ari ka sui na'a. Sa Dorite'e nia saena mae nai'ari. Kaili ka tua, sa Laugere ka fata 'uri "Maniramo, leka sofiloa sa Iro'ima kwa! 'Uri ma, unu ne'e ke dao 'i angita nini? Ma kulu leka fani mae ne'e ma unu ne'e ke ladafia sa tai nini, ki saungia 'i māna sa Kwasufo'oa?" Ma'a nau sa Maniramo ka leka go'o ka tua fa'inia sa ngwane'e Iro'ima, ka fata 'uri, "Iro'ima, kulu fiku ka sui na'a, ma unu ne'e ke dao angita nini?" Sa Iro'ima ka 'uri "Kwalitai, kira ke labua ma'i 'i Maku loko, ka fafaro ma'i saena asi ka dao 'i ne'e, sa'ulafi na'a, ka ta'ea na'a mae ne'e, unu ka donga na'a."

See, Tongala, Laua'a and Lafua lived at 'Aitanga, they lived at 'Aufaolu. There was a band they gathered. Iro'ima gathered that band, on the death of Kwasufo'oa. Kwasufo'oa married Kalifaka, Gwagwaofilu was angry and put sorcery magic into a water-bamboo up at Makwasi, Kwasufo'oa drank it and then he died. Iro'ima, Geobauta and Kwa'ilalamuadoe felt angry and when they'd deposited him they went down to Lalibubu.

They stayed there and they went to a seance at Talakali where they revealed it was him. They gathered a band, the magic from Talakali arrived, they set up a flare way over at Maku and they set a day for it to arrive. So then, Tongala went in your band, Laua'a went in the band, Lafua went in the band, and they gathered at Lalibubu. Alaisae was in the band, Diosi was in the band, Kwalemanu was in the band, that man Salofafo was in the band, Talaumae was in the band, Fangamae was in the band, that man Manukao was in the band, the man Kekea was in the band, Ngūta was in the band.

They gathered the band and Iro'ima shouted for my father and La'ugere. They'd fled and were staying at Ngalimatanga. La'ugere said "Maniramo, let's go and see Iro'ima." Kwa'ioloa went to listen, Fatangasi went, Kele went, and that man Kwasite'e who begot Defene, who begot that man Niufilia. They set out, Galisu'u went, and me, I went.[1] On getting into the shelter, I saw those people, all of them. Dorite'e was in the band. We sat down and Laugere said "Maniramo, go and ask Iro'ima! So then, when is this flare to arrive? If we go with this band, who is the flare to attack, to kill on account of Kwasufo'oa?" My father Maniramo went and sat with that man Iro'ima and said "Iro'ima, we have all gathered, so when is this flare to arrive?" Iro'ima said "In four days they'll set it up over at Maku, float over the sea and arrive here, and in the evening when the band is raised, the flare follows."

1 Of the men whom Alasa'a accompanied to this meeting, Maniramo was his father, La'ugere (who attacked the ship *Sybil*) was a brother's son of his grandfather Kamusudoe, and Kwa'ioloa (after whom Michael Kwa'ioloa was named) was a son of Kamusudoe's younger brother.

Iro'ima and Gwagwaofilu

When Alasa'a was old enough to accompany his father to important meetings, he witnessed the beginning of a feud which he described to his sons. This was probably around 1910.

Alasa'a told the story as part of the history of Fairū, to show how his community had given refuge to people fleeing from the feud. But it is included here because it illustrates the violence of Kwara'ae local politics which Alasa'a describes as his childhood experience before the British imposed colonial law.

The instigator of this feud, Iro'ima, whom Alasa'a also refers to by his other name Si'au, was a notorious warrior, who appears again in Chapter 5. He was one of the 'Ere'ere group, which included Alasa'a's future father-in-law Arumae Bakete, as well as Iro'ima's target in this feud, Moses Gwagwaofilu.

Gwagwaofilu's story as a former Queensland Christian was recalled by his son Clement 'Au'au in 1999:

I'll talk about my father Gwagwaofilu going to Queensland. When he went to Queensland he stayed for eight years, then he brought the mission, called the SSEM. When he brought the gospel he came to stay at Onepusu. Then they [the mission] bought the ship called the *Evangel* and they came down to Faumamanu. While he was staying at Faumamanu they made the mission there, and at that time his father and the others were all living as heathens [*uikiti*, from English 'wicked']. They said "Oh, it's not right for our son to talk about the mission, the mission is a mistake. It's not suitable. No, stay heathen, son, we don't want to do the mission."

Then they stayed there for a year, they cleared gardens, then they planted coconuts, the coconut trees they called the Faumamanu [plantation] Company. When they planted them the sea people wanted to kill them but because they were true to god, they couldn't kill them. They stayed there and his father and the others bespelled him and he went back to being heathen, he was backsliding. He returned to live as a heathen, then he killed someone. So then the Christians, their leader preached to him, they wanted him to go to the mission again. What he said was "Listen, it's not fitting for me to return to the mission, because there's a man's life on my hands. That's why I won't return to the mission with you. However you preach, I'm not going back."

Well, while he was there as a heathen he was also a tabu-speaker, he went back to baking to the ghosts. When he returned to pig-baking he took over our tabu-sanctum at 'Ere'ere, so he was a senior man, a tabu-speaker. Well then, his father asked for my mother for him, a girl from Auluta, they paid for my mother with a hundred moneys. Then he begot me.

Translated from Kwara'ae and abridged

Clement 'Au'au, son of Gwagwaofilu, 1999

Sorcery divination

The kind of seance divination (*adaada*) and sorcery detection (*labua unu*) which Iro'ima used to track down Gwagwaofilu comes from north Malaita. Iro'ima commissioned it from Talakali, across the Fokanakafo inlet in East Fataleka.

The Anglican missionary Walter Ivens wrote about this magic from his research among the sea people of Lau in north-east Malaita in 1927. (What he refers to as the 'beu' is a shrine, equivalent to the Kwara'ae tabu-sanctum or *feraābu*.)

When it is desired to find out the man who is guilty of causing a death by malevolent magic, a diviner is put in charge of the investigation. He first erects a fence of sticks at the side of the beu of the chief who is said to have been killed by magic. He takes the leaves of certain trees along with leaves of the green dracæna, and puts them into the enclosure thus made along with a coco-nut. As he works he keeps on repeating the proper incantations. The proceedings are carried out at dead of night, and at a time when there is no moon. The diviner keeps watch over the charms till he begins to see a small light proceeding from them, like the light of a firefly. He points this out to his helpers, and they and he follow it wherever it leads them. ***

The party then is led to a certain house, and the light is seen to settle on it. Inside the house a man is heard talking in his sleep ; he wakes up and says that a ghost is eating him (he has nightmare). The diviners say that the " light has entered him." He protests his innocence, or rushes out of the house and enters another house in the village. The light follows him wherever he goes and his people acquiesce in the test.

When the diviners return and make their report, a war-party sets out to kill the accused man.

From *The Island Builders of the Pacific* by Walter G. Ivens, 1930, page 227

Nia ka "Ma kulu ke alasia sa tai nini kui saungia?" "Unu alasia sa ngwae nai'ari Gwagwaofilu Mosisi, kuke saungia na'a māna sa Kwasufo'oa. Unu kulu daofa'i liu ka alasia sa ngwane'e Raraakalo kulu ka saungia na'a māna sa Kwasufo'oa. Kera'a ne'e kira folia ma'i kelema, nini'a sa Gwagwaofilu ka saeta'a ne'e sa Kwasufo'oa ba'ea 'i Kalifaka, ka tuarani ka liu go'o ka sui, so'olafi sa Kwasufo'oa ka sofongani ka'o nia saena fi'i folota, nia ka dangulua akalo 'i saena ka saungia aiburiku."

Go'o ma'a nau ka oli na'a ma'i, oli ka dao go'o ka 'uri "La'ugere kulu leka." Sa La'ugere ka 'uri "Fa'ua?" "Ō, mae ne'e tata'e na'a 'uana sa Gwagwaofilu go'o nini'a. Ma di'ia kira ka taraunasia sa Gwagwaofilu ma tai adaro'o ka rao 'uana ma kulu mae na'a. Kira ka saungia sa Gwagwaofilu fāfi kulu, kulu mae na'a. Koro ke oli go'o." Nia nai. 'Unari, sa Si'au lia ma sa La'ugere tata'e na'a, ka "O, Si'au, uka ne'e 'oko fikua ka sui na'a, 'oke afua na'a namo ne'e. Bore ma ī'a nini 'oke afua ke mae 'i saena, nia ābu kero'o kesi fanga ana, 'oke sasia na'a 'amu." Nia ne'e, go'o kaili ka oli, akwala 'i Talakali ne'e nia 'i nai'ari.

'Una'ari unu ka dao, kira ka leka na'a 'i sulia, kira ka alasia ne'e unu radafia fera gwa'u. Sa Gwagwaofilu nia 'i Tatafe'ai, saena maoma sa Gwalua kira 'oi'oi sango kira ka teo na'a. Na unu ka daofa'i liu, ka radafia sa Raraakalo, buira sa Raraakalo nia 'i Tatafe'ai saena babala 'i maoma sa ngwane'e Gwalua. 'Unari unu ka daofa'i liu, ka radafia sa Raraakalo ma sa Mosisi Gwagwaofilu saena babala 'i maoma lo'oba. Akwa'a ka tolo na'a, ka "Sai, tae ne'e 'uri, tae ne'e 'uri? Sai, unu nini'a radafi koro'o." La'a ka la'a ka dangi, sa Iro'ima ka 'ada kokolana "Ō, Gwalua, kwatea ma'i rō fa'i ko'oko'o nau kī ni'i saena maoma 'oe." Sa Gwalua ka tata'e ka 'uri "Ō, mango basi 'ana Iro'ima, nau kui 'isia sango nai, nau ku fi'i kwateda kwau."

Mae fuiri ka tua na'a, tua na'a, tua na'a ma'akwalia ala'anga nai'ari. Kira ka 'isia sango fuiri. Sa 'Oigaula ka tata'e, sa Nare ka tata'e, sa Galiamanu ka tata'e, sa Tole'a ka tata'e, sa Gwalua ka tata'e. Tata'e kira ka sisira'i kwangana go'o sa Iro'ima na ramo baera, kira ka a'oa'o ana kwanga kī kira ka dangalu, sa ngwane'e Alaisae ka fele a'oa'o ana ta kwanga ka dangalu, sa Kwalemanu ka 'ao'ao ana ta kwanga ka dangalu, sa Diosi ka dau 'ao'ao ana ta kwanga ka dangalu. Go'o kira ka foto'ia go'o

He said "And who are we to trap and kill?" "If the flare traps that man Gwagwaofilu Moses, we'll kill him for Kwasufo'oa. If our flare comes on past and traps that man Raraakalo, we'll kill him for Kwasufo'oa. It's those two who purchased the sorcery; it was Gwagwaofilu being angry that Kwasufo'oa led away Kalifaka, he bade his time and afterwards, one evening when Kwasufo'oa hid his water-bamboo in a clump of gingers, he dropped the magic into it and killed my younger brother."

Then my father returned and when he got back he said "La'ugere, let's go." La'ugere said "Why?" "Oh, this band is setting out for Gwagwaofilu, that's what. And if they let Gwagwaofilu get away, whichever of the two they reach for, we're dead. If they kill Gwagwaofilu through us, we're dead. Let's go back." That's what. So then, Si'au looked and La'ugere got up: "Oh, Si'au, you've already gathered the derris, now you'll poison the pool. But the fish you'll poison to death in it, it's tabu for us two to eat them, you do it yourself." That was it, we returned, and the ten from Talakali were there.

So then, the flare arrived and they went along with it and ambushed where the flare flashed on an empty sanctum. Gwagwaofilu was at Tatafe'ai, at Gwalua's festival, they were performing a dance and sleeping there. The flare came past and flashed on Raraakalo, when Raraakalo was at Tatafe'ae in the festival shelter of that man Gwalua. So then, the flare came past and flashed on Raraakalo and Moses Gwagwaofilu in the festival shelter over there. There was a hue and cry: "Hey, what's this, what's this? Hey, it's the flare flashing on them." Dawn became day and Iro'ima shouted a call "Oh Gwalua, bring out my two owls [sorcerers] that are at your festival." Gwalua got up and said "Oh, wait a bit Iro'ima, I'll finish my dance and then give them up."

The band stayed and stayed and stayed, waiting for the word. They finished the dance. 'Oigaula got up, Nare got up, Galiamanu got up, Tole'a got up and Gwalua got up. Getting up, they drew out their guns and that warrior Iro'ima and them raised their guns and let them off, that man Alaisae held up a gun and let it off, Kwalemanu raised a gun and let it off, Diosi held up a gun and let it off. Then they slammed a bullet at Olisito'ona. So 'Oigaula

bolo ana sa Olisito'ona. Nia ne'e, sa 'Oigaula kwa'ila'inia go'o fa'i bolo lo'oko ka 'uri "'Oe ne". Dikoa saena tafe ka ru'u saena karona sa Olisito'ona, ka teo go'o 'i Lalibubū. Sa Tole'a kwa'ila'inia kwanga ka 'uri "'Oe ne" ana sa Fare, ngwae Talakali nai'ari, ka ru'u 'i bo'obo'osi limana, kula ki sa'isa'i gwaro ana, suli ka teo. Sa Dori ta'e ka laua ka tafi na'a 'ana fa'inia. Nia ne'e, go'o kira ka kame na'a 'i sulida, sa Tongala ka dila na'a, sa Lafua ka dila na'a, sa Laua'a ka tafi na'a, rū nena kaulu tafi go'o 'i 'osiana nai, lisia. . . . Sa Fangamae ke fele a'oa'o ana ta 'oko sua ka tafi na'a, sa Ngūta ka fele ana ta kwanga ka tafi na'a, sa Kekea ka dau ana ta kwanga ka tafi na'a, sa Manukwao ka tafi na'a. Kira ka tata'e kira ka 'ui laelae suli kaumulu, kira ka to'osia mafula ka do'ofia fera sa Diosi, lo ki saea 'ania 'i Ferasungia, ka do'ofia kwaru ābu kaumulu. Kaulu tafi go'o ma'i nai, tafi go'o ma'i kaulu ka ma'a mauri go'o saena ano nau. Kaulu ka 'ania go'o fanga saena ano nau. * * *

just levelled and shot a bullet off and said "There you are." Smashing into the bench, it entered Olisito'ona's ribs and he lies at Lalibubū. Tole'a levelled his gun and said "You there" to Fare, a Talakali man, it entered his upper arm at the place we wear an armband, the bone remained. Dori got up and grabbed him and fled with him. That's it, they seized hold of them, Tongala escaped, Lafua escaped, Laua'a fled, the reason you all fled was because of that, see. . . . Fangamae held up a bundle of spears and fled, Ngūta grasped a gun and fled, Kekea held on to a gun and fled, Manukwao fled. They started running and shooting after you, they set fire and burnt Diosi's men's house, where they call it Ferasungia [Scorched-house], and burnt your tabu rocks. You all fled here, fled here and you remained alive in my land. You just ate food in my land. * * *

An impression of Moses Gwagwaofilu, as described by his son Clement 'Au'au and by Japhlet I'ana, who also remembered him as an old man. This is how he would decorate for festivals in ornaments typical of the times: a comb and cowrie shells in his hair, nose-pin, pearl-shell crescent, shell-bead armbands, embroidered cane girdle and shell-bead garters. The otu *stud at the tip of the nose is often said to be the sign of a man who had killed.*

5
Niusamolaku ma Daolana Lō

Aia'a, nau ku ala'a la'u sulia nau'a nai. Nau ku niusamo, ku rao go'o 'uana wan selene fuana rō asoa kī, hafakeraon. Twelf baoni fuana rō fa'i ngali kī, nau 'i Katere, ka ra'e ma'i ka leleka, nau ku saene la'u 'i buri, nau ku ngalia faef selene, twende foa baoni fuana rō fa'i ngali kī. Aia'a, ka nau 'i taisina, mae ana Diamani fa'inia Biritis kera'a ka fu'a. Ara'i nai ka fata 'uri aku, sa Misita Solda, ngwae 'i Birisbini; "Ō di'ia nia le'anga'a la'u 'oko oli 'i fanoa kamu. Di'ia ne'e Diamani uinimi kaili na'a, kaulu ta'a na'a." Ta ma nau 'i taisina nai. Di'ia ngwae kira to'o ana buka kī kira ke lisia ne'e niusamolaku ne'e 'unari.

Nau ku dao 'una'ari fuana misis nai'ari, Misis Solda, nia ka fata mala faka nau ku fata mala tolo. Nia saea ti rū nau ku rao lala 'uana ti rū. Nau ku rao go'o sulia na ulu madamo kī, faina madamo, go'o 'i Maringa, si basisi 'i Maringa ne'e faka nai'ari teo 'i saena ne'e kira ke saea 'ania Maringa. Faka 'i Katere nai'ari, kaili ka leka. Kabitana ne'e ka fata 'uri fuana, sa Misita Makselo, "O Misita Solda, na kuki te'ete'e nai'ari, nia leka kuki basi aku, nau kui lekaleka 'i Tulake kui lisia kutu kuki, koro ka dao nia ka fi'i koso. Aia'a kuki 'a'ana 'oe nini'a eta kuki ka daua basi 'ana ma'akwalia."

Aia'a go'o koro ka leka na'a. Nau ku kuki na'a, leleka ka dao 'i Tulake, kaili ka lutimi kako fuiri, kaili ka oli na'a 'uana 'i lo'oba 'i Bukutu. Dao 'i Sanafulae, Waitisibi ka eta age, go'o Maringa dao logo 'i nai'ari ka age logo. "Ō, ofodangi kulu fi'i to'ofolo." Aia'a ki teo go'o 'i nai'ari, na ara'i kaili ka kwa'ubia ka daranga go'o, ka tara unasisi fū sekese raono 'ania, ka ta'e ka afutaka go'o 'aimili. Bosokuru kī kira ka tafi kira ka koso 'i asi, kira ka ago go'o 'ania, nau ne'e ku tafi ku ru'u 'i to'oba 'i fokoselo, fa'i bolo ka ta'e ka tafangia fa'i tagi to'oba ka limata logo. Nia liliua go'o, ka 'uri na'a rō fa'i bolo kī loko ana Waitisibi lo'oko, tafangia go'o 'i lo'oba, bosokuru kī kira ka abuli 'i ninimana faka lo'oba.

5
My Recruitment and the Arrival of Law

Well, I'll talk more about myself. When I was a new recruit I worked for one shilling for two days, half-a-crown [two and sixpence per week]. Twelve pounds for two years while I was at Gatere and it went up eventually when I signed on again afterwards, and I took five shillings, twenty-four pounds for two years. Well, while I was at the station the war of Germany with Britain was fought. My master said to me, Mr Schroder, a man from Brisbane: "Oh, if all goes well, you'll return to your home. If Germany defeats us, it will be the worse for you." But I was at the station. If people read the books they'll see my recruitment there.[1]

I came there for the missis, Mrs Schroder, she spoke really foreign and I spoke really local. She'd say something and I'd work at something else. I just worked for three months, and the fourth month at Maringe, the Maringe passage in which lay the ship they called the *Meringe*. That was the Gatere ship which we went in. The captain said to him, Mr Makselo, "Oh Mr Schroder, that little cook, he can come and cook for me a bit, while I go to Tulagi it doesn't look good for me to cook, and when we arrive he can step down. Well, your senior cook, the first cook, can hold on and wait for him."

Well, then off we went. I cooked until we arrived at Tulagi, we loaded the cargo and we went back over towards Bugotu. Arriving at Sandfly, the *Wheatsheaf*[2] anchored first, then the *Meringe* arrived there and anchored too. "Oh, in the morning we'll go across." Well, we rested there and our master drank beer and got drunk, he pulled out a winchester with six rounds in it, he got up and took shots at us. The crew fled and got down into the sea, they hid there, and me, I fled up into the forecastle, a bullet came and pierced a tank up there and it spurted out. He continued with two bullets over at the *Wheatsheaf*, piercing it over there, and the crew rolled over the side of the ship.

1 As a new recruit, Alasa'a describes himself as *niusamo* or 'new chum', an expression going back to the days of the Queensland plantations. Colonial regulations required recruits to be officially registered.

2 Bogotu is at the eastern end of Isabel island and Sandfly Passage is a route through the Gela island group. The *Wheatsheaf* was a trading and recruiting ship owned by the Buffet brothers who had a plantation on Florida in the Gela group (Golden 1993:82).

Gatere plantation

Chapter 5 begins in 1918, at the end of the First World War, with Alasa'a's first journey overseas as a migrant worker, to Gatere plantation on the north coast of Isabel island. It continues with the imposition of colonial law on East Kwara'ae in 1919, after his return home.

By the time Alasa'a was old enough to work abroad the labour trade which employed his fathers in Fiji and Queensland had ended and Europeans were opening plantations in Solomon Islands. Alasa'a's employer or 'master' (*ara'i*) at Gatere on the north coast of Isabel island was John Schroder. His story, told by Graeme Golden in *The Early European Settlers of the Solomon Islands*, illustrates the colonial economy of Alasa'a's youth.

John Schroder was born in Karageio, Norway in 1885. When he was five his family migrated to Australia and settled in Brisbane . . . John had two brothers Leif and Niels and a sister Henrietta, who was to marry the Solomons businessman Oscar Svensen. It was at Svensen's invitation that John made his first voyage to the Solomons in 1903. . . .

In 1911 Svensen bought John's shares in the rubber company for 4,500 Pounds and with the proceeds, and in partnership with his brother Niels John registered a lease of 1,000 acres at Gatere Bay for a term of 99 years. In 1912 John took the steamer to Sydney to have a boat built to service the plantation. The schooner Meringe was built to his specifications at a cost of 1,250 Pounds. John also had plans to marry Nellie Berg, the daughter of a Norwegian ship's Captain and a good friend of Oscar Svensen . . . In 1913 Nellie Berg sailed to Tulagi and the couple were married. . . . Gatere plantation was developed through his own hard work and consisted of land at Gatere east and west and at Sikali. The property had a five mile continuous stretch of beach front and the lease included three small islands a short distance out to sea. The islands of Bane and Legahana were also planted with coconuts, giving a total area of 1,355 acres. . . . During 1912 John was heavily occupied in planting young coconut palms at Gatere and that planting program continued through until 1919, by which time 35,079 trees had been planted on 701 acres. In 1914 John incorporated Gatere Plantations Ltd. and registered the company in Brisbane.

From *The Early European Settlers of the Solomon Islands* by Graeme Golden, 1993, pages 315-6.

John Schroder at Gatere plantation in 1920.
With thanks to Graeme Golden

Recruiting in Malaita

An extract from a letter from the first Malaita District Magistrate, Edge-Partington, to the Resident Commissioner in 1911 shows the conditions under which Schroder recruited his Malaitan employees in the days before government controlled their island.

In the case of the "Maringe", Mr Schroder, thinking the place was quite safe, sent one boat ashore to the market with a native recruiter. This market is a friendly lot, and have caused no trouble, and done no murders the whole time I have been here. He only sent one gun in the boat. The bushmen called out to the native recruiter, who went ashore, leaving the gun in the boat, covered with a bag. A bushman walked up to the boat, took the gun, and bolted into the bush with it. The remaining bushmen, seein there were no more guns in the boat, naturally acted chee and pointed all their guns at the crew, who fell down in the bottom of the boat. If the bushmen liked they could have killed the lot, but they did not fire, only showed them what fools they ~~are~~ were. The boat got away, and ba back to the ship, and the bushmen fired three shots at the ship at a distance of about 100yds, hitting nothing, just showing their contempt for a vessel that sends a boat ashore recruiting, with no white man in it, and only one gun which they had stolen with out any trouble.

From Solomon Islands National Archives Mala 1911 No 9

Aia'a, bosokuru kaili kī, sa Ri'a, ngwae saena 'Oba ne'e nia sekon mait. To'oa go'o kira ka ra'e kira ka lobā na'a ara'i. Teo go'o dangi, kaili oli 'i Tulake. Dao go'o kira ngalia ara'i nai'ari saena kwauta, kwauta ka leleka nia ka lusu, kaoni doe nia la'u ana, la'u nia ka 'uia la'u Waitisibi.

'Unari, kaili ka oli ma'i kaili ka tua go'o 'i safitana 'i Tulake fa'inia 'i Makabu. No kaili 'iri tua ana ta uafa. Rodo ka rodo, ara'i nai'ari ka so'olafi bore ma ta bosokuru ngalia na'a kwau, fo'o sulia rō bongi kī, ūla bongi go'o ana farere. Dina ka sui na'a, kaili ka koso saena tabalau doe fuiri. 'Unari nau ku alua na'a ketolo saena ofini ka 'akofia na'a fuana tu kiloko nia ke kwa'u ti. Nau ku ra'e ma'i ku lia 'ala'a saena ngwasi ma nia kwata tu tu, go'o nau ku sasia ma'e ti ka teo go'o nau ku koso toli saena tabalau. Ara'i kwa'u ti ka keresia leta fuiri leleka ka sui go'o, ka alua leta soso ka alua banikini ka teo fafia, nia ka ngalia sitili naefi kwao nai'ari kī, ki la'umi'i lala. Koso toli ta rō reba 'ai teo toli, ta rō reba 'ai ka teo 'ala'a, limana reba 'ai fu nia kwatea gwauna 'i olofana, 'ena luana ka ba'u mala fi'i nangata'i resa fuiri. Musia luana te'e 'uli'uli sulia īla ne'e teo. Gwauna ka lafua ifi'ai fuiri ka 'asia ka teo 'i fu'ufu'una, nau ku rongoa ne'e nia 'uri "Ē" go'o nau ku ra'e na'a. Ku ra'e ku lia na'a, 'abu fūri utakataka na'a ma ke mamafusi ana, go'o nau ku āko na'a ku 'uri "'Ai rela, mulu lae ma'i! Mulu ra'e ma'i!"

Na bōso kaili ka ra'e ka lia go'o ka 'uri, "O kulu ma'afu na'a." Sa Ri'a ka dudu 'i nai'ari, sa Kirio ka dao ka lia logo ka 'uri "'Ai, kulu mae na'a." 'Unari, sa Ugulu ka ra'e, tala'i bosokuru kira lia kaili ka noto mili ka tua na'a 'aimili. Tuatua 'i nai'ari, sa Ri'a ka "Rela, kulu leka fa'arongo 'ania." Kira ra'efia bauta ka dao 'i māna uafa lobo 'I Tulake kira ka ribauta go'o, māna uafa lo'oba ka kwao ka gwa. To'a ne'e kira solodia kaida'i nai'ari kī, to'a i' Alu kī, na ngwae kī ta ngwae kī ne'e kwa'a. Kira fiku 'i lo'oko ka sui go'o, bauta ka leka, lanisi ka leleka ka saete go'o. Dokota liu na'a, ekselensi ka liu na'a, kira'a ta'ifau kira ra'e na'a ma'i, kira dao go'o 'i nai'ari, dokota ka koso na'a. Nia dau nama 'ana fafia sirana 'iri dangulua, nia ka "Ō, nia tala saungia kwa'ae, na resa ne'e nia dau fafia."

Well, in our crew was Ri'a, a man from 'Oba who was the second mate. Counting [the shots], they climbed up and seized the master. Resting until day, we returned to Tulagi. On arriving they took the master to court and the court went on until he lost and had an extra big fine, as he'd also shot up the *Wheatsheaf.*

So then, we returned and stayed between Tulagi and Makambo. We didn't stay at a wharf. Night came and the master, in the evening one of the crew took him out, he was bound for two days, the third day was Friday. Dinner was finished and we went down into the large cabin below deck. Well then, I put the kettle on the stove and heated it for two o'clock for him to drink tea. I came up and looked up at the clock and it was quarter to two, then I made a cup of tea and left it while I went down below deck. The master drank the tea and wrote a letter and then when he'd finished he put the letter on the saucer, put the cup on it and he took a white steel knife, one of those you fold up. Going down, with two steps below and two steps above, at the fifth step he put his head under it, pressed his neck and when it swelled, struck it against the razor. It cut through his neck, only the flesh at the back remained. His head lifted the timber and it fell and lay on his chest, I heard him say "Ee", then I climbed up. I climbed and looked, the blood had sprayed around and run down, then I shouted "Hey there, everyone come here! Climb up here!"

Our bosun climbed and just looked and said "Oh, now we're done for." Ri'a squatted down there, Kirio arrived and looked too and said "Eh, now we're dead." Well then, Ugulu climbed up, the whole crew looked and we were dumb-founded and just sat there. We sat there and Ri'a said "Hey, let's go and tell the news." They climbed into the boat, arrived at the wharf over at Tulagi and reported, where the wharf was black and white. The people who were soldiers [police] at that time were people from Alu, men who were strong men. They'd gathered over there and then a boat came, a launch came alongside. The doctor came, his Excellency came, all of them climbed aboard and when they got there the doctor went down. He had to hold onto his belly and couldn't let go, he said "Oh, he's killed himself with the razor he's holding."

The whiteman's suicide

A letter from the Acting Resident Commissioner to the High Commissioner for the Western Pacific (the 'Excellency' referred to by Alasa'a) names the man who killed himself on the *Meringe* and confirms the details of Alasa'a's story. As a 'returned Soldier' in 1918 at the end of the First World War, he was presumably suffering shock from his experience of the fighting in Europe.

WPHC Inwards Correspondence 2479/18.
With thanks to Judith Bennett

2479/18

Office of the Resident Commissioner,
British Solomon Islands,
TULAGI, 13th September,1918
Recd 22.10.18.

W.P.H.C.
No. 204/1918.

Sir,

I have the honour to enclose particulars for entry in your Register of the death of David Edward Davies, a returned Soldier, who was found dead on the 11th instant in the cabin of the schooner "Maringe" of which he was in sole charge.

2. The deceased had been suffering from hallucinations and the Government Medical Officer, who arrived on board whilst the body was still warm, reports that the internal jugular vein and wind pipe were severed by a razor which was lying close to the corpse.

I have the honour to be,
Sir,
Your Excellency's most obedient
Servant,
Charles Workman
Acting Resident Commissioner.

His Excellency,
the Acting High Commissioner
for the Western Pacific,
SUVA. FIJI.

This early photograph of Solomon Islands plantation workers has only the documentation written upon it, but it shows how Alasa'a and his workmates might have looked at Gatere (in the days when Europeans called all native men 'boys').
With thanks to Graeme Golden

Oli ka ra'e, tarā go'o leta fu kira ka lisia saena, ka "O ara'i nai'ari, nia ka mango'abusu'a 'ania ne'e nia lusu nai, ka saungia na'a. Ai, ki 'iri sai la'u ana reba 'ai fu teo 'i fu'ufu'una." Kira alua lala fasi kaili 'isia 'ania mongona.

Kira ka ngalia ma'i tede to'oba kika dao, kira ka 'agā ara'i kira ka leka fadilangani 'i Bangai, ka teo ka dangi 'ofodangi, lanisi ka saete: "Mulu lae ma'i." Kaili koso go'o nai, dao go'o 'i lo'oba, kwauta ka istata na'a. Kaida'i nai'ari nau ku "Mifala" go'o, nau ku 'iri sai ana ta angilisi le'a. Kira ka dau nau kika daofa'i liu na'a fa'inau. Nau ku koso sa kilu nai'ari ku tata'e ku tata'e nai'ari ku ū 'i gwauna gwa'i simede nai'ari, gwauku ka ra'e 'ala'a. Kira ka tuafia go'o 'i fera loko 'i māna uafa lo'oko, 'i ofisi lo'oko, haoso kwauta lo'oko nia fungu. Ngwae gwā go'o, 'afe gwā go'o, 'afe kwao kī na'a, tua kira ka ada na'a ana kwauta lo'oko, mala nau ku fi'i sasia kwauta lo'oko. Kira ka sasia ma'e kwakwa 'i fu'ufu'uka, ta ara'i lia logo fuana. Ara'i nai'ari fū, māna busu na'a 'i fu'u-fu'uka. Tai nini'a lia go'o 'i kukūka fa'inia sa māka, tai loko ka ala'a. Nai saea go'o ta rū kira ka "Geaman," nai saea la'u go'o ta rū kira ka "Geaman." Nau ku 'uri "Rela nai fata go'o fa'ua?" Nau ku kwauta sulia asoa nai'ari leleka ka rodo, kaili kwauta leleka go'o, miki oli mili ka teo saena faka.

Teo ka dangi, kaili ka tata'e 'i kwauta ka leka, kwauta fūri ka leleka ka rodo, kaili saena sela. Teoteo saena sela fūri ka dangi ofodangi, kaili ka tata'e ana aiti kiloko. Nau ku teo saena sela nai, sela nai'ari teoteo 'i Tulake, 'uri kira fa'alia na'a. Te'e bali ne'e 'oke teo 'ania, kira ka kanusua toro fa'asi'o. 'Oke ru'u go'o mala, ko ū nama ana kula abitako ko fa'ita'i ana ta bali ko teo 'ania. Leleka mimimu ka fī, onimu ka fī, 'oko tata'e ko mimi logo saena ta'e soso fuiri. Ofodangi kira ka kwatea go'o te'e 'uli bisikete fa'inia te'e banikini kafo, 'oko kwa'ufia, logo 'oko ta'e fuana kwauta fūri.

Kwauta ka leleka, tōsode na'a. Ara'i saungia ana ta wiki, ana farere, ka le'a fuana ne'e nau ku lisia nama ne'e kaida'i nau ku sai ana ngwasi, nau ku sai ana taeme ne'e nia saungia ana.

He came back up, got out the letter and they looked at it: "Oh, the man was overwhelmed that he'd lost and killed himself. But we don't understand the plank lying on his chest." They suspected we'd stopped his breath with it.

They brought a coffin up, they came and shouldered the man and went with him to Bangai, they stayed till morning next day and a launch came alongside: "You all come here." We got down, arrived over there, and court started. At that time I'd just go "Mifala,"[1] I didn't know any good English. They held me and went past with me. I went down into the pit and I got up, got up and stood on top of the block of cement, my head held up. They were sitting in the sanctum over by the wharf, at the office, the court house was full up. Black men, black women, and white women, they were already sitting watching the court when I came to do the court. They made holes in our chests, when a master looked at us. The master's eyes burst our chests. Whoever it was, he looked at our throats and into our eyes and talked. I'd say something and they'd say "Liar," I'd say something else and they'd say "Liar." I said "Hey, what can I say?" I was in court all that day until night, we went on in court until we returned and slept in the ship.

Sleeping till next day, we got up and the court went on, the court went on until night, and we were in a cell. Sleeping in the cell until morning next day, we got up at eight o'clock. I've slept in the cell, the cells at Tulagi, which they've now destroyed.[2] There was a side you lay on, they took your clothes from you. Once you entered you had to stand in the clear space and turn to the side you lay on. Eventually when you were aching to pee or shit you got up and peed into a dish. In the morning they just gave a biscuit and a mug of water, you drank it and you set out for the court.

The court went on until Thursday. The master was killed a week ago on the Friday, and fortunately I'd seen when it was, I knew about watches, and I knew the time when he was killed.

1 'Mifala', Pijin for 'we', illustrates the lingua franca Alasa'a had learned on the plantation.

2 Tulagi was destroyed by Japanese bombing during the Second World War in 1942.

Tulagi, the colonial capital

S.G.C. Knibbs, Commissioner of Lands for the British Solomon Islands Protectorate, describes Tulagi as it was when he first arrived by ship from Sydney in 1913:

Next Tulagi appeared, with red-roofed bungalows standing out conspicuously against the green background of coconut-palms. The Union Jack flying from a tall flag-pole at the Residency on the top of the hill denoted that the territory was part of His Majesty's Empire. As we rounded the point to enter the harbour cheers rang out from natives on the island of Makambo who had come in from Malaita to work the cargo which the ship carried. Here she was at last! They had been there for several days in anticipation of her arrival, for at that time there was no wireless station, and communication with civilization was entirely by steamer.

With a rattle of chain the anchor plunged into the water, and simultaneously a whaleboat flying a large blue ensign bearing the legend "H. O." (Health Officer) left the shore, bringing off the medical officer to grant us pratique. To the left lay the island of Tulagi, some two and a half miles in length, forming one side of the harbour. To the right was the small island of Makambo, where Messrs Burns, Philp have their chief depot in the Solomons. Astern, at a distance of two or three miles, was Gavutu, the local headquarters of Lever's Pacific Plantations. White paths ran spiderweblike over the island of Tulagi, linking up the various houses, and on the foreshore lay the Government offices, the Post Office close to the concrete jetty.

***

Beyond the Post Office were the labour lines, now long since gone, and farther on a small concrete-floored native hospital, where the hotel now stands. The concrete still remains, and may be seen forming a courtyard on the far side of the present building.

The old gaol and a gaoler's house were in course of erection. Of the former the concrete cells still stand, used now as store-rooms. The house is occupied by another official. The gaol fence, which consisted of a ten-foot-high galvanised iron wall, has been dismantled and turned to other uses.

From *The Savage Solomons as They Were and Are.* by S.G.C. Knibbs, 1929 pages 22-3, 264-5

A view of Tulagi in the 1930s, looking over Chinatown and its wharfs, with small traders' ships like the Meringe *and the* Wheatsheaf, *towards the island of Makambo in the middle distance.*

Photo by L.P. Kendall in British Museum Ethnography Dept. pictorial collection, with thanks to Andrea Bannatyne.

'Una'ari go'o, sa Misita Diake, inifekta, ka aotim kwauta ka 'uri "Iu, las kwauta kaumulu nia ana farere. Kaulu uini mulu uin na'a, kaumulu ka lusu mulu lusu na'a, kaulu ka mae na'a, ka noa'a rū gafamanu kī." Kaimili ka oli, so'olafi, to'a 'a'ana kira ka 'uri "'Ua, rorodo kulu ke mae." Na'a kaili ka nē na'a fuana saitana, ka mango ana faka fuiri, kaida'i saitana ngasingasi'a liu. Faka fuiri ka gelo ka to'oto'o ana ta bali saena asi fuiri ma ke to'oto'o ana ta bali, ma ka ra'e ka ta'e. Nia ka 'uri "Noa'a, kira ka fonefone kaulu saena fera 'i sela lo'oko ma nau ku dikoa na'a. Luamulu ke mū luaku ka mū." Rū ne'e, rū ne'e nau ku ti'iti'i ku leka ana faka ku sai ani kī nai.

So then, Mr Jack the inspector [?], cleared the court and said "Yes, your last court is on Friday. If you've won, you've won, if you've lost, you've lost and you're dead, it's nothing to do with government." We returned and in the evening the senior people said "Tomorrow we'll die." Now we invoked satan[1] and he breathed on the ship, a time when satan was very powerful. The ship rolled over onto one side and into the sea and then onto the other side, and rose back up. He said "No, if they shut you all in that cell-house I'll break it apart. If your throats are cut, my throat's cut." This, when I was young and went abroad, this is what I experienced.

'Unari ka dangi kaili ka dao go'o 'i lo'oba, kira ka ūria ringi fuiri, ka ta'i nau'a go'o kira makimi nau go'o nai. Aia'a, sa Kabingtana ka tara ma'i rō lima nia kī fa'inia gwa'i noto kī. Ka le'a nai nau ku lisia ne'e nia fa'ata'inia limana 'uri, 'u'una ka oli fa'asia ta gwai'ai nau ku lisia. Gwa'i rū kwao fu saena roto kī, nia tara limana ka fata 'uri ana "Tae nini kwa?" Nau ku "Gwa'i noto kī ne'ana kwa." Nia ka "Fita rū?" "Fai gwa'i rū kī ne'ana." Na rū ne'e kī, ki ala'a bore suli'i ma madakwala'a saitana lala na'iri'a. Nia ka tarā ma'i ta lima saena tarasisi, ka "Tae la'u nini?" Nau ku 'uri, "Gwa'i noto kī logo ne'ana," nia ka "Ma fita rū?" "Fai rū." Go'o nia ka fata 'uri "Taeme tae nini?" Nau ku lia saena ngwasi nini nau ku liu ma'i, nau ku lia 'ala'a ma nia kwata tu aiti. Nau ku lia 'ala'a saena ngwasi ne'e teo 'i gwauna sinamā. To'oko kira ūria ringi lo'oko, te'e nau'a ne'e ku ru'u, to'a nau ka tua na'a 'i mā. Go'o nia ka fata fuana solodia fu ū, ka 'uri "Taeme tae nini?" Solodia nia ka lia ka "O, barafa aiti kiloko." Nia ka 'ui 'ania fai gwa'i noto kī ka to'o go'o 'i lo'oba, loea ka lafua kifi lōri, ka daua 'i langi ka alua saena gwauna. Ruana ka lafua ka daua 'i langi ka alua saena gwauna. Ūla nia lafua ka ra'e go'o 'uri ka 'ui 'ania saena gegeo, go'o fera fuiri ka foga na'a, kira ka bubu ana āko'a, ngwaiselo ke ringiringi 'ana ma, tini ke kokoke 'ana ma, darama lo'oko ke angi 'ana ma, biukili lo'oko ke angiangi 'ana.

So then, day came and we arrived over there, they stood in a circle and I was the one they picked out. Well, Carpenter pulled out both his hands with pebbles in them. Fortunately I saw him show his hands, his finger moved back from a stone and I saw it. They were white ones from the road, he pulled out his hands and said "What's this?" I said "They're pebbles." He said "How many?" "There's four stones." Those things, although we were talking about them this was satan's knowledge. He pulled out a hand from inside his trousers and "What is it now?" I said "They're pebbles too," he said "But how many?" "Four." Then he said "What time is it?" I'd looked at the clock as I came past, I looked up and it was quarter to eight. I'd looked up at the clock at the top of the doorway. There they stood in that circle, only I went in and my people stayed outside. Then he spoke to a soldier standing there, he said "What time is it?" The soldier looked and said "Oh, exactly eight o'clock." He threw the four pebbles away and they landed over there, the lawyer lifted a hat, he held it high and put it on his head. A second time he lifted it high, held it up and put it on his head. A third time he lifted it, went up and threw it into the dust, then the sanctum broke up, they let out shouts, the whistle shrilled and the tin banged and the drum cried and the bugle cried.

Aia'a, 'unari nau ku 'uri "Se! Kaimili lusu go'o nai." Bore ma kaida'i nau ku sasia kwauta nai'ari rela, nau ku sasia go'o saena angi'a, nau ku manata ka ngiri na'a, sulia nau ku sasi 'uana

Well, so then I said "Hey! We've lost then." But while I was doing that court-case, well, I was crying as I did it, I thought how hard it was because I tried going abroad and this was the

1 Alasa'a uses the Christian term 'satan' to mean nothing more nor less than 'ghost' (*akalo*).

faka ku sasi to'ea na'a reala. Nia nai rū nau ku te'ete'e ku leka ana faka ku sasi'i kī nai. 'I ta'ena nau ku ngwaro na'a, ne'e ngwae ke fata fafi nau 'ania kwauta, ngwae sukadi nau kero'o ke sasi logo kwauta.

Aia'a, nia nai nau ku uinimi kwauta nai'ari fuana kaimili go'o kaili ka ra'e mili ka rao na'a fuana Mastaman, Disi. Nau'a ne'e ku sanasimi kuki nia, to'a nai kira ka kwa'i karasi na'a. Aia'a, ala'anga lae ka dao 'i Katere, sa Misita Solda ka ra'e saena lanisi 'i Katere ka nia na'a ma'i. Nau ku lia go'o toli ku 'uri "Selo! Katere lanisi dao." Fulake leleka ka nia na'a 'i fafona dek. Dao ka saete go'o, Solda lofo ka to'o go'o ka daofa'i liu na'a fa'inia hanbak fuiri. Nia ra'e ka alua 'i to'oba, rō tiba kī teo go'o 'ala'a nia ka nangalangani silifa fuiri saena fulau, go'o nia ka ra'e ka sae nau "Koso ma'i, koro leka. Lia, rū nau ku sasia nai." 'Unari kaili fi'i oli 'uana 'i Katere. Di'ia ne'e nau ki bolebole'a i'ira kaimili lusu na'a, bore ma ne'e nau ku nekea nama 'aku fuana ne'e nau ku uinimi kwauta nai'ari fuaimili, na hae kwauta nari nau ku eta ana hae kwauta nari.

Ruana kwauta aku 'i Tulake, io. Na rō ngwae Makira kī, nau ku selo 'ania 'aba kaleko sulia bali loko 'uana 'i Maringa ta'u. Kera'a ka dole ma'i, nau'a nau ku dole 'aku kira ka lisia 'uri, bōso ka ākoāko 'uada. Kira loko kira tuku ru'u no'o 'adaro'o fa'asida, kira ka dao, kira ka taofi nau. 'Unari, ngwae nai'ari sa Laufo'oa, ngwae 'i Uru nari, 'i Sinaragu, ka rongoa ka ogata'a. Ka teo ka leleka, kaili ka ngalia la'u gwata ara'i. Kaili ka kōngia ana sarere, tefolo naifi kaili ka fa'asia ana kula ne'e kaili kōngia ana, na umu ka teo toli saena kafo, kira likisia 'ai ka 'asia fafia. Ngwaefuta nai go'o sa Le'abulu, kira saea 'ania sa Defene, alua sa Suka, nia lulua gwata fuiri ka leleka ka ngalia naifi fuiri. Nia isu kaili ka lisia gwata ne'e kaili alua saena baola, ka dao 'i fanoa ka lisia go'o sa'esa'erū saena sosobini nai'ari, go'o nia ka leka fa'ata'inia na'a ana ara'i. Ara'i ngali nau, nau ku kwauta fa'inia ma nau ku liliua ana gwata kwasi. Leleka nau ku uinimi 'i nai'ari. Na kwauta 'ato nai'ari nau ku sasia rō kwauta nai'ari kī ana hae kwauta 'i Tulake.

result. Those are the things I did when I was small and went abroad. Today I'm old, and if a man threatens me with court, if a man forces me we'll go to court too.

Well, that's how I won that court-case for us, and then we went up to work for Masterman, the D.C. [District Commissioner] I replaced his cook and my people cut the grass. Well, word reached Gatere and Mr Schroder climbed into the launch at Gatere and here he was. I looked down and said "A sail! Gatere has come in the launch." There was a flag above the deck. It came alongside, Schroder jumped off and came over with a carrying-bag. He climbed up and put it up there, and two steps from the top, he banged the silver on the floor[1] and then he climbed up and told me "Come down, let's go. See what I've done." So then, we returned to Gatere. If I'd been stupid then we'd have lost, but I pressed on with it and so I won that court-case for us all, and that High Court case was my first time in the High Court.

My second court case at Tulagi, yes. Two Makira men, I waved with a cloth in the direction of Maringe far away. They delayed coming and I, I was delayed, the others saw this and the bosun shouted to them. The two of them continued cuscus [possum] hunting and left and when they arrived they swore at me. So then, that man Laufo'oa, a man from Uru, from Sinalaagu, heard and was angry. It lay until we took the master's pig.[2] We baked it on a Saturday, we left a table knife at the place where we'd baked it, the ovenstones lay below in the stream and they cut trees to fall on top. My kinsman Le'abulu, called Defene, who begot Suka, he searched for the pig and eventually took the knife. He traced us and saw the pig which we'd put in a banyan, he arrived home and saw meat in the saucepan, then he went and showed it to the master. The master took me, I went to court for it and I passed it off as a wild pig. Eventually I won there. Those are the difficult court cases I've been in, two court cases in the High Court at Tulagi.

1 The 'bag of silver' could mean that Schroder had collected their wages due from the government.

2 The pig seems to have been a sacrifice to the ghosts to make good for the defilement of being sworn at.

Iu, nau ku ala'a la'u sulia lō. Sa Misita Belo ka dao 'i Rarasu furi kira saea 'ania 'i 'Aoke, go'o sa Kabolo ka oli. Nia dao fa'inia lō. Dao 'unari, ka saenimi na hetemanu'anga ne'e kira saea 'ania bilisimanu, ana sa Manibili, ma'a nau na'iri'a, ka leka kwau ka tua 'i Gwaubusu. 'Una'ari lō ka dongā na'a nai, sa ngwane'e Nafiramo, sa Gulu'i, kira 'uia 'i Maefa'ikwala, 'afe sa Rara'omea, kira tua 'i Na'oasi. * * * Sa Gulu'i ka 'uia 'i Maefa'ikwala, ka akwa 'ani ne'e 'afe nia kwasala'i ngela. * * * Leleka faka ne'e kira [Misita Belo fa'ida] leka 'i saena ne'e Mala, ka dao 'i māna uafa, go'o sa Manibili ka ra'e na'a. Na etangilana lō ana saungwae'a na'iri'a, ne'e osia na mae. 'Unari kira ka ra'e go'o, kira ka teo ka dangi ofodangi, rō bauta kī ka leleka ka ōlo 'i Su'usao. Kira ka alu'i nai'ari solodia kī ka ra'e na'a, ra'e 'uana 'i Na'oasi.

Kira ka dao ana ofodangi nai'ari, fasi kira ke loba sa Gulu'i fa'inia sa Nafiramote'e, go'o Nafiramodoe ka 'uida 'ania unasisi. Nia kwa'ia ta fa'i bolo ka nekea ana sa Misita Belo, ka mae, ka kwa'ia ta'eta'erū ka alua ta fa'i ai ka nekea ana sa Misita Belo, ka mae. Ūla go'o, sa Misita Belo ka "Sut!" Solodia 'ui go'o nai, kira ka foto'ia sa ngwane'e Nafiramo ne'e 'uida, Nafiramodoe. Rō fa'i maelo kī ka ru'u saena ilina, ka teo saena fu'ufu'una, ka 'iri saka, 'asi ka teo na'a. Kira ka kwa'ia ta fa'i bolo kira ka 'uri, "'Ae'o sa Nafiramote'e ne, ngwae ne'e 'oko saungwae." Ma'a nau nairi'a. Tata'e ka tafi, ka feoa fa'i saina. Maelo ne'e fālia go'o fa'i saina ne'e na fa'i 'agena, nia ka leka ka ruru'u na'a 'i to'oko saena 'oni'oni karai buira fuli fera 'i Na'oasi saena keketo. Ngela nai'ari sa Tua, Liu'aubulu, tona 'anida ka lada go'o ana sinamā ana safisi ana mā 'olofolo lo'oko, kira ka dangulua bolo saena merona, leleka ka tata'e tafa na'a 'i olofana luana, ka 'asi ka teo na'a. Aia'a, ngela nari 'i Suaranamae, tona sulia 'ui'a fūri, te'a nia 'ifi go'o, nia ka ngalia fifinga'i kwake ka alua, ka kedea mafula, ngela ka kalifa'i go'o, bolo ka leka saena māna, nangata'inia saena fifinga'i kwake, 'abuna ka luasa na'a, butamemena ka 'asi na'a.

Yes, I'll talk more about the law. Mr Bell arrived at Rarasu, which they called 'Aoke,[1] then Campbell went back. He came with the law. When he arrived he signed the headmanship, which they called policeman, to Manibili, who was my father, he went off to live at Gwaubusu. So then the law followed him, that man Nafiramo, and Gulu'i, they shot Maefa'ikwala, the wife of Rara'omea; they lived at Na'oasi. * * * Gulu'i shot Maefa'ikwala and proclaimed that his wife had aborted a child. * * * Eventually the ship they [Bell and others] travelled in, the Mala, arrived at the wharf and Manibili went aboard. That was the beginning of the law on killing, which broke down feuding. So then, they went up, they rested till morning next day, and two boats went and landed at Su'usao. They left them there and the soldiers went up, went up to Na'oasi.

They arrived that morning so as to seize Gulu'i and Nafiramote'e, then Nafiramodoe shot at them with a winchester. He fired a bullet directed at Mr Bell, it was dead: he knocked out the shell and put in another one and directed it at Mr Bell, it was dead. On the third, Mr Bell said "Shoot!" The soldiers shot and struck that man Nafiramo who'd shot at them, Nafiramodoe. Two bullets entered his back and stayed in his chest and didn't come out, he fell and lay there. They fired another bullet and said, "You Nafiramote'e, you're the man who's the killer." That was my father. He got up and fled and it mangled his buttock. The bullet destroyed his buttock and his abdomen, he went through up there into the chicken shit behind the sanctum-site at Na'oasi, in the bamboos. The boy Tua, Liu'aubulu, was startled by them and rushed through the opening of an upper-floor doorway, they let off a bullet into his anus, it went up and came out under his neck, he fell and lay there. Well, the girl Suaranamae was startled by the shooting, her mother opened the door, she took a bundle of taro leaves and put it down, kindled a fire, the child looked up and a bullet went into her eye, knocking her onto the bundle of taro leaves, her blood flowed and her brains fell out.

1 Rarasu is the original name of the place where the government built its station, named after the island of 'Aoke in the bay.

William Bell

In 1915 William Bell was appointed District Officer for Malaita and by the time of his death in 1927 he had imposed government authority on most of the island. With a small force of paramilitary police (commonly known as 'soldiers'), he took determined action against anyone who refused to recognise government law, in particular its prohibition on killings. Bell's raid on Na'oasi, on a hilltop in 'Aita'e, was the crucial incident which subdued the warriors of East Kwara'ae, as Alasa'a explains.

William Bell with two policemen at 'Aoke in 1917, photographed by Martin Johnson.
From the Martin and Osa Johnson Safari Museum

The killing of Maefa'ikwala

In June 1918 Maefa'ikwala of Fauboso in Latea became another innocent victim of the need for restitution by bloodshed. Gulu'i of the Sakwalo clan had to remove the defilement which his wife had inadvertently caused to himself and his ghosts. Rather than kill his own wife, he killed Maefa'ikwala and made a public announcement of the reason in the customary way.

Almost a month later, the victim's husband Rara''omae reported the killing to Bell, who took a statement from him, of which this is a part.

My name is Raromia. I now live at Saulana. Before I came to Saulana I was living at Fouboso. I left Fouboso because my wife was killed. A man named Galui killed my wife. My wife's name was Mehekwala. She was killed at Fouboso. She was killed twenty seven days ago. When Galui shot Mehekwala Mehekwala fell down. Galui then ran away.

***

Neparamu was holding a Winchester rifle and Galui shot Mehekwala with a Snider rifle. The reason Galui shot Mehekwala was because Sainali, the wife of Galui, defecated in Galui's house and Galui was angry and shot Mehekwala. Galui lives at Kanasi. Kanasi is very close to Fouboso and is not very far from the sea at Kwai.

From the Solomon Islands National Archives

The raid on Na'oasi

William Bell wrote a report of his police raid on Na'oasi which confirms many of the details recalled by Alasa'a more than sixty years later. Alasa'a's knowledge of the incident was aided by the fact that his fathers disposed of the dead, although he himself was working overseas at the time.

BRITISH SOLOMON ISLANDS PROTECTORATE.

A U K I. 17th. MAY 1919.

Sir

In reference to your letter No.39 of the 14th.of August last authorizing action against a native named Gului for the murder of a woman named Nehekwala, I have the honour to report that soon after receiving your letter the message demanding the surrender of Gului was sent to Nauasi but the demand was ignored, at least, as far as the surrender of Gului, but they endeavoured by threats to intimidate all natives whom they thought might show the police the way to Nauasi, and I have had no favourable opportunity to try and effect the arrest until quite recently. Then the husband and near relatives of the murdered woman failed me and a native without any personal interest in the murder offered to show me the track. Late on the evening of the 30th.ultimo I went into Kwai Harbour in the "Mala" and early the following morning proceeded with the police inland. We travelled some distance before daybreak although there was no moon, the guide lost the track and it was about 7.30.a.m. before we reached Nauasi. The village has thick undergrowth on three sides with a stone wall enclosure at one end. I divided the police into two parties to try and surround the houses which the men were supposed to occupy and prevent their escape. When the police were making the movement the Nauasi natives fired on them. The result

and

H.B.M's.ACTING RESIDENT COMMISSIONER.

T U L A G I.

A policeman or 'soldier' of the British Solomon Islands Protectorate armed constabulary, which enabled Bell to impose colonial rule on Malaita.
From British Museum Ethnography Dept. pictorial collection, with thanks to Lady Patricia Garvey

2.

And consequences were that two of the police were wounded and four of the Nauasi natives killed and two wounded. Lce-Corp.Famoa who was leading the party on the left was shot through the thigh, the bullet luckily missing the bone. Constable Jimi Kako was shot through the front of the ankle, apparently not damaging the bone. The names of the Nauasi natives who were killed are two men both named Nefaramu and one named Lioa and a small boy who was killed in a house by a bullet passing through it. I did not see the wounded men, but natives who saw them later informed me that one was named Oganimai, wounded in the hand and forearm, and the other was named Harry Tewani, wounded in the calf of the leg. One Nefaramu who was killed is the Nefaramu mentioned in the daposition by Raromia, the husband of the murdered woman, as having stood by Gului with a Winchester rifle while Gului committed the murder. It is fortunate that a number of women and children were not hit as the shooting was in the midst of the houses. The shooting lasted only a matter of seconds and the police fire on the whole must have been well directed.

From Solomon Islands National Archive Resd.Commr.No.17 1919

Why Gulu'i failed

Ngunu, a descendant of the Na'osi people, dictated these comments on the raid in 1983, explaining how their defence failed because of another incident of ritual defilement.

Bell killed us because of this: they'd defiled the home, the women's seclusion house burnt and it smoked into the home, so that there was no protection for our family. When they shot up the home my grandfathers Oda, Gulu'i and Areta'ingwane wanted to fight, they wanted to shoot, but it was hard to do because the ghost abandoned our family. So it was they killed us in the home at Na'oasi, as a result of this.

Translated from Kwara'ae

Malaitan men discussing guns. This photograph was probably taken in central Malaita by the missionary Northcote Deck, within a few years of the raid on Na'oasi. The unusual two-storey house is reminiscent of the one at Na'oasi where the boy Tua was killed.
From *Pearls from the Pacific* by Florence Young, 1925, facing page 46

Etangilana ofotalana fanoa 'i Malaita nai. Sa Misita Belo ne'e dao, ka ofota, nia ne'e kira eta go'o 'i Na'oasi. Sa Gulu'i tafi ka teo saena kilukilua burina bobo 'ai. Sa Misita Belo saka go'o, nia ka kwa'ia ta fa'i maelo, ta fa'i unasisi go'o, ka mae. Ka kwa'ia ta fa'i ai ka mae, kwa'ia ta fa'i ai ka mae. Ka dangulua go'o fa'i bolo ka dūrua go'o ururuna ta solodia, ka kwa'ia ta fa'i ai. Kira 'olonga'i kwanga ma nia toli sa kilu. Ka kwa'ia ta fa'i ai, ka 'uri "Bo'obo'osi 'aemu ne'e" ana ta solodia, kira ka tafi na'a nai. Leleka kira dao ka tua lo'oba 'i māna uafa, kira ka tua ka leleka rō bongi kī ka sui ūla bongi, solodia ka ra'e 'i Ma'usunga. Ra'e 'uana sa Si'au, ne'e kira saea 'ania sa Iro'ima. Nia saungia ngela sa ma'a nau Una, sa Lao, maelana sa Maelisua.

Sa Manibili tata'e ka ra'e na'a, solodia ra'e na'a. Ra'e kira ka donga 'i Tatalimara, kira ka saka 'i Ngwa'angwa'afoloa, kira ka oli ma'i kira ka alasida 'i to'oba 'i fanoa sa 'Ima lala 'i Ludangwanole, 'i Ma'usunga, ka noa'a. Kira 'are'areta'inia, go'o sa Si'au ka tata'e ka 'aga kwanga ka "'U!" tafi go'o nai, kira ka dao ka alasia fanoa 'o'ō lōri. Fu'anga'a lōri ka leka. Sa Ko'oūa dao ka fu'a na'a, ngela kini nia 'i Ngwasa ka dao ka fu'a na'a, sa Kuru ka dao ka fu'a na'a. Fu'alia tala'i solodia lōri, kira fu'alia sa Misita Belo. Ngela kini nai'ari 'i Ngwasa ka agā sa Misita Belo ka to'osia saena gwa'i kunu gwata, ne'e ki saea 'ania kunu sa Belo teo go'o 'ana nini'ari.

Sa Ra'ua ne'e mae, sa Sausaungia ka mae ana rodo nai'ari. Sa Sausaungia ne'e mae ka teo 'i fera. Sa Ra'ua ne'e alua sa Timana Mangeo, Timana ne'e alua sa ngwane'e Maelekisi, nia fū mae kira ka 'afua ka teo saena luma. Solodia kī ka ladafida go'o 'i nai'ari, kira ka fu'alia te'a sa Timana 'i Robolaungia fa'inia ngwa'i. Kira ka bulia kelasia 'afu'afu'a fuiri, kira ka laua ngwa'i ana te'a sa Timana kira ka tafi fa'inia.

'O'a fuiri ka angi go'o nai, 'Ere'ere koso go'o 'i lo'oba 'i Gwaunafauango, kira ka 'olonga'i, kira ka 'uri "Maelada nini 'i ne'e. Kira oli kira ka liu 'i ne'e ta'ena ma kulu olonga'inia na'a umu ne'e ada." Kira ka 'uia umu kī ka teo ma'akwalia solodia ne'e kira ra'e 'uana 'i 'Ere'ere.

This was the beginning of subduing the country of Malaita. Mr Bell came and subdued it, and this is how they began at Na'oasi. Gulu'i fled and lay in a hole behind a log of wood. Mr Bell came out, he fired a bullet, a winchester bullet, it was dead. He fired another, it was dead, fired another, it was dead. He let off a bullet and it dislocated a soldier's knee, he fired another one. They readied their guns but he was down in the hole. He fired another and said "That's for the calf of your leg" to a soldier, and they fled. Eventually they came and stayed down at the wharf, they stayed for two days and then on the third day the soldiers went up to Ma'usunga. They went up for Si'au, who was called Iro'ima. He'd killed the son of my father Una, Lao, for the death of Maelisua.

Manibili set out and went up and the soldiers went up. Going up, they followed the Tatalimara [stream], they came out at Ngwa'a-ngwa'afoloa, they came back and ambushed them up at 'Ima's home at Ludangwanole, at Ma'usunga, but no. They called out for him, then Si'au got up and shouldered his gun and "Hup!" he fled, they arrived and ambushed the empty home. There was fighting. Ko'ou'a came and fought, his daughter Ngwasa came and fought, Kuru came and fought. They fought all the soldiers and fought Mr Bell. That girl Ngwasa grasped Mr Bell and threw him into the pig swamp, which they still call Bell's swamp even to this day.

Ra'ua was dead and Sausaungia died that night. Sausaungia was dead and lay in the sanctum. The Ra'ua who begot Timana Mangeo, the Timana who begot that man Maelekisi, it was he who died and they bundled him up to lie in the house. The soldiers forced their way in there, they fought Timana's mother Robolaungia for a bag [of shell-money]. They kicked over the bundle, they seized the bag from Timana's mother and fled with it.

The gong cried out and the 'Ere'eres came down over at Gwaunafauango, they made ready and said "This is where they die." When they return and pass here today we'll have these stones ready for them." They threw together stones and lay in wait for the soldiers who'd gone up to 'Ere'ere.

The raid on Ma'usuunga

The second paragraph of Bell's report, on his pursuit of Gulu'i to Ma'usunga in 'Ere'ere, is less informative.

Sia'au Iro'ima of 'Ere'ere, who Gului was said to be staying with, was the warrior who had led the attack on Gwagwaofilu over the sorcery accusation, and his people were formidable opponents of the government. Maybe Bell did not report his confrontation with them because they got the better of him, or because of the misbehaviour of his police.

Although both Gulu'i and Iro'ima escaped this time, Bell returned six months later and arrested Gulu'i without trouble. He found Iro'ima dying of sickness, probably a victim of the global influenza epidemic.

2. I remained at Kwai for several days and endeavoured to find out the whereabouts of Gului. It was reported that he had gone to the village of Mausunga to live with a man named Eroema who had quite recently committed a murder. I left Kwai and two days later returned in the night. I made a patrol to Mausunga the following morning but but did not find any one that I wanted. The people I saw said that Gului had never been there and that Eroema had not slept in the village since he heard of the visit of the police to Nauasi. There had been rumours of traps and an ambush prepared for the police, but we encountered neither nor did we see any signs of hostile natives.

I have the honour to be,

Sir,

Your most obedient servant,

District Officer

From Solomon Islands National Archives, Residt Commr. No.17/1919

John Langi of 'Ere'ere heard about Bell's raid on Ma'usunga from his father, who heard it from his own father, Iro'ima's son Kwa'ilalamua. Langi dictated the story in 1999.

John Langi, great-grandson of the warrior Iro'ima, 1999.

Iro'ima was in our clan at 'Ere'ere, where the main clan which I'm descended from is called Dilikwanga. ... Well, it was Manibili, grandfather of Billy Toina, who brought the soldiers and Mr Bell. They wanted to go up and kill Iro'ima, because Iro'ima, even after the law had arrived, he went on to burn a village at Fiu, on the Kwaibaita river. He burnt a whole village up at Tasisi in Kwaio, then burnt a whole village there, then came back and was hiding up at Ma'usunga, inside a palisade. Well, a few days after the killing, Manibili brought the police, but heard rumours that they were waiting to attack them. Manibili said, "We won't follow the stream, lest when we get up there, they kill us." Because he'd already heard the news. "We must go round up above Anofiu, climb up and eventually we'll come down and we'll look down on Ma'usunga. That's the easiest way for us to track down this man." But that day, as they'd told him, everyone was ready down at Nangananga Pool, along the A'arai stream, with stones, spears and guns.

They arrived above Ma'usunga and took hold of the women in the village there, one woman fought with the policeman, and they took a package of money which contained all the red shell-money of the clan. Then they burnt all the houses, but Iro'ima was down in the palisade, pointing his gun, he wanted to shoot that man Mr Bell. But the two or three men with him stopped him. Kwa'ilalamua said "Father, don't kill this man." So Iro'ima broke through the palisade, went down into the bamboos and broke the bamboos and went down into the stream and ran away up to 'Ere'ere and hid in a cave called Sisila and stayed there. They put up a reward for them to kill him, but it was difficult and eventually he died of a cold, pneumonia, he died there. His gun and club, they'd put enemy-magic on the club, they remain until the present, with Sosoke at Taba'akwaru.

Translated from Pijin

To'a fuiri ka bōfolo 'i fu'uba, sa Manibili ka ba'ea ngwa'i 'afe fuiri ma ngwa'i kini fuiri, kira ka tata'e 'ofodangi. Leleka kira ka ra'e lala 'i 'Aimela kira ka gwalinga 'i Ngongora, kira ka saka lala 'i fu'uba 'i sakalana ta'i tala 'i 'Ere'ere 'i fu'uba 'i Darifaubako. Leka na'a fa'inia sa Ū'a, ka leka na'a fa'inia sa Kwa'ioloa, ka leka na'a fa'inia sa Kuru. Kira leleka kira ka kwatea 'aeda saena bauta kira ka fi'i oli. Oli kira ka ra'e kwau 'i Latea kira ka dao, ko'o nau ne'e kero'o tua, ko'o nau sa Fiu'adi nia ngwaro na'a. Sa Ū'a dao go'o ka 'uri "Fiu'adi 'ae! Nau ku maemae ma 'oko rongo nau na'a. Solodia ngalingali nau ka dao 'i fafona asi ku fi'i oli ma'i ku ra'e." Ko'o nau fi'i 'arefo logo 'ana.

Nai'i lō ne'e dao ka lomota fanoa kia nai, ka fonea saungwae'a. Kira lisia mala ne'e mae leka 'i Na'oasi, kira fi'i ma'u. Buri'ana nia ka ra'e 'i Lama, ka 'uia ulu ngwae kī, sa Dausabea, sa Kisita, sa ngwae ne'e Refo. Ofotā na'a fanoa 'i Malaita kira ka ma'u sulia kisi saungia na'a ta ngwae nai. 'Una'ari mala sa Misita Belo ka fi'i dao 'i Faumamanu, fuana sa Manibili. Dao 'unari sa Manibili fi'i gania fu tuatua 'i Gwaubusu, ra'e ma'i ka fulia fanoa 'i nai'ari nini 'i Faumamanu, nia gania ana to'a 'i Fairū. Sa Sausaungia, ngwa'i to'a ne'e nia ganida nari mae na'a, sa Kalakini, sa Ata'i, sa ngwane'e Busuka, sa Arasimae, sa Sili'ota, sa So'ofia. Kira ka ala 'ania fuana nia fi'i oli ka tua la'u 'i Faumamanu. Tua ka fi'i etangia na'a fera 'i kanaselo ka fi'i fulia 'i Faumamanu. Nia fulia 'una'ari ma nau ku doe na'a. Go'o, buri'ana nau ku leka na'a ana faka, nau ku leka ku tua ma'i 'i Katere sulia fai fa'i ngali kī.

Leleka nau ku dao fera 'i kanaselo ka fi'i fuli. Nau ku dao 'i ne'e, nau'a ne'e ku etangia diasa'anga ana sa Misita Belo 'i Faumamanu. Du'ungana sa Fafo'i, saka ana 'i Fusiga, kini 'i Fairū, nia rata'ia to'a 'i Funilofo fa'inia kakamo 'i Alakwailiu. Kira ka fu'a fa'inia ka leleka ka rodo, ala'anga ka ra'e 'i Malanga, ma'a nau fa'ida kira ka 'uri "'Oko koso toli ko fadā go'o." Nau ku koso fuana sa Misita Belo, ma ngwae kwa'i ngwae mala.

While those people laid it out down there, Manibili summoned a group of women and a group of girls and they set out in the morning. Eventually they went up to 'Aimela instead and reached the top at Ngongora, they emerged down at the end of the 'Ere'ere path down at Darifaubako. They went with U'a, went with Kwa'ioloa, went with Kuru. They went and set foot in the boat and then returned. Returning, they went up to Latea and when they arrived my grandfather and I were there, my old grandfather Fiu'adi. U'a arrived and said "Oh Fiu'adi! I was good as dead, but listen to me. The soldiers took me to the sea-side and I returned and came up." My grandfather was astonished.[1]

That's how the law came and spread over our country and stopped the killing. When they'd seen death come to Na'oasi, then they were afraid. Afterwards he went up to Lama and shot three men, Dausabea, Kisita and that man Refo. Subdued the country of Malaita, they were afraid and wouldn't kill anyone. So it was that Mr Bell then came to Faumamanu for Manibili. When he came Manibili asked, while living at Gwaubusu, to come up and make a home there at Faumamanu, he asked the people of Fairū. Sausaungia and the group of people he asked are now dead, Kalakini, Ata'i, that man Busuka, Arasimae, Sili'ota and So'ofia. They allowed him to return and live at Faumamanu again. He then started the Council house and founded Faumamanu. He founded all this when I was already big. It was after I'd been abroad, I'd been to stay at Gatere for four years.

Eventually I arrived and the Council house was founded. When I arrived here, it was I who began the judgments of Mr Bell at Faumamanu. It was because Fafo'i, born of Fusiga, a girl from Fairū, he disputed the Funilofo people over the swamp-taro at Alakwailiu. They fought over it until night, a message went up to Malanga and my father and others said "You go down there and explain it." I went down for Mr Bell, a real man-beater.

1 Kuru and Ko'ou'a (apparently a namesake of Alasa'a's great-grandfather) who had fought the police, and Kwa'ioloa (one of Alasa'a's 'fathers') were evidently taken as prisoners or hostages.

The raid on Lama

The killing of three men who resisted arrest in 1919 at Lama, near Mount Alasa'a in south-central Kwara'ae, including the notorious warrior Kisita, seems to have confirmed the effect of the police raid on Nao'asi. (The reward collection described by Osifera on page 71 was another consequence of this incident.)

A letter from William Bell to the Resident Commissioner gives some background to this raid.

BRITISH SOLOMON ISLANDS PROTECTORATE.

A U K I. 19th.MAY 1919.

Sir

I have the honour to report that there is now no doubt that the three runaway prisoners from Tulagi named Maisala, Suiasi and Kesita returned to Malaita about three months ago. There was much talk among the natives concerning their return about that time but the reports differed so much that I did not feel certain that they had returned.

2. I presume I am at liberty to take the police inland to try and arrest any of them if there is a favourable opportunity without any preliminary measures. They belon to the same community as Otea who recently committed a murder, vide my letter No.4 of the 6th.of February. I am also informed that they belong to the same clan as Gului and the Ereere people, so there is a pretty tough lot in a small area which is directly across the island from the Government Station. There has been a great deal of boastful and impudent talk from that part during the last few months, most of it undoubtably with the object of intimidating other natives to try and prevent them assisting the Government. The are well informed of my movements from somewhere, probably one of their countrymen at the Mission villages close by here is responsible for

From Solomon Islands National Archives, Residt. Commr. No.22/1919

Local government

As part of Bell's programme of colonial government, East Kwara'ae and the neighbouring islands of the sea people became the administrative sub-District of Kwai. In 1922 he formally appointed Bejamin Manibili, who had guided the raids on Na'oasi, Ma'usunga and Lama, as the first government Headman of Kwai.

The Council house which Manibili founded at Faumamanu, also known as the Court house and Tax house, was where government officers conducted business on tours around Malaita. The dispute over the swamp taro at Alakwailiu was typical of their work to resolve the kind of conflicts which so often led to feuds, as shown by Alasa'a's history.

The Fairū senior men whom Alasa'a lists as giving permission for the Council house are those who allowed Keret to be built in the same place in 1906. In describing these demonstrations of leadership for the land, Alasa'a was no doubt thinking of his dispute with Ramo'itolo of Latea over the land at Faumamanu (see page 81).

This photograph shows District Officer Ronald Garvey at work in the sub-District immediately to the south of Kwai in 1928. It is labelled:

Taking the native tax at Uru just one year to the day after Bell & Lillies had been murdered by these natives kinsmen about 1½ miles from RHG.

This is much as Bell would have appeared to Alasa'a at Faumamanu a few years earlier.

From British Museum Ethnography Dept. pictorial collection, with thanks to Lady Patricia Garvey

Sa Manibili lisi nau go'o ka 'uri "Lae ma'i, lae ma'i. To'a baera kira 'iri koso ma'i? Ngwa'i fataābu ne'e kira teo gwari ka dangi na'a, ki diasimi kakamo lōri." Nau ku, "Noa'a, ta'i nau'a go'o." Go'o nau ku ala'a 'i sulia. "Iu, kakamo noa'a la'u rū to'a Fairū, ka noa'a la'u rū to'a 'i 'Ere'ere, ka noa'a la'u to'a Funilofo, rū ngwae liu alua nini, sa Kwalaingwa nini'a, fasia kakamo ne'e." Go'o sa Misita Belo ka 'uri, "'Ae 'ira ma, nia fa'uta?" Nau ku 'uri "Nia fasia fuana ta ngwae fiolo ka liu, ke 'ilia ke do'ofia ka 'ania. Noa'a la'u rū ulu fū'ingwae na'ikiri." Go'o sa Misita Belo ka 'uri "'Ira ma sa ta'i ne'e ke ngalia?" Go'o nau ku 'uri "'Ere'ere ne'e ke tabu 'afia", go'o nia ka 'uri "'Ira rū to'a 'i 'Ere'ere." Nau ku etangia diasimi go'o nai. 'Una'ari sa Misita Belo ka 'uri aku "'Oke tua, 'oko daua kanaselo sa Manibili ka hetman". Go'o nau ku 'uri "'Oke foli nau?" Go'o nia ka 'uri "'Ae noa'a". Go'o nau ku 'aila, ruana nau ku oli ana faka.

Isitatalana ra'o na'i, kira saungia sa Misita Belo, sa Binkofo nau ku etangia na'a, nau ku sifi na'a. 'Una'ari ka leka ana sa Misita Sada, nau ku sifi na'a, ka leka ana sa Fosta nau ku sifi na'a, ka leka ana sa Adisina nau ku sifi na'a, ka dao ana sa Kokorolo nau ku mango. Nia nai nau ku ū na'a ma'i 'ua ku sai na'a ana rū kī 'i fanoa kia. Aia'a, nau ku te'ete'e nau ku 'ania 'uligwata ana fo'oa, nau ku lisia na'a ngwae saungi'a, nia nai nau ku ala'a saena kasete nini ngela nai ta'ena, fuana ne'e ta ngwae ke lisia ka rongoa ka 'uri, "Ma'a nau ne'e eta ū, ma'a nau nini'a 'ua." Na ku oli logo 'uana kasatomo nai 'i Kwasibu, fuana nai ūa 'ani fanoa nai ka ū. Lō rū nai na'a, gafamanu ne'e dau na'a fafi nau, bore falafala nai ke liu logo 'ana, gafamanu ka lia fāfi nau. Fatalaku dao na'a 'unari ana so'olafi ne'e. * * *

Manibili saw me and said "Come here, come here. Aren't those people coming down? That group of tabu-speakers who lie in the cold till day while we judge that swamp-taro." I said "No, there's only me." Then I talked about it. "Yes, the swamp-taro doesn't belong either to the Fairū people or to the 'Ere'ere people, or to the Funilofo people, its something a passer-by put there, it was Kwalaingwa who planted the swamp-taro." Then Mr Bell said "Well if so, what then?" I said "He planted it for any hungry person passing by to dig and roast and eat. It doesn't belong to these three clans." Then Mr Bell said "So then, who is to get it?" Then I said "The 'Ere'eres clear around it," and he said "So it belongs to the people of 'Ere'ere." I'd started judging. So then Mr Bell said to me "You stay and hold the council of Manibili, the headman". Then I said "Will you pay me?" Then he said "Not you." Then I declined, and for the second time I returned abroad.

That was the start of my work, they killed Mr Bell and with Bincock I began to be a chief. So then, going on to Mr Sanders I was a chief, going on to Foster I was a chief, going on to Anderson I was a chief, and when it came to Cockeral I left off. So I'm still here and I know all about our country. Well, when I was small I ate pig-flesh from rewards, I saw people killed, and that's why I'm talking into my son's cassette today, so that if anyone sees or hears it he can say "My father was here first, and this is my father." I'll also return to my custom work at Kwasibu, so that I can maintain my homeland with it. The law belongs to me and the government holds on to me, but my tradition will go on and government watches over me. That's as far as my talk goes this evening. * * *

The achievements of William Bell

Bell's biography and his death are documented by Roger Keesing and Peter Corris in their book *Lightning Meets the West Wind* (1980). They make this comment on his achievements just before the Na'oasi raid.

Bell, by 1918, had begun to command a respect no European had ever won from the Malaitans. In the north around Malu'u and Bita'ama, in Kwara'ae and Langalanga along the west coast, and even along the south-western coast among the feared 'Are'are, Bell had begun to be a presence to be reckoned with. To the Malaitans, he was 'Misa Bello', tough, respected, increasingly feared by the strong as he was turned to by the weak and aggrieved. But most of the mountainous interior, and most of the eastern coast, almost out of reach of Bell's twenty-foot whaleboat, remained sovereign and defiant.

From *Lightning Meets the West Wind* by Roger Keesing & Peter Corris, 1980, page 65

Memories of Mr Bell

Silas Sangafanoa remembered meeting William Bell, and in 1987 he dictated some personal impressions of his work.

I saw him, he was always around and sometimes at 'Aoke he had a white jacket and white trousers too, he'd have a walking stick, and a pair of glasses. . . . Mr Bell's way was like this. If he was holding court he didn't want a man to look away, you had to look him straight in the eye before you could come to court.

Formerly with us there were rough men in the bush, they were rough and muscular. And when Mr Bell recruited police, it was rough police he recruited. Because when they heard of a killing inland, it took all their strength to go, the police were strong men. Well, his recruits, Mr Bell had to feel the man's arm or feel his body and he had to be muscular before he could be in the police. Because there were musclemen elsewhere and they were bad lads. At present we see children in the police, but not formerly. When the police began, formerly, they still looked like the wild forest which we cut down in the inland. Mr Bell would knock them down, it was his way to strike like that. That's how they viewed him. When he spoke he wouldn't talk kindly to anyone, he was really very hard.

Well, first of all he made laws, built roads and things, and maybe taxes too. The two things I think he died from were roads and taxes. Because for all the pagans before it was tabu, they wouldn't follow a road. Roads were for women to walk on. But at that time he said to make a road around the coast, called a government road. Some of the men from the inland had to come down and build it. The chiefs looked after the road, and the headmen. When it came to the day for building the road, well they'd call the chiefs in the inland, "Alright, everyone must come down."

Well, even when he visited the plantations, he'd go for the whitemen too. Eh, if you didn't treat people well, the labourers, or you didn't give them good food and we labourers reported the damage as his visit came round, he'd strike the master. He'd say "Why aren't you treating the boys well, with food to make them strong for work, for hard work?"

I'm one who liked him. I liked him for this; he came and made the place quiet and safe, and he came and made the people start to increase as at present. He said "You people, civil war must end." That's what I liked. If he hadn't come and the law with him, eh, there'd be no people now. We're not plentiful in Solomon Islands.

Translated from Pijin

The death of Bell

In 1927 Bell, his white deputy and thirteen police were killed at Sinalaagu in Kwaio, along the coast from East Kwara'ae. Their Kwaio attackers were objecting to government, and particularly to recently imposed taxes. Joe Ngwaki of 'Ere'ere, a one-time Christian at Keret, had attempted to do the same thing at Faumamanu a year earlier but was overpowered by the police.

The government's brutal retaliation on the Kwaio for Bell's death put a conclusive end to anti-colonial resistance throughout Malaita.

6

Ta 'Ala'anga La'u sulia Kasatomo

Nau ku kwa'i sulia doelaku, kwa'i sulia lekalaku, nini'a nau ku saea ta'ena. Nini nau ku sai ana rū nai'ari kī, tala 'i ngwae 'i nini'ari kira kinā na'a. Nau ku daua kasatomo, leleka nau ku leka ana lō, nau ana sukulu, ta'ena. Na ne'e nau ku 'ala'a ana.

Io, ta 'ala'anga la'u, nau ku te'ete'e nau ku 'iri rongo lili ana ma'a nau fa'inia te'a nau, du'ungana kasatomo ne'e saea. Di'ia nau ku taigere ana ma'a nau fa'inia te'a nau, nau ngwae ta'a go'o. Noaima nau ku aburongo ana ma'a nau fa'inia te'a nau ku lae kwailiu go'o 'aku, kira saungi nau na'a. 'I ta'ena nau ku lisi kaumulu ko'o nau kī, kira su'ungenge ana ma'a kira kī fa'inia te'a kira kī. Ma'a nia fata bore nia nangata'i gwau ka liu na'a. Du'ungana ta tae nini? Ana faka ne'e 'uri. Kasatomo nia 'ato, to'o ta'i ngwae kesi leka liana, to'o ta'i ngwae kesi ro'o 'i ngwae, to'o ta'i ngwae kesi ulu suli tai. 'Oko ulu sulia ta ngwae, 'oko leleka kira ka saungi'o, noiama 'oko 'aila 'ania fatalana ma'a 'oe, 'ae'o ngwae siroro go'o. Aia'a, ka faita'inia ma'i 'i ta'ena, kaela ngwae nini'ari ma kaela kini 'i nini'ari, ma'a kira ke fata kira ka nangata'inia gwauda kira ka liu lala ana ta kula. Te'a nia ka fata nia kesi gerea go'o.

Aia'a, saena sukulu ka 'uri logo, god ne'e fatalana 'uri "'Oke rongo sulia ma'a ma te'a 'oe, ngwaefuta 'oe kī, 'oke ro'o sulia fatalaku. 'Oko 'iri lisi nau, fatalaku go'o ne'e 'oko rongo, bore ma ngwae 'oko lisia di'ia 'oko su'ungenge ana ma 'oko su'ungenge logo aku. 'Oko 'aila si rongoa fatalada ma 'okesi donga ala'anga kira kī, ma nau'a bore noa'a logo, si ne'e 'oko rongo nau go'o. Ta'ena ta kini, ta ngwae, kira 'iri ro'o go'o sulia ma'a kira kī ma te'a kira kī. Ka leleka ka nia go'o ana ko'o nau fa'ida ne'e. Lisia, nia ne'e nau ku saea go'o 'i ta'ena. Ai nini'a 'afe kwau ma ngela nai ka fata sulia ma nau ku ofota fata-lana ka leleka ka gwari ne'e, nia su'ungenge ka 'afe akala'i fau. Ngela ne'e ka su'ubota ka 'uri "Nai sasia rū 'uri," nau ku "Noa'a, koro sukulu na'a, koro na'a saena lō. Safa'i ala'a sulia. 'Oko su'ubota ta ma mae ne'ana." Leleka nini'a ka gwari. Sulia ne'e su'ungenge logo aku ka su'u-ngenge logo ana ngela nau, ka fata ka ridi saena sulina, nini'a nia kesi ro'o sulia fatalana ma'a nia ka 'afe kwau. Noa'a kira kesi folia 'ua nai.

6

A Further Talk about Custom

I've related my growing up, related my travels, that's what I've told today. That's why I understand things which the present generation are ignorant of. I held to custom, later on I went to the law, and I belong to the mission, today. That's what I'm talking about.

Yes, a further talk, when I was small I didn't disobey my father and my mother, because of what the custom says. If I don't care about my father and my mother, I'm just a bad person. Or if I don't listen to my father and my mother and I wander about on my own, I'll be killed. Today I see all of you, my grandchildren, resisting their fathers and their mothers. His father speaks but he shakes his head and wanders off. What's the reason? That's like abroad. Custom is difficult, an individual can't do as he likes, an individual can't obey just anyone, an individual can't be persuaded by whoever. If you're persuaded by just anyone and you go on, you'll be killed, or if you reject your father's words, you'll be a pauper. Well, it applies today, small boys and small girls at present, their fathers speak but they shake their heads and wander off somewhere. His mother speaks and he doesn't care.

Well, it's the same as in the mission, god's word says "If you obey your father and mother, your relatives, you'll be obeying my words. You can't see me, you just hear my words, but with a person you can see, if you resist him you also resist me. If you refuse to listen to their words and don't follow what they say, I'm denied too, because it's only me you're hearing." Today some girls and boys don't obey their fathers and their mothers. Eventually it's come to be my grandchildren. Look, this is what I'm saying today. There's the one who married away and my son spoke out about it and I calmed him down until he cooled off, she insisted on marrying, ten times. My son was forceful and said "I'll do so-and-so," I said "No, we're in the mission now, under the law. Talk it over calmly. If you force it there'll be a feud." Eventually he cooled off. Because she resisted me in resisting my son, he spoke and it slid off her back, so she didn't obey her father's words and married away. They still haven't paid [bridewealth] for her.

A Christian conclusion

Alasa'a concluded one of his recorded talks with a family counselling session on traditional values, which provides an appropriate conclusion to his book. His call for obedience and chastity probably echoes the concerns of Kwara'ae elders for many generations past. As he says, and his own stories show, formerly people who ignored such teachings risked being killed for their misbehaviour. Alasa'a makes it clear that he endorses the government law and Christian religion which put an end to such killing, so it is rather ironic that these developments also removed the ultimate sanctions for parental authority and sexual morality.

As Alasa'a says, he was brought up in the religion of his ancestral ghosts, 'praying to bones'. He joined the church some time in the 1940s, after the ghosts had failed to prevent the deaths of four of his children. But he was not always firm in his Christian faith and, as he says, he reverted to using the power of ghosts, or 'satan' as a warrior (*ramo*). Like most Kwara'ae Christians, including his sons, Alasa'a was pulled by the ups and downs of life between Christianity and the religion of his ancestors, changing his allegiance several times during his life.

There is no doubt that Alasa'a continued to believe in the power of the ghosts, who he so graphically evokes in the image of Satan as an old-time Kwara'ae warrior. But in his last years he seems to have accepted the superior power of God. His chronicle ends with a prayer to the deity which, as he says, his ancient ancestors originally worshipped when they first arrived in Malaita.

*A fine SSEM church of the early 20th century, in the style of the Kwara'ae 'patterned sanctum' (*fera gwaroa*) sometimes built as a shrine for the ancestral ghosts.*
From the SSEM archive, precise date and place unknown

Rū nau ku saea fuana ngela ngwane ne'e kī, "'Oko kwaikwaila'i gwau ko fulia rū ma ma'a 'oe go'o na'a. 'Ae fasi 'oke sasi ne'e noa'a go'o. 'Unari 'oke ro'o go'o sulia ma'a 'oe fa'inia te'a 'oe, 'i 'oke alua ngwae, ma 'oko le'a. Di'ia 'oko ro'o sulia ma'a 'oe fa'inia te'a 'oe 'i 'oke la'u. 'Oko rongo lili ke leleka, nau ku 'iri sai amu. Fa'amanata'anga 'i na'o, ko'o nau fa'inia ma'a nau kera'a fata 'uri, "Nia ke dangi nau ku fa'amanata 'ofodangi. Asoa ne'e, ta ngwae 'oko gonia titiu 'oe, ta kini 'oko gogonia titiu 'oe. Ngwae 'oko dauta'a sulia titiu 'oe, kira kwa'ia dikoa na'a ta'ena. Kini 'oko dauta'a sulia titiu 'oe nia agwa'i na'a ta'ena, sulia kira ke 'usu ana nai." Nini'a ne'e nau ku tua ku fa'amanata 'ania ta'ena. Nau ku maemae, kaulu kaela ngwae ne'e mulu ke ro'o sulia ma'a kaumulu kī, 'i ne'e 'oko le'a. 'Oko taigere ke leleka 'oko fa'alia rū ta ngwae, ma'a 'oe ne'e ke ru'u ana, 'oe noa'a go'o. 'Oko ro'o ngwae ka leleka 'oko usu ana kini ta ngwae, ma'a 'oe ne'e ke ru'u ana, 'ae'o ne'e noa'a go'o, nia'a ne'e ke fa'alirū. Fatalaku nai, nau ku fa'amanata na'a nini.

Nau ku fa'amanata sulia kastomo ne'e ngwae kira ke ro'o sulia te'a nia ma ma'a nia ma ngwaefuta nia kī, ka tata'e ke leka o'o fa'inida nia kesi leka olobauta. Bore ma 'i ta'ena ana sukulu ne'e, nau ku fa'amanata sulia god saea ne'e ngwae kī ke ro'o sulia te'a nia ma ma'a nia ma ngwaefuta nia kī, kira fi'i ro'o sulia fatalana god. Fasi fatalana god ne'e 'oke ro'o go'o sulia, noa'a. God fadā na'a, "'Oke ro'o sulia ma'a 'oe, ngwaefuta 'oe, te'a 'oe, 'oko fi'i ro'o sulia fatalaku. Fatalaku 'oko rongoa go'o. Di'ia 'okesi ro'o sulia fatalana ma'a 'oe, te'a 'oe ma ngwaefuta 'oe kī, ngwae ne'e 'oko lisida ma kira ka ala'a fuamu, ta ma 'okesi ro'o logo sulia fatalaku." Ala'anga nau ku fa'amanata 'ani'i fāfia ala'anga nini nau ku sae'e ana so'olafi ne'e nini'a. Ta ne'e nau ku fa'asia ngela nau kī ma ko'o nau kī ku oli 'uana 'i Malaita, nau ku maemae ma kastomo nai nau ku fa'amanata ana. Kastomo nai nau ku ala'a sulia ta'ena, rū fuli kī. Ita ma'i ka leleka nau ku ngwaro na'a, fatalaku dao 'unari ka sui. * * *

Bubunga nau eta 'ania god, ta'ena akalo ka fa'alia. God ka dao go'o ka dadā la'u go'o. Kōgwata'a ke noa'a na'a, noa'a kisi kōngia na'a ta gwata nini'ari. Kaida'i nia teo ana fanoa ne'e, saitana ka dao 'i saena. Saetana ka fo'osae

What I say to the boys is, you toss your head and start something, but it's up to your father. If it's you doing it, you can't. So then, obey your father and your mother, so you'll have sons and be alright. If you obey your father and your mother, you'll be safe. If you go on disobeying I don't know what will become of you. In teaching formerly, my grandfather and my father said "Your day is coming and I'm teaching in the morning. In the daytime, as a man, safeguard your virtue, as a girl, safeguard your virtue. As a man, if you mishandle your virtue, they'll strike and smash you presently. As a girl, if you mishandle your virtue, it will fall away presently, because they'll fornicate with you." That's what I'm here to teach about at present. When I'm dead, you children who obey your fathers, you'll do well. If you don't care and eventually you damage some-one's belongings, your father will have to deal with it, not you. If you obey someone else until you fornicate with someone else's girl, your father will have to deal with it, not you, and it's he who'll be damaged. Those are my words, that's what I'm teaching.

I'm teaching about the custom that people obey their mother and father and relatives, they set out and go to work with them and don't wander about. But today, with the mission, I teach how god says that if people obey their mother and father and relatives, they'll be obeying the word of god. It's not just the word of god you're obeying. God has explained, "Obey your father, your relatives, your mother, then you'll be obeying my words. Just listen to my words. If you don't obey the word of your father, your mother and your relatives, people who you can see and who talk to you, then you are not obeying my word either." I'm teaching about this on top of the talk that I gave this evening. So I'm leaving my sons and my grandchildren and I'm returning to Malaita, and if I die I'll have taught about my custom. I've talked about my custom today, things which happened. From the start until I'm old, that's where my talk has come to. * * *

My island began with god, today ghosts have spoiled it. God came and levelled it out again. Pig-baking is no more now, we don't bake pigs at present. While he was in this country, satan came in. Satan girded on his 'ania fo'osae gwaroa nia, ka felesia fofo sima nia, ka fa'ā ngwa'i faolo nia, ka fasira'i ana fa'i ua ne'e ta 'o'a ka angi. Ta linga 'i ākoa. Ka fasira'i ka ra'e ana ta fa'i ua, ta mafula ka gafu. Ka leleka fanoa ne'e ka funi'ai'a 'i nai god ne'e mamana liu fuakulu.

Nini'ari 'ae'o ngwae, 'ae'o kini, 'oke manamanata'a go'o. Kadi kaida'i 'i na'o 'oko dauta'a kira saungi'o na'a, 'oko dauta'a suli'o 'oko ina sala go'o, ngwae 'oko dauta'a suli'o 'oko usu. Nia nai nau ku ala'a saena kaset ne'e, nau ku 'ita ku tua ma'i ka leleka ka dao 'i ta'ena, sataku 'iri fū fa'inia ne'e nai 'usu ana 'afe ta ngwae, ma nau ku fa'ainā kini ta ngwae. Nau ku galia fanoa ne 'i Honiara nau ku tuafia ka leleka ka dao 'i ta'ena, nia ne nau ku ala'a 'i saena kaset nini ngela nau fuana nau oli na'a. Nau ku oli ku tua ku maemae saena fanoa nau. Nau ku saea ne'e nau ku tua tau na'a, ala'anga nai ana so'olafi ne'e ne, nau nini'a farere nai oli na'a fa'asia ngela nai. Nau ku fa'ada, kira ka tua 'i ne'e saena fū'ingwae nai, saena tua'a nai nia 'i ne'e nau ku oli ku inamae'a na'a 'aku, saena bubunga nau. Nau ku oli ana kastomo, fuana nai ta'ea. Ta ngwae 'oko rongoa 'oko dao, ngalia ngwae 'oe, fata sulia fanoa 'oe, 'i ke saga. Ala'anga nai ne'e dao 'unari.

Nau ku fa'ala'ua na'a fatalaku 'ani god, nai fo'o na'a. O god eternal father, god almighty, nau ku tage'o'ana 'ae'o du'ungana god na ma'a, god na ngela ma go na ano'irū. Ngela 'oe sa Jesus nia koso ma'i ka mae fuaku ana 'ai faifolo. Nia ka olita'i nau ma'i ta'ena nau ku kuru saena 'abuna, ana 'ai faifolo 'oe. Nau ku saele'a liu nau ku ti'iti'i ma'i nau ku fo'osia suli. Nau ku ngali'o sa Jesus sulia fai fa'i ngali kī nau ku dao sa Saitana ka ma'u 'ani nau, nau ku ramo 'ani. Nau ku tua 'ani ka leleka nia ka olita'i nau ma'i fani ngela nau kī, ta'ena nau ku 'inamae'a. God ngalia 'afe nai fa'asi nau, nau ku inamae ka dao 'i ta'ena. Nau ku siroro fani ngela nau kī ka leleka nau ku saele'a fafona ne'e ngwa'i ngela nini nau kira ū na'a fuana o'onga'a 'oe. Michael 'uana o'onga'a 'oe, sa Mae[satana] nini'a ka koso bore 'oko ta'ea logo. Nau ku saele'a fafona rō ngwae ne'e kī kira didifuliku kira ka 'abe 'ani 'ae'o, kira ka fata suli'o, fuana 'oko suraadaro'o, ma 'oko lafu-ta'inidaro'o fuana o'onga'a 'oe. Ko'o nau kī kira ke donga'o. Nau ku mae na'a, nau ku su'uma'inau logo. Di'ia nau ku dauta'a suli nau, naisi lisi'o god, kaida'i nai sui saena fanoa nini 'i ano.

patterned girdle, grasped his bundle of arrows, put on his new bag, stepped out on the hill and a gong cried out. There was a sound of shouting. He stepped out and climbed another hill, a fire smoked. Eventually the country was laid waste, as it's god who was so true to us.

At present you men and women should be thoughtful. In former times if you misbehaved they killed you, if you misbehaved and you got pregnant, or if you were a man who misbehaved and fornicated. That's what I'm saying into this cassette, from when I began until today, my name wasn't well-known from fornicating with men's wives or making men's daughters pregnant. I've been all around the community of Honiara and live there till today, that's why I'm talking into my son's cassette so I can return. I'm returning to stay and die in my home. I said that I've lived a long time, that's my talk for this evening, and on Friday I'll return and leave my sons. I'll leave them, they can stay here with my clan, with my family here, and I'll return and be all alone, on my island. I'm returning to custom, to revive it. Anyone who hears can come, bring your men, talk about your homeland, to get it straight. That's where my talk comes to.

I'll cover my talk with god, now I'll pray. Oh god eternal father, god almighty, I give thanks to you for god the father, god the son and god the spirit. Your son Jesus came down and died for me on the cross. He brought me back today and I'm immersed in his blood, on your cross. I know well that when I was small I prayed to bones. I took you Jesus for four years and when I came Satan frightened me, I was a warrior with him. I lived by it until he brought me back, with my children, and today I'm bereft. God took my wife from me, I'm bereft until today. I struggled with my children and eventually I'm happy for these children of mine to stand up for your work. Michael is for your work, it was Mae[satana] who dropped out, but you restored him. I'm happy for these two men to take my place and attend to you, they speak according to you, so you'll bless them and lift them up for your work. My grandchildren will follow you. When I'm dead, I'll concentrate on myself. If I behave myself badly I won't see you god, when I'm finished in this home on earth. If I concentrate on you and I trust in you by night and day, and I talk with you until today.

Di'ia nau ku su'uma'ini'o nau ku fīto'omu ana rodo ma na dangi, nau ku ala'a fa'ini'o ka leleka ka dao 'i ta'ena.

Nau ku fa'asia ngela nau kī ma ko'o nau kī ma funga nau kī saena fanoa nini 'i Kobito nau ku leka bore fa'asida 'oke sufida 'ania ngasingasi'anga 'oe. Kwatea kira ke ratai ana 'ae'o, 'oko tata'i nau nau ku tua fuana 'ae'o, nai ego amu faulifu ana mauria, ma ku ma'a ana 'ae'o god mauri, 'i na'o ma'i nau ku ma'a lala ana suli. Nau ku ābu nau fanga ana suli, ta'ena nau ku saele'a liu. Ta'ena nau ku saele'a liu fafona god 'oko liufi nau fani ngela nau kī kaili ka tua fuana 'ae'o noa'a kaili kesi do'ofia ta gwata, nau kesi resia ta alo, nau kusi akalota'e, du'ungana ne'e 'ae'o nini'a, 'oko olita'i nau ma'i fani ko'o nau kī 'i roki'i ngwae nai doe na'a 'oke tala'ida fuana o'onga'a 'oe. Kira ke kwairo'oi ana 'ae'o ma kira ka fata suli'o, ma kira ka ū fani o'onga'a 'oe 'i olofana salo ka leka 'i fafona asi kira liu fani o'onga'a 'ae 'oke lia suli kira'a. Blesim nau fuana olilaku kwa'ia ta'itala nau, ko 'abe 'ani nau, nai oli fuana bubunga nau. Aberata'i kaimili fo Jesus sai amen.

KA SUI NA'A

I'm leaving my children and my grandchildren and my in-laws in this home at Kobito, although I'm going from them, bless them with your power. Let them stick by you, you guide me to live with you, I lean on you, the rock of life, and I call you father, living god, whereas formerly I called bones my father. When I was tabu I had food from bones, today I'm very happy. Today I'm very happy that god, you excel for me and my children, we live for you, we don't bake pigs, I don't scrape taro [for offerings], I don't get ghost-possessed, that's because of you, you brought me back, and my grandchildren, my whole lineage you have led to your work. They are obedient to you and they speak of you, and they stand with your work under the sky and on the sea they go with your work and you look after them. Bless me while returning on my way, attend to me, I'm returning to my island. Take care of us for Jesus say amen.

THE END

References

Aihunu, A. et al. (eds) 1978 *Custom Stories Vol.4 Six Stories of Rapu 'anate from 'Are 'are, Malaita.* Solomon Islands Cultural Association, Honiara

Akin, D. 1999 Compensation and the Melanesian State: Why the Kwaio Keep Claiming. *The Contemporary Pacific* Vol.11:35-67

Akin, D. n.d. *Good Women and Bad Women: Ancestors, Menstruation and Inequality in Contemporary Kwaio Society.* (ms. in preparation)

Burt, B. 1994a *Tradition and Christianity: The Colonial Transformation of a Solomon Islands Society.* Harwood Academic Publishers, New York

Burt, B. 1994b Land In Kwara'ae and Development in Solomon Islands. *Oceania* Vol.64:317-35

Burt, B. 1998 Writing Local History in Solomon Islands. In J. Wassmann (ed) *Pacific Answers to Western Hegemony: Cultural Practices of Identity Construction.* Berg Publishers, Oxford and New York

Cooper, M. 1972 Langalanga Religion. *Oceania* Vol.43:113-22

Coppet, D. de 1981 The Life-Giving Death. In S.C. Humphries & H. King (eds) *Mortality and Immortality: The Anthropology and Archaeology of Death.* Academic Press, London

Coppet, D. de & Zemp, H. 1978 *'Are 'are: Un Peuple Melanesien et sa Musique.* Seuil, Paris

Corris, P. 1973 *Passage, Port and Plantation: A History of Solomon Islands Labour Migration 1870 - 1914.* Melbourne University Press

Denoon, D. & Lacey, R. 1981 (eds) *Oral Tradition in Melanesia.* University of Papua New Guinea and Institute of Papua New Guinea Studies, Port Moresby

Fifi'i, J. & Keesing, R.M. 1989 *From Pig-Theft to Parliament: My Life Between Two Worlds.* Solomon Islands College of Higher Education & University of the South Pacific, Honiara

Fox, J. 1993 Introduction to J. Fox & C. Sather (eds) *Origins Ancestry and Alliance: Explorations in Austronesian Ethnography.* The Australian National University, Canberra

Gegeo, D. & Watson-Gegeo, K. 1996 Priest and Prince: Integrating Kastom, Christianity and Modernization in Kwara'ae leadership. In R. Feinberg, & K. Watson-Gegeo (eds) *Leadership and Change in the Western Pacific.* London School of Economics Monographs on Anthropology No.66

Golden, G. 1993 *The Early European Settlers of the Solomon Islands.* Privately published, Melbourne

Guideri, R. 1980 *La Route des Mortes.* Seuil, Paris

Hogbin, H.I. 1939 *Experiments in Civilization: The Effects of European Culture on a Native Community of the Solomon Islands.* Routledge & Kegan Paul, London

Hviding, E. 1995 *Vivinei Tuari pa Ulusaghe / Custom Stories of the Marovo Area.* University of Bergen and Solomon Islands Western Province.

Ivens, W.G. 1927 *Melanesians of the Southeast Solomon Islands.* Kegan Paul, London.

Ivens, W.G. 1930 *Island Builders of the Pacific.* Seeley Service, London

Johnson, O. 1944 *Bride in the Solomons.* Houghton Mifflin, Boston

Keesing, R.M. 1978 *'Elota's Story: The Life and Times of a Solomon Islands Big Man.* University of Queensland Press

Keesing, R.M. 1992 *Custom and Confrontation: The Kwaio Struggle for Cultural Autonomy.* University of Chicago Press.

Keesing, R.M. & Corris, P. 1980 *Lightning Meets the West Wind: The Malaita Massacre.* Oxford University Press.

Knibbs, S.G.C. 1929 *The Savage Solomons as they Were and Are.* Seeley, Service, London

Kuschel, R. 1988 *Vengeance is Their Reply part 2: Blood Feuding and Homicides on Bellona Island.* Dansk Psykologisk Forlag

Kwa'ioloa, M. & Burt, B. 1997 *Living Tradition: A Changing Life in Solomon Islands.* British Museum Press, London & University of Hawaii Press, Honolulu

Ma'aanamae (of 'Ai'eda) 1993 *Mae Suria Waawane.* J. Laete'esafi & D. Akin (eds), Kwaio Cultural Centre, Malaita

Maranda, P. & Maranda, E.K. 1970 Le Crane et l'Uterus: Deux Theoremes Nord-Malaitans. In J. Pouillon & P. Maranda (eds) *Echanges et Communications: Melanges Offerts a Claude Levi-Strauss.* Mouton, The Hague, Paris

Not In Vain Annual report and later quarterly newsletter of the South Seas Evangelical Mission, commencing 1887, Gordon, NSW (Mitchell Library, State Library of New South Wales)

Rannie, D. 1912 *My Adventures Among South Sea Cannibals.* Seeley, Service, London

Research in Melanesia 1975 Vol.1 University of Papua New Guinea

Ross, H.M. 1973 *Baegu: Social and Ecological Organisation in Malaita, Solomon Islands.* Illinois Studies in Anthropology No.8

Southern Cross Log. Journal of the Melanesian Mission (Anglican) commencing 1898, Auckland and London

Young, F.H. 1925 *Pearls from the Pacific.* Marshall Bros., London